D0429126

PLEASE
LET ME
KNOW
YOU,
GOD

Books in the Minirth-Meier Clinic Series

Passages of Marriage
Dr. Frank Minirth, Mary Alice
Minirth, Dr. Brian Newman,
Dr. Deborah Newman,
Dr. Robert Hemfelt, Susan
Hemfelt

Imperative People
Dr. Les Carter

The Lies We Believe
Dr. Chris Thurman

*Love Hunger: Recovery for Food
Addiction*
Dr. Frank Minirth, Dr. Paul
Meier, Dr. Robert Hemfelt,
Dr. Sharon Sneed

*The Love Hunger Weight-Loss
Workbook*
Dr. Frank Minirth, Dr. Paul
Meier, Dr. Robert Hemfelt,
Dr. Sharon Sneed

Love Is a Choice
Dr. Robert Hemfelt, Dr. Frank
Minirth, Dr. Paul Meier, Don
Hawkins

Love Is a Choice Workbook
Dr. Robert Hemfelt, Dr. Frank
Minirth, Dr. Paul Meier, Don
Hawkins

The Path to Serenity
Dr. Robert Hemfelt, Dr. Frank
Minirth, Dr. Richard Fowler,
Dr. Paul Meier

Serenity Meditation™ Series
Day by Day Love Is a Choice
Jerilyn Fowler, Richard Fowler,
Dr. Brian Newman,
Dr. Deborah Newman

Food for the Hungry Heart
Cynthia Rowland McClure

Free to Forgive
Dr. Paul Meier, Dr. Frank
Minirth

The Man Within
Ted Scheuermann, Dr. Brian
Newman, Dr. Larry
Stephens, Bob Dyer

One Step at a Time
Cynthia Spell Humbert, Betty
Blaylock, Dr. Frank Minirth

Pace Yourself
Ric Engram

Setting New Boundaries
Mark MacDonald, Kevin J.
Brown, Raymond R. Mitsch

Time Out
Gary Hurst, Mike Kachura,
Larry Sides

A Walk with the Serenity Prayer
Dr. Frank Minirth, Dr. Paul
Meier, Dr. Janet Congo,
Dr. David Congo

The Woman Within
Jan Congo, Jan Meier, Julie L.
Mask

Steps to a New Beginning
Sam Shoemaker, Dr. Frank
Minirth, Dr. Richard Fowler,
Dr. Brian Newman, Dave
Carder

The Thin Disguise
Pam Vredevelt, Dr. Deborah
Newman, Harry Beverly,
Dr. Frank Minirth

Truths We Must Believe
Dr. Chris Thurman

*I Can't. God Can. I Think I'll Let
Him.*
Jane Cairo, Sheri Curry, Anne
Buchanan, Debra Klingsporn

*You Take Over, God. I Can't Handle
It.*
Kevin Brown, Dr. Raymond
Mitsch

PLEASE LET ME KNOW YOU, GOD

How to restore a true image
of God and experience
His love again

Dr. Larry Stephens
with
James D. Denney

THOMAS NELSON PUBLISHERS
Nashville

Dedication

To God in honor of His holy and perfect image.

To all who desire to truly know God and experience His love in
their hearts.

Published in Nashville, Tennessee, by Thomas Nelson, Inc., and
distributed in Canada by Lawson Falle, Ltd., Cambridge, Ontario.

Scripture quotations are from the NEW KING JAMES VERSION of
the Bible. Copyright © 1979, 1980, 1982, Thomas Nelson, Inc.,
Publishers.

Scripture quotations taken from The Holy Bible: NEW
INTERNATIONAL VERSION are marked NIV in the notes.
Copyright © 1978 by the New York International Bible Society.
Used by permission of Zondervan Bible Publishers.

Library of Congress 92-50830   ISBN 0-8407-7731-6

Printed in the United States of America

1 2 3 4 5 6 — 97 96 95 94 93

Contents

Part One: The Distorted Image

An Open Letter from God 3
Chapter 1: The Distorted Image 5

Part Two: Assessing Our Image of God

Chapter 2: Symptoms of Distortions in Our
            Image of God 23
Chapter 3: Diagnosing Our Distortions 30
Chapter 4: Where Distortions Begin 42

Part Three: Who Does God Say He Is?

Chapter 5: The Four-Dimensional Image 73
Chapter 6: God's *True* Image 92
Chapter 7: Spiritual Decontamination 108
Chapter 8: Reparented by God 133

Part Four: Knowing God Intimately

Chapter 9: Obstacles to Knowing God Intimately 147
Chapter 10: Giving Your Children a Hug from God 169
A Letter to God 188
Notes 192
The Thirty-Day Image of God Restoration Program 195

Acknowledgments

First and foremost I would like to acknowledge my wife Donna. The personal insights and practical suggestions which she shared with me throughout the development of this book were invaluable to its success and completeness. I also appreciate all of the work she did, from helping me to prepare the original proposal to her intuitive and insightful editing. Finally, I appreciate all the sacrifices she made in allowing me to devote the time and energy to this book.

I would like to acknowledge Janet Thoma for first supporting the Image of God Concept, for her commitment to putting out a book that would honor God, and for her God-given gift of editing. I would like to acknowledge Susan Salmon for her diligence in producing the manuscript, for her commitment to excellence in editing, and for her personal support and encouragement throughout the development of this book. I acknowledge Jim Denney for collaborating with me on the development of the manuscript. His abilities and talents are better than any I have experienced.

≈§ **PART ONE** §≈

The Distorted Image

AN OPEN LETTER FROM GOD

My dear child,

It has been a long time since I've heard from you. You haven't let Me hold you in My arms lately.

You may not understand this, but I really do get lonely when you are away from Me. I miss you very much. I miss being able to encourage you and help you with your problems. I miss sharing your joys and your sorrows. I miss the talks we used to have. It seems you come around only when you celebrate holidays or when you really get in a bind. Or when you get angry with Me or think I'm being unfair.

I understand how you feel. I know it's difficult for you to trust Me, given all the things people say about Me these days. I also realize how hard it is for you to understand all the pain and suffering you've had to endure in your life. And there's so much injustice in the world.

Believe Me, I understand.

And I want you to know how much I love you.

Ever since you were born, I have loved you. You never saw Me, yet I taught you to walk. I provided your first nourishment. I was so proud of you when you took your first steps, when you spoke your first words.

My plan was for you to receive My love through your parents when you were little. Maybe your parents didn't follow My wishes. Perhaps you didn't receive the love I intended you to have. Perhaps the pain you've suffered in the past few years has caused you to lose sight of Me.

Even so, I have continued to love you. Year by year, I have drawn you to Me with gentle cords of love. I gave up My Son for you so that we could be together, now and forever.

I will never cease to love you. I will never let go of you. I will never leave you or forsake you.

You may find this hard to believe, after all you have been through, but it is true.

You can learn to trust Me.

You can experience My love for you.

You can *experience My presence with you in a real and intimate way.*

My dear child, come a little closer. Let Me show you the tenderness of this Father's heart.

Please let Me love you.

Chapter One

The Distorted Image

Rick Hanks was the picture of a big, husky Texas cowboy—rugged features, ruddy complexion, clear blue eyes and sandy hair, a ready smile, and a strong handshake. Standing over six feet tall in his snakeskin boots, he would have looked right at home on the range, but Rick spent most of his workday on the sixth floor of a Dallas high-rise, running the successful advertising agency he founded ten years ago. On the outside, he looked like a guy without any troubles or complications in his life. Inside, he was hurting. Bad.

Rick had come to the Minirth-Meier Clinic for counseling because of problems in his marriage. But as we met together in my office for the first couple of weeks, it became evident that his marital conflict was just a symptom of some deeper issues. I sensed that he had some very deep emotional wounds in his inner self—and probably in his image of God. So, when I felt it was the right moment, I asked him, "Rick, how is your relationship with God?"

"Great!" he said with just a little *too* much emphasis. "That's one thing I have to be thankful for. Even with all the problems Jennie and I are having, we at least have the Lord. In fact, my relationship with God has never been better!"

I had heard such answers many times before: "I feel really close to God"; "He is really blessing me"; "I'm really growing in the Lord." Clearly, many Christians are reluctant to admit that they have struggles and frustrations in their relationship with God.

The fact is, at any given time in their lives *most* Christians experience some hindrance or dissatisfaction in their relationship with God, in their understanding of who He is, and in their sense of what His purpose is in their lives. When we gather together as Christians in church, in Bible studies, or in homes for fellowship, there seems to be an unspoken rule: *never admit inadequacy in your relationship with God!* The result is a gnawing sense of spiritual isolation from other Christians. We look around and see all these happy, fulfilled, godly Christians, and we ask ourselves, What's wrong with me? Why can't I be like they are? Why do I feel so distant from God?

If that is your feeling right now, I want you to know you are not alone. If there is one truth I have learned from the hundreds of hours I have spent counseling Christians with spiritual and emotional problems, it is this: the *majority* of believers, as faithful and devoted to Christ as they may be, feel frustrated by their lack of closeness to God, and they feel confused about who God really is. They seem to know all *about* God in their minds, but they are frequently unable to *feel His presence* in their hearts.

As Rick and I talked further, I learned (as I suspected) that was also true of him. Why, then, did he tell me that everything was great, that his relationship with God had never been better?

Rick wasn't lying to me. I'm certain of that. He thought he was being honest. But he had never admitted the truth to himself. He had never stopped to analyze the true state of his image of God.

"Show Me How to Find God!"

Carrie Bishop turned the Styrofoam™ cup around and around in her hands, worrying at it with her fingernails, poking little dents all around the rim. Her voice trembled. I could see the wounded little girl in her as she looked around the room with childlike eyes. A lifetime of pain and loneliness glistened in those eyes as she told me and the others in the group why she had come to the Minirth-Meier Clinic.

"I've been unhappy for as long as I can remember," she said, absently twisting a strand of her long straw-colored hair around her fingers. "I feel numb inside, like I don't exist. I have no spiritual life. I haven't read my Bible or prayed in years. I thought I knew God when I was a child, yet I just don't feel close to Him. When I find the courage to go to church, I struggle to get any meaning out of the sermon or the songs. It's hard to be in church, surrounded by all those smiling faces while I just feel empty and lonely inside. Sometimes I just wish I could disappear."

"Disappear from church?" I asked.

6

"Yes," she said, looking up at me. Now the pain in her eyes didn't just glisten. It *spilled*, running down her cheeks. Someone next to her handed her a Kleenex.™ She dabbed at her face and went on. "When the pastor gives the benediction, I dash for the exit. I don't want to talk to anyone. I don't want to put on a plastic smile and say, 'Hi! How are you! Isn't it wonderful to be a Christian!' Because everything *isn't* fine. I'm not sure who God is anymore or if He really loves me. I feel like a freak—like I'm the *only* Christian who feels lonely and rejected by God."

"No, Carrie," I said, "you're not the only one who feels that way. I've encountered a lot of people who feel that way. Many of them have come to the clinic with an empty heart and a broken image of God. Some have tried to fill that emptiness with material things or their careers or years of therapy. But they always end up feeling empty and incomplete until they can see God clearly and accept His unconditional love."

Her brow furrowed. "What do you mean by 'unconditional love'?"

Agape - God's Love

"Unconditional love is love that accepts you no matter how you look, what you do, or who you are," I explained. "That's the way God loves us. That's the kind of love God meant for us to receive from our parents. From the time you were born, God meant you to feel loved whether you were beautiful or plain, successful or unsuccessful, brilliant or backward. But some of us didn't get that kind of love from our parents. Carrie, I think you're one of those people."

The Styrofoam™ cup fell from Carrie's fingers to the floor. She put her face in her hands and doubled over, her shoulders heaving with uncontrollable sobs. The woman next to her leaned close and put an arm around her.

Later, when she had regained her composure, Carrie told all of us in the group about her father and the incestuous sexual abuse he had inflicted on her from the time she was a preschooler until she was eight years old. She told us of a mother who was cold, distant, and unloving—and often given to explosive outbursts of rage. She told us of the ex-husband who had sexually abused her and physically assaulted her during their fourteen-year marriage.

As Carrie talked, there was a far-off look in her eyes; she seemed to be watching old events replayed on a video screen inside her mind. When she finally finished her story, she seemed to drift back into the present, as if she were emerging from some horrible dream of the past. Her eyes pleaded with me. "Dr. Stephens," she said, "please help me! I'm broken, and I don't know how to put myself together! What can I do? I will not leave this room until you show me how to find God!"

This book exists because of people like Rick Hanks and Carrie Bishop and the hundreds of hurting people I've met who are just like them. At this point, I should make it clear that Rick Hanks and Carrie Bishop are real people in the sense that their stories have been assembled from bits and pieces of the lives of people I have known. Their stories, and the stories of other people you will meet in this book, are composites of actual case histories, with details, names, places, and events altered to protect the privacy of my clients.

The emotional and spiritual issues I address in this book are common and widespread. I am convinced that as you read the stories of Rick, Carrie, and others, you will recognize personality patterns, emotional issues, and spiritual principles from your life. You will recognize these patterns, issues, and principles *because they are true*. I have seen them played out again and again in hundreds of lives—including my own.

I believe you are reading these words because, like the people whose stories are woven through this book, you long to experience the fruit of the Spirit—love, joy, peace, patience, kindness, goodness, faithfulness, gentleness, and self-control. But you are prevented from this rich experience of the goodness of God because your image of God has become distorted or broken. Yet I sincerely believe that if you honestly, prayerfully walk the journey of self-discovery with me in these pages, you *will* find a deeper, more satisfying relationship with your heavenly Father.

Our Image of God

At the very outset, let me be clear about what I mean by *our image of God*. I define this term as "the way we experience God, view God, relate to God, and feel about God." Our image of God is not the same thing as God's *true* image, which is revealed in the

Bible. The portrayal of God in the Bible is perfect and undistorted; however, your image of God and my image of God can easily become clouded by our human emotions, by our limited understanding, by the painful experiences of the past, or by sin. When our personal, inner experience of who God is becomes distorted, we lose sight of God's truth about Himself.

It is easy to see how people like Rick Hanks and Carrie Bishop—people who have experienced serious emotional traumas such as childhood abuse—can have distortions in their image of God. But what about people who have never experienced the catastrophic pain that Rick and Carrie have suffered? Can people who have lived relatively safe, happy, "ordinary" lives experience distortions too?

The answer, as I have witnessed in my counseling practice, is yes. I have talked with many people who, despite having been raised in nurturing and secure homes, have emerged into adulthood with significant distortions in their image of God.

Wear and Tear

For some people, their image of God gradually becomes distorted because of neglect and general wear and tear. Many Christians maintain a relatively positive and comfortable image of God throughout childhood and adult life. Some may have grown up in the church and even attended a Bible college or a seminary. But they have become complacent and a little lazy, and they have neglected their relationship with God. Their devotional life has slacked off. At the same time, they have unthinkingly exposed themselves to entertainment media and other influences that seek to tear down their image of God—and those influences have taken their toll.

Such a person was Patrick. "My childhood was straight out of 'Leave It to Beaver,'" he recalls. "A full-time homemaker mom and a dad who was strict but wise and always caring. An older brother who watched out for me and helped me out of jams, even though we fought from time to time like brothers do. We went to church every Sunday, we learned about God in the home, and my parents set a good example. I got a good start in life. But somewhere along the way, my image of God took a bit of a beating."

Patrick remembers doubts about the goodness and the reality of God entering his life during his college days. "I attended a state university and was a member of the Campus Crusade for Christ chapter at school. At the same time, I was studying all these agnostic philosophers—Bertrand Russell, Albert Camus, Voltaire, Nietzsche—and for the first time in my life I began to question the reality of God. My faith survived, but it had taken a few hits."

Patrick's image of God continued to suffer as he got out of college and into the "real" world. "After graduation, I pursued my career and became successful," he recalls, "but I was not happy. Money and promotions became very important to me, and God took a backseat. I thought if I just had enough money and prestige, I'd be happy. But I wasn't.

"I still went to church, I still considered myself a Christian, but I was experiencing a lot of doubt and fear. I started having sleepless nights where all I could think about was, *Someday I'm really going to die, it's really going to be all over, and everything I have will be gone.* I knew that a Christian shouldn't be afraid to die. I didn't understand it then, but I had allowed my relationship with God to become tainted by a massive dose of worldliness. I just knew that something was wrong between me and God, and that I needed spiritual counseling."

Patrick's healing began when he made a new commitment to get serious about his relationship with God. By working on some of the same exercises and strategies that you are about to encounter in this book, Patrick was able to begin restoring an image of God that had become tarnished by neglect and everyday wear and tear.

Rolls-Royces and Yugos

Many other Christians experience distortion in their image of God because they are willing to settle for a second-rate relationship with God, or they are unaware that a first-rate relationship with God is possible. They have not experienced a major emotional trauma as have Rick Hanks and Carrie Bishop. Their lives have been safe and uneventful, and their Christian faith has been neatly tucked into one compartment of their lives. They go to church and they try to live good lives, yet they are vaguely aware that their relationship with God is not satisfying.

I would compare these people to car owners. It is as if God offered to give them a beautiful gold-plated Rolls-Royce and they refused His offer, saying, "No, thanks, I'm just going to keep driving this beat-up old Yugo." You might say that such people are satisfied with a dissatisfying relationship with God. They're not particularly happy with their experience with God, but they're not unhappy enough to seek improvements in that relationship.

Throughout most of her life, Deborah has been content with a Yugo experience with God. Raised in an upper-middle-class neighborhood, she never lacked for either love or material things. Throughout her childhood and adolescence, Deborah's parents took her to church and Sunday school every week. God, however, was pretty much confined to Sundays; very little was said about God the rest of the week.

Deborah might have been content to roll through life with her Yugo image of God had it not been for what she calls the Scare. She explains, "The moment I found this lump in my breast, I felt a cold chill pass through my body. I felt like I was going to pass out. I was absolutely certain I had cancer and I was going to die. I lived with that fear for almost a whole week. Then the doctor told me it was just a fibroid tumor—benign.

"Well, after the Scare, I got very serious about my life and my relationship with God. During that week when I thought I was going to die, I bargained and pleaded with God to let me live. That was also the first time I realized I didn't really know who God is. I had gone to church all my life, so I knew a lot *about* God, but I didn't feel I really *knew God* at all!"

As part of Deborah's process of getting serious about her relationship with God, she started meeting God every morning and evening for prayer and Bible study. The Bible study plan she followed was much like the "Thirty-Day Image of God Restoration Program" you'll find at the end of this book. "It was a struggle at first," she admits. "It was something I had to force myself to do. But now my devotional experience with God is an essential part of my life. I wouldn't dream of starting any day without stopping to talk to my heavenly Father and to listen to what He has to say to me that day."

Today, I would compare Deborah's relationship with God and her image of God to a shiny new luxury car—no battered old Yugos for her! "The difference in my life is incredible," she says. "To me, God used to be a character in a Book. I thought I knew God, but I really only knew *about* God. Today, God is my *Friend*."

God's Desire for Us: Knowing Him

In his book *Knowing God*, J. I. Packer tells about a friend, a Christian scholar who decided to take a stand for Jesus Christ, even though by doing so he ruined his chances for career advancement. Packer and his friend were walking in the sunshine, talking together about the difficult decision the scholar had made. Near the end of their conversation, Packer's friend looked up and smiled. "Ah, but it doesn't really matter," he said, "for I have known God and they haven't."

"The remark was a mere parenthesis," Packer observes,

> a passing comment on something I had said, but it has stuck with me, and set me thinking. Not many of us, I think, would ever naturally say that we have known God. The words imply a definiteness and matter-of-factness of experience to which most of us, if we are honest, have to admit that we are still strangers.[1]

And yet, Packer concludes, that is just the personal, intimate experience God intends for us to have with Him. "What were we made for?" he asks. "To know God. What aim should we set ourselves in life? To know God. What is the 'eternal life' that Jesus gives? Knowledge of God. . . . What higher, more exalted, and more compelling goal can there be than to know God?"[2]

God eagerly desires that we come to know Him as our Friend and as our loving, nurturing Father. As Jesus said, "And this is eternal life, that they may know You, the only true God, and Jesus Christ whom You have sent."[3] My hope, my goal, and my prayer for you as you journey through this book is that you might find some key, some insight, that would bring you closer to a genuine trust relationship with God.

What the Research Shows

Again and again as I counsel people regarding their emotional and spiritual problems, I hear such statements as:

- "God can't forgive someone like me."
- "I'm not sure I can really trust God."
- "God has favorites. It's obvious that God loves some people more than He loves me."
- "I know God loves everyone unconditionally, but He doesn't love me that way."
- "Even though I'm a Christian, I secretly wonder if God really exists."
- "God isn't the same today as He was long ago."
- "God promised to protect me, but for some reason He doesn't."
- "God is always punishing me or testing me. He seems to enjoy seeing how much suffering I can take."
- "You have to do certain things to get God's attention. You have to fast or perform religious rituals or pray in just the right way or He won't hear you."

Perhaps you have made some of these statements. The fact is that *none* of these ideas about God have any basis in the Bible.

I have seen the emotional pain and spiritual suffering of hundreds of people—all caused by tragically mistaken ideas about God. It saddens me to realize that only a tiny fraction of people with emotional and spiritual needs actually go to a pastor or counselor for help. Most just struggle along the best they can, managing to survive day by day. Some, unfortunately, *drown* in their pain and confusion, never knowing the abundant life God meant them to have as His children.

Having witnessed so much emotional and spiritual pain as a counselor, I decided to devote my doctoral dissertation to this subject, and out of that research came this book. Let me share with you the results of some of the research I conducted at the Minirth-Meier Clinic.

In 1990, under the auspices of the clinic, I conducted a study of Christians and their image of God. The participants formed a representative cross section of Christians from across the country;

from various backgrounds, age levels, and education levels; and from a wide spectrum of denominations. When those Christians were asked to honestly and anonymously describe their conception of God, their experience with God, and their feelings toward God, the answers that resulted were disturbing. Some of the questions we asked were:

- Do you see a difference between the Old Testament God and the New Testament Jesus?
- Do you see God as a judge or as a father?
- Do you see God as flexible or inflexible?
- Do you see God as a shepherd or as a dictator?
- Do you feel that God is reachable or unreachable?
- Do you consistently experience God as reliable?
- Do you sometimes feel God has abandoned you when you need Him?
- Do you consistently experience God's complete forgiveness?

Out of a possible score of 80, the average score of those tested was 48.8. A score below 58 indicated that the subject had significant difficulty in consistently experiencing God as good and loving.

The study revealed that *less than 50 percent* of the Christians questioned were able to claim they had a consistently positive relationship with God. That would seem to be a startling fact all by itself.

But the study uncovered an even more startling fact. The study was designed to reveal a factor called the halo effect—a response bias in which subjects may tend to be idealistic rather than realistic in their answers to questions. I expected to find a difference between the way people consciously described their relationship with God and the way they actually experienced that relationship on an emotional level.

In other words, many people—like my friend Rick Hanks—tend to describe their image of God in terms of how they idealistically think it *should* be rather than how it realistically *is*. As Christians, we have been programmed to think we *ought* to have a certain kind of relationship with God, so when we are asked about that relationship, we automatically respond with all the right spiritual-sounding clichés. We give off a halo of spirituality rather than admit—even to ourselves!—that something may be wrong between us and God.

In the clinic study, questions asked for responses that subtly indicated the individual's *feelings* toward God, while other questions indicated the individual's *beliefs* about God. Any discrepancy in those two indicators tended to show that a person's beliefs about God were more positive than their feelings toward God—and that discrepancy was *proof* of the halo effect.

As expected, the clinic study revealed a significant halo effect: two-thirds of those who reported a positive image of God were actually fooling themselves. Once the halo effect was factored in, it was clear that *three-fourths* of the participants had a negative or distorted image of God—and many didn't even realize it!

Where does this halo effect come from? Why is there such a disparity between how people think they experience God and how they really experience Him? There are several explanations.

First, many people have grown up with the belief that it is not okay to share negative feelings. Perhaps, as children, they were corrected by their parents whenever they expressed anger or sadness or disappointment. "You shouldn't feel that way," they were told. As adults, they may experience God as a parent who continues to correct them for their negative feelings, so they choose to repress, rather than express, those feelings.

Second, many Christians choose to mask their negative feelings toward God out of fear that other Christians will think critically of them or scold them. They are convinced that other Christians will not accept them and their honest feelings.

Third, some Christians are simply in denial. They are not in touch with the way they truly feel toward God. Consciously, they want to believe everything is okay with the relationship. At a hidden or preconscious level, however, hidden sorrow, resentment, confusion, or neurotic fear is at the core of the relationship. Persons in denial need to have the Holy Spirit uncover those hidden feelings about God and reveal them to the conscious mind.

Again, I don't think anyone involved in the study lied or fudged the answers. They all answered as truthfully as they knew how. A part of our natural human defenses is to avoid any truth about ourselves that would cause us pain or anxiety.

I have met many Christians who had absolutely orthodox theology, could quote a dozen verses from memory about God's love and forgiveness, and strongly believed that their God was a forgiving God—yet they confessed to me, "I just don't *feel* God can ever forgive *me*." Such people are a walking contradiction! Yet we all, at various times, walk around with these irreconcilable differences between what we believe and what we feel. To be human is to be full of contradictions—contradictions about God, about ourselves, and about life.

So, when someone asks us about our image of God and our relationship with God, our natural and understandable tendency is to give the spiritually correct answer rather than an answer that comes honestly out of our feelings and experience. As we examine the Scriptures, however, we see that God truly wants our *honesty*, not our pious answers.

What the Bible Says

The Bible clearly shows us that God *encourages* us to express our true feelings—including the way we feel toward Him. Jesus set the ultimate example of honesty in expressing His feelings when He cried out from the cross, "My God, My God, why have You forsaken Me?"[4]

There is nothing wrong with expressing our honest emotions. God gave us those emotions so that we could fully experience life. Our emotions are a distinctive part of our humanity, and God built them into us when He created us in His image.

Our relationship with God does not change just because our emotions change. He is our heavenly Father, and we are His children. Our relationship with God is not an all-or-nothing experience. It is a lifelong, growing, dynamic, *personal* relationship. As such, it is much like a *family* relationship.

All families experience emotional ups and downs, times of anger, disappointment, withdrawal, and sorrow. These emotions don't have to destroy the family ties—*if* they are faced and dealt with in a healthy way. The same is true of our "family ties" with God the Father.

God welcomes your honest emotions. He does not judge you or punish you when you cry out in pain and confusion. Rather, He

16

invites you, as 1 Peter 5:7 states, to cast all your care upon Him because He cares for you.

Assessing Your Image of God

I have developed a checklist that will help you assess your image of God. I would encourage you to do this exercise right now. Answer these questions by placing a check mark in front of each statement that expresses your feelings.

Most important of all, answer these questions carefully and honestly on the basis of your *true feelings,* not on the basis of what you have been taught, what you think you should feel, or what other Christians might think of your answers.

After you've completed the checklist, I will show you how to interpret your answers.

What Is Your Image of God?

_____ 1. Sometimes I do not feel comfortable praying to God.

_____ 2. At times it is difficult for me, emotionally, to read the Bible.

__✓__ 3. I often feel alienated from God.

__✓__ 4. If I were honest, I would have to admit to myself that at some level I feel resentment against God.

__✓__ 5. I cannot trust God as much as I would like to.

_____ 6. Sometimes I have difficulty experiencing God's unconditional love and acceptance.

__✓__ 7. Sometimes I do not feel God loves me.

__✓__ 8. Sometimes I feel God must be punishing me.

__✓__ 9. I would be embarrassed if anyone knew how I actually feel about God.

_____ 10. I feel some anxiety or apprehension when I think about going to church.

__✓__ 11. If I am honest with myself, I must admit I have felt spiritually empty for a very long time.

__✓__ 12. I have trouble relating to God on a personal level.

_____ 13. I frequently doubt my salvation.

_____ 14. Though I call myself a Christian, I inwardly question God's existence more than I am willing to admit.

_____ 15. God expects me to be perfect, and I can never be perfect.

__✓__ 16. I often question God's fairness.

_____ 17. At times I have trouble accepting God's complete forgiveness.

__✓__ 18. At times I feel that God has abandoned me and that He is nowhere to be found.

_____ 19. Another Christian has caused me to stumble spiritually, and I am having difficulty regaining my spiritual stability.

__✓__ 20. I divide God's character into traits I like and traits I dislike.

_____ 21. God is responsible for most of the suffering I experience in my life.

_____ 22. I have sinned greatly, and I feel I can't go back to church.

_____ 23. The church is full of hypocrites. I don't want to be around people who claim to know God but don't live like it.

_____ 24. Poor Christian leadership in the church makes me believe God must be a mediocre God.

_____ 25. I believe God will love me only if I tithe or give sacrificially to Him. He does not accept me merely on the basis of my acceptance of Jesus Christ as Savior.

Now, count the number of check marks.

Did you score a perfect 0? Then you scored better than I do! A score of 0 would indicate that you have an absolutely *spotless* image of God—no questions, no doubts, no problems, no distortions of any kind. Quite frankly, if you scored 0 or 1 on this checklist, you should question whether you are being honest with yourself. Or you should examine whether you have answered these questions according to what you *believe* about God rather than what you genuinely *feel* toward God.

Anyone who is human is bound to experience some confusion or doubt regarding a personal relationship with God. So a score from 2 to 7 would indicate a fairly healthy image of God—some areas of struggle, some areas of tension, some questions that are honestly being faced as part of the process of growing more mature as a Christian and as a human being. In the coming chapters of this book, you will learn ways of resolving those areas of tension, strengthening any areas of weakness, and generally maintaining the healthy, stable relationship with God you already enjoy—even if hurts or trials come into your life that might threaten the relationship.

If you scored from 8 to 14, you are probably experiencing a significant negative distortion in your image of God. You have some genuine hurts and questions that need to be addressed. These hurts and questions are interfering with the way you understand, experience, and relate to God.

Scoring in this range indicates that you probably have a history of both positive and negative experiences with God. You may have received some inconsistent messages about God in childhood—either direct messages such as "God won't love you if you do that" or indirect messages in the form of parents or other caregivers who did not consistently model godly love and acceptance to you. These inconsistent messages about God continue to reverberate within you in adulthood, creating a noticeable dissonance between what you *believe* and what you *feel* about God. This book will help you develop habits and strategies that will resolve the dissonance and inconsistencies in your image of God so that you can enjoy a deeper and more secure trust relationship with God.

If you scored more than 14, you are most likely experiencing some major painful distortions in your image of God. But please understand this: there is no shame in having a broken image of God. You *can* rebuild that image, and you *can* experience the joy of an intimate and vital relationship with God. In coming chapters, you will discover specific steps and strategies you can undertake *right now* that will enable you to rebuild your image of God and enhance your experience with Him.

Don't feel judged by God because of those distortions in your image of Him. For now just believe me when I say that He loves you and accepts your honest feelings. Most of all, He wants to heal you and to have a close, nurturing relationship with you.

What is important about your score on this checklist is that you now have a starting point in your journey toward a new and vital relationship with God.

The Path Ahead

It's time to begin bringing your beliefs and your feelings into conformity. Together, in the coming pages, we can uncover the hidden distortions in your image of God—distortions straining your relationship with Him, distortions keeping you from experiencing the abundant, joyful life God truly wants you to have.

In the rest of this book, you will

- discover the deep emotional sources of the distortions in your image of God, especially those distortions you carry from childhood.
- do some revealing exercises that will help you uncover the hidden distortions in your image of God.
- discover the keys to rebuilding your image of God on a reliable, biblical foundation.
- discover how you can be reparented by God, your loving heavenly Father.

Don't expect the path ahead to be easy or painless. Honest self-examination is never easy, but it is always rewarding. It is a path I have walked and continue to walk. Daily, as I grow in my experience with God, I continue to find new depths to His character—and I find previously undetected flaws in my understanding of Him.

My prayer for you as you read this book is that God will reveal Himself to you, page by page, day by day, in all His amazing love and grace. As you read these pages, I ask you to open your heart to Him. Feel His supportive arms around you. Look into His eyes of love. Listen to His voice—a voice that is gentle, yet strong. Hear what He is whispering to you.

He is saying, "Please let Me love you."

PART TWO

Assessing Our Image of God

Chapter Two

Symptoms of Distortions in Our Image of God

When Rick Hanks first arrived at the clinic, it took him a while to get to his reasons for coming. He talked about how his advertising business was going (great), how the Dallas Cowboys were doing (not so great), what the weather was like (cold and cloudy). Finally—and reluctantly, it seemed—he got to the point. "My marriage isn't going too well," he said at last, "and then there's this problem I've been having with depression. It's hard to sleep nights. And I just feel so empty during the day. Like nothing really matters."

Over the next couple of weeks, we continued to talk about his marital problems and his depression, but we were having a hard time getting to the source of his problems. He deflected questions about his faith and his religious upbringing with brief replies and a change of subject. Finally, I said, "You know, I hardly know anything about your religious training as a child. I often find this to be an area that holds the key to a lot of emotional and psychological problems."

"I don't see what that has to do with—"

"Well," I said, "you never know. It may not get us anywhere, but why don't you share with me a little bit about how you were brought up and the kind of religious instruction you had as a boy?"

He sighed deeply and shook his head to show he didn't think much of this line of inquiry. "Well," he said, "my dad made us all go to church every Sunday. Every single night he would line us up in the living room—my mother, my two brothers, my three sisters, and me—and he would read to us out of this great big Bible and preach at us. I mean, he was nothing but a hardware salesman, but he could preach just like a pulpit pounder in a revival meeting. Hellfire and brimstone and the judgment of God, that sort of thing. We kids would sit on the couch or on the floor, and we'd shake with fear while he shouted at us. His favorite theme was how God would punish us if we broke any of His laws."

"Did you feel your father lived a consistent Christian life?" I asked.

"Are you kidding? He beat Mom up all the time. Beat us kids too. He cursed and swore a blue streak—but if he caught us kids swearing, he'd mop up the floor with us." He told me that his father had once struck him in the face for asking how we know the Bible is true. All of that was Rick's model of Christian fatherhood and of the fatherhood of God!

In his early twenties, Rick married a Christian young woman named Jennie. She was able to drag him to church two or three Sundays a month, but he resisted with all his might. When their children were born, Jennie insisted all the harder that he go to church "for the sake of the kids."

"I believe in God," said Rick, "but I don't like to go to church. I don't have much use for the kind of God you find in churches. The kind of God who's always threatening you with hellfire and damnation."

"Don't they talk about the love of God in your church?" I asked.

He was silent for a moment. "I guess so," he said. "But I still don't like churches. Churches are full of hypocrites."

"I can understand that you would want nothing to do with that terrifying, threatening God of your childhood. And I can understand why you want nothing to do with religious hypocrisy. But the God your father modeled for you is not the God of the Bible."

His face darkened with anger at the mention of his father. "But my old man's God came *straight* out of the Bible! He always had this big black King James Version, and he was always preaching hellfire and damnation at us!"

"Sure, the Bible talks about hell," I answered. "But God doesn't want people like you to go to hell. That's why He sent His Son Jesus—to pay the ultimate sacrifice so that you don't have to pay it yourself. God loves you, Rick. He accepts you right where you are. I think it's time you learned to let God love you."

As you and I journey through this book together, we will learn more of Rick's story—the pain that caused his image of God to become so tortured and the process he followed on the path to

24

healing. A large part of Rick's healing is due to the courageous way he has faced the various problem areas of his life—his troubled marriage, his compulsive outbursts of anger, his low-self-esteem, his struggles with anxiety and depression, his avoidance of God, both in his personal devotional life and in his infrequent church attendance. Those problems in Rick's life led him to seek counseling at the Minirth-Meier Clinic.

Yet—as Rick discovered during our counseling sessions together—the problems were only the *symptoms* of a much deeper disorder in his life: a distorted image of God.

Symptoms of a Distorted Image of God

The same disorder became apparent early in my counseling sessions with Carrie Bishop, the woman we met in Chapter 1. In the lives of Rick Hanks and Carrie Bishop, the symptoms of a distorted image of God were apparent in their marriage and family relationships, their interpersonal relationships, their personalities, and their spiritual lives.

The symptoms in Carrie's marital life were painfully clear. She had lived in an abusive marriage for fourteen years. Her husband had beaten her and emotionally abused her. Finally, after one beating that left her unconscious and put her in the hospital, Carrie summoned the will to leave her husband. She had been divorced for two years when she first came to the clinic for counseling, and she still felt guilty about leaving her husband.

As we examine the lives of Rick Hanks and Carrie Bishop, we become aware of this stark reality: our image of God has profound and definite effects on our lives, our relationships, and our personal psychology. Our image of God affects how we think, feel, make choices, respond to life, and relate to others.

In my counseling sessions with Rick, Carrie, and hundreds of other Christians, I have suggested they take a brief written inventory of their relationships. By taking this inventory, they have been able to identify various symptoms that point to a distorted image of God. As you read through this inventory, you might want to check the symptoms in each area that apply to you.

Symptoms in Marriage and Family

_____ Staying in an abusive marriage
_____ Poor sex life
_____ Codependency
_____ Unrealistic expectations
_____ Control issues

A note of explanation before continuing: you may wonder how a distorted image of God could result in symptoms such as a poor sex life. There are several explanations.

For example, couples who engaged in premarital sex may have experienced feelings of guilt at the time, which were healthy messages telling them they needed to abstain until marriage. In many cases, however, the feelings of guilt and shame continue even after marriage and are carried into the marriage bed, inhibiting the couple from fully enjoying God's gift of sex. On a subconscious level, the couple believe they are being directly punished by God when in reality they are experiencing the effects of unresolved guilt and shame.

In other cases, people are brought up from childhood to feel guilty about their sexuality, and they project these feelings onto God. They feel God doesn't want them to experience sex, even in marriage. They feel God is watching everything they do, and they feel dirty engaging in sex. Most of this misplaced guilt over sexuality is rooted in early childhood, as children are forced to have sexual experiences against their will. Or sexual shame may come when children first experience their sexuality through curiosity, exploration, and natural development and then are shamed by their parents for being who they are as sexual beings. They believe that God, as a parent, condemns them as well. These feelings and attitudes toward sex may persist well into adulthood, robbing them of the pleasure of one of God's most beautiful gifts to humankind.

Christians who have few or no inhibitions about expressing their sexuality in marriage usually have better sexual experiences and are less likely to believe that God thinks sex is bad. Thus, they are less likely to have distortions in their image of God.

Symptoms in Interpersonal Relationships

_____ Problems with trusting others

_____ Fear of abandonment

_____ People pleasing

_____ Martyr syndrome

_____ Failure to be assertive

_____ Taking the role of victim

_____ Compulsive caretaking

By taking this inventory, Carrie Bishop was able to recognize a pattern in her relationships with others. She realized that she had no close friendships because she had problems trusting other people. And because she saw herself as a martyr and a victim, she continually placed herself in the victim role with others.

Symptoms in Personality

_____ Low self-esteem

_____ Compulsive perfectionism

_____ Compulsive or addictive personality

_____ Generalized fear, anxiety, and worry

_____ Depression

_____ Feelings of guilt and shame

_____ Compulsive outbursts of anger or violence (rageaholism)

Carrie clearly saw herself in many of the symptoms on this list. She was a compulsive perfectionist; she demanded perfection of herself in her housekeeping, her performance at work, and her performance as a mother—and she became very depressed and angry with herself when she failed to meet those standards of perfection. She also demanded perfection from her son Jeremy, and (like her rageaholic mother) she was given to unpredictable outbursts of anger whenever Jeremy fell short of perfection. Carrie had strong obsessive-compulsive tendencies. She was addicted to Valium™, and she continually struggled with feelings of depression, anger, fear, and shame.

Rick Hanks also saw himself in this list of symptoms. He realized that he had a driven, workaholic personality, and that his workaholism was fueled by low esteem. He was frequently subject to depression, worry, feelings of shame, and sudden, inexplicable outbursts of anger.

Symptoms in Spiritual Life

_____ Decrease in church attendance

_____ Decrease in prayer

_____ Decrease in Bible study

_____ Doubting one's salvation

_____ Unresolved anger toward God

_____ Feeling rejected by God

_____ Spiritualizing

_____ Pharisaism or legalism

_____ Avoiding talking about God

_____ Hiding from God

Carrie felt she *ought* to go to church, pray, and read her Bible, but she found it difficult—and even painful—to do so. She continually doubted her salvation and God's love and acceptance of her. She told people, especially people in her church, that she loved God and had a wonderful relationship with Him. Yet inwardly, she was angry with God.

This inventory helped Rick recognize that his avoidance of church, his lack of personal devotions, his frequent bouts of anger toward God, his blaming God whenever things went wrong, and his tendency to slip into legalistic thinking and behavior (even though he openly hated his father for being so rigid and legalistic!) were all symptoms of a distorted image of God.

As you read through these lists, did you identify any of these symptoms in your life? Then you should know that these symptoms are strong indicators that something may be wrong with your image of God and your experience with God. The *good news*, of course, is that most of us, by experiencing healing in our image of God, can also experience dramatic improvement in the symptoms I have just listed. There is enormous hope for you—and you can take that hope with you as an encouragement as you journey through the rest of this book.

At this point, you may not understand how these symptoms in your marriage and family, your interpersonal relationships, your personality, and your spiritual life relate to your image of God. But as we move through the next few chapters, you will gain insight into the way your image of God affects your relationships, your decision making, your responses to problems, your feelings, and your behavior. In fact, I am convinced that no single factor has a greater impact on our lives than our image of God.

In the next chapter, we will learn how to diagnose the various distortions that can affect our image of God.

Chapter Three

Diagnosing Our Distortions

Mr. Hanks, Rick Hanks's father, sat at the head of the table, a long stainless steel carving knife in one fist, a big two-pronged meat fork in the other. A roasted Sunday chicken lay on the platter before him, ready to be whacked and sliced and divided up among the two adults and six children. It was a dry, hot June day in 1965—a Sunday much like any other Sunday in the white clapboard home of the Hanks family, just outside Sweetwater, Texas. The entire family was gathered in the room, which reeked of tension and fear.

"Fine sermon at church this morning," said Rick's dad as he began to carve. "Hope the preaching wasn't wasted on you kids. Jim, what did you get out of the sermon this morning?"

Ten-year-old Jim's voice quavered as he answered, "God's always watching, Daddy. He sees everything we do. He hears every thought we think."

"And don't ever forget it, Jim-boy," said Mr. Hanks, sawing a leg and thigh apart at the joint. He turned toward the six-year-old girl at his elbow. "Annie, how do you know God's always watching?"

"'Cause it says so in the Bible, Daddy," she replied.

"That's right, Annie," said Mr. Hanks, hacking at the chicken wing.

"How do we know the Bible's true, Daddy?"

All eyes turned in horror toward fourteen-year-old Rick, sitting at the corner of the table nearest his father's right hand. Mr. Hanks turned a withering stare in Rick's direction, and his thick black brows knitted together. "What did you say, Rick?"

"All we know about God is what it says in the Bible," Rick continued. "How do we know that what the Bible says is true?"

Mr. Hank's fists tightened around the utensils, whitening his knuckles. Rick glanced toward the foot of the table and saw a look of panic in his mother's eyes. His brothers gave him a pitying look, as if to say, "Couldn't you keep your stupid mouth shut?" His sisters just looked away.

There was a loud clatter as the carving knife and fork fell from Mr. Hanks's fists. Rick turned toward his father and opened his mouth to say something. He never got the chance to speak. He got the back of his father's hand instead. It struck him full in the face, leaving his lip stinging and his ears buzzing.

Rick's mother rose from her chair.

"Leave him!" Mr. Hanks shouted hoarsely. "The boy will learn not to blaspheme if he wants to live under my roof!"

Mrs. Hanks sat down, looking pale and miserable.

Rick put a hand to his mouth. It came away stained with a trickle of blood.

Mr. Hanks bowed his head. Mrs. Hanks and the children bowed their heads in response. Rick bowed his head too—but not in respect. His head was bowed in shame. Tears squeezed from his clenched eyes and dripped onto his plate. His face burned red with humiliation.

"O Lord," Rick's father intoned, "for the bounty we are about to receive, make us truly thankful. In Thy holy name, Amen."

"I had many worse beatings than that from my dad," Rick recalled sometime during our third or fourth appointment, "but that one rap in the mouth really sticks in my mind. My dad hit me for asking a question about God. I wasn't being a smart aleck. I really wanted to know. But he just hit me, then he thanked God for the food. I was crying, and my whole family just prayed, then ate their dinner like nothing had happened. I never forgot that."

It's hardly surprising, given his childhood, that Rick Hanks would grow up with a seriously distorted image of God. I have identified ten basic categories of distortions, which I've shown on page 32. Rick fit *several* of these. As you and I examine these ten common distortions together, I would encourage you to consider prayerfully whether any of them have affected *your* experience with God.

THE TEN MOST COMMON DISTORTIONS IN OUR IMAGE OF GOD

1. God has good and bad traits.

2. God is undependable.

3. God is unfair.

4. God is a religious institution.

5. God is a controller.

6. God is too demanding.

7. God does not exist.

8. God is a critical parent or a condemning judge.

9. God holds grudges.

10. God is not holy and perfect.

The Ten Most Common Distortions in Our Image of God

Distortion 1: God has good and bad traits. Many people tend to relate to God as if He were a human being, possessing desirable and undesirable traits. They compartmentalize His attributes and say, "I like some things about God, and I dislike others." For example, Rick Hanks once told me, "I know God loves everyone, He's a personal God, and He wants to be involved in our lives. But He's also all-seeing and all-knowing, and that makes me feel like God is always looking over my shoulder, always on my back, always ready to nail me if I make a mistake."

Carrie Bishop shared with me that she felt God has good traits (He's loving and holy) and bad traits (He's distant and unjust). "I know God loves people because He sent Jesus to die for the world," she said. "But it's not fair the way God just sits up there in heaven and lets innocent people suffer the way He does. It's not fair that God lets good people get cancer or that He lets good people get killed on the highway by drunken drivers. It's not fair that God lets little children be molested or abused by grown-ups."

It's true that we can't fully understand why bad things happen to good people (although we do know that the world's suffering can at least partially be understood in terms of human free will and human sin). But we know that the Bible tells us that God is completely good and has no bad traits.

"You are my God," asserted David. "Your Spirit is good."[1]

"No one is good but One," said Jesus, "that is, God."[2]

And James wrote, "Every good gift and every perfect gift is from above, and comes down from the Father of lights, with whom there is no variation or shadow of turning."[3]

Clearly, the Bible leaves no room for sidestepping the issue: God is entirely good and has no bad traits whatsoever. Equally clearly, many people will have an easier time *believing* the biblical truth about God than *feeling* and *experiencing* that truth on a moment-to-moment basis—particularly if they or someone close to them is going through a painful trial. But that is our goal: *to bring our feelings and experience of God into conformity with what the Bible says about God.*

Distortion 2: God is undependable.   Many people find it difficult to put their entire trust in God. They feel that God doesn't
always hear them when they pray. Or they believe that God
sometimes reneges on the promises He made in the Bible. Very
early in her life, Carrie came to believe that God was undependable because she prayed and prayed for God to stop her father
from molesting her, yet his abuse continued for several years.

One source of this distortion is a practice called prooftexting—
that is, taking verses of Scripture out of context and twisting them
to support a theological bias.

For example, Jesus promised, "If you ask anything in My name,
I will do it."⁴ Perceiving that verse to be a blank check, some
people pray, "Lord, in the name of Jesus, give me a million dollars." When the money doesn't arrive by return mail, these people
conclude that God's promises are undependable. They fail to realize that this promise of Jesus must be understood within the context of the entire Bible. Then it becomes clear that the name of
Jesus is not some magical formula (like abracadabra), which we
attach to our prayers to coax God to do our bidding like the genie
of Aladdin's lamp. When we pray in the name of Jesus, we ask
according to His will. The purpose of prayer is not to bend God's
will to ours but to conform our will to His.

When we have a realistic and biblical understanding of prayer
and the promises of God, we can be assured that God is depend-
able, and we can trust Him with every detail of our lives.

Distortion 3: God is unfair.   This is one of the most common
complaints against God: "If You are just, loving, and all-powerful,
God, why do You allow suffering?" Or as Rick Hanks once told me
during a time when he was experiencing problems in his business
and personal life, "I've always tried to do what's right, and I've got
nothing but problems. Yet my business competitors cheat and
steal and my peers live an immoral life-style—and God seems to
bless them!" Or as Carrie once asked me, "Why does God allow
evil people to abuse innocent children, then get off scot-free?"

These feelings are understandable, given the massive injustices
that go on around us and in our lives. Yet the Bible makes it plain
that God is just, even though evil reigns for the time being in this
world. In this present age, as Jesus said, God "makes His sun rise

on the evil and on the good, and sends rain on the just and on the unjust."[5] God views human beings and human events from a much larger perspective than we do. Though this present life is unfair, a time will come when God's justice and wisdom will be made known to those who love Him and to those who do evil.

Distortion 4: God is a religious institution. Many people mistakenly identify the institutional church with God Himself. Rosemary was such a person.

Some years ago, Rosemary, a woman in her early forties, went to her pastor for counseling. About twenty years previously, she had been involved in a brief extramarital affair, which continued to cause her a great deal of guilt and stress. She hoped the pastor would give her insight into her guilt feelings so that she could feel forgiven by God. Instead, her pastor savagely condemned her for her past sin.

For a full year after that traumatic experience, Rosemary was unable to pray or go to church—not because she was angry with the pastor but because she accepted his condemnation of her. She believed her pastor spoke for God, and she felt unworthy of a relationship with God or with the church.

The fact is that God created the church as His representative on earth. But the church is made up of imperfect human beings who do not always represent the nature of God. There are a few bad pastors, just as there are bad mechanics, bad politicians, and bad psychiatrists. And even a good pastor can have a bad day.

The institutional church is a reflection of *our image* of who God is, and sometimes that reflection can become distorted. The institutional church should never be confused with God Himself.

Distortion 5: God is a controller. Many people feel that if they commit their lives to God, He will take away their freedom and choices. Dan could not bring himself to place his trust in Jesus Christ. "I like my life the way it is," he said. "I don't want to be a puppet for Jesus. I want to be in control. I have my own opinions, my own view of morality, my own career, my own friends. If I become a Christian, God might want to change all of that."

The issue of control presents us with a beautiful spiritual paradox: the Bible urges us to give our lives over to God's control,[6] yet God is *not* a controller! He never forces us or manipulates us into doing anything. God only *invites*. God encourages us to surrender to Him because He knows we can never be happy and fulfilled apart from Him, but He will never control us or take away our freedom.

God's gracious, inviting character is illustrated in these words: "Behold, I stand at the door and knock. If anyone hears My voice and opens the door, I will come in to him and dine with him, and he with Me."[7]

Distortion 6: God is too demanding. This was a major distortion in Carrie's life. From her harsh and critical mother, Carrie acquired an obsessive-compulsive drive for perfection. She drove not only herself but her young son Jeremy. Part of her drivenness was rooted in her fear that if she fell short of perfection, God would reject her and punish her, just as her mother had so often rejected her and punished her in childhood.

Many people see God as a cosmic critic, always looking over our shoulders, always saying, "Not good enough." This distorted image of God can lead to religious addiction—the compulsive need to do religious works to the point of exhaustion and burnout. People who see God as a demanding critic have set their expectations higher than God's. They fear God's displeasure, and they feel that God's yoke on them is heavy, which results in depression, defeat, and paralysis.

Jesus came to give comfort to the weary and defeated, and to introduce them to a God who is accepting, not demanding. He came to rescue those who stagger under the heavy yoke of legalism. "Come to Me, all you who labor and are heavy laden," He said, "and I will give you rest. . . . For My yoke is easy and My burden is light."[8]

Distortion 7: God does not exist. I would include in this category not only atheists—those who believe there is no God of any kind—but also those who believe that although there may be *some* kind of god, he (or it) is not a *personal* god—and certainly not the God of the Bible.

When Einstein was asked if he believed in God, he replied that he believed in a god that was nothing more or less than the sum of all the laws of the universe. He did not believe this god was personally involved with humankind or with individual human beings. He did not believe in the God of love or the God who sent His Son to die for our sakes.

Many other people believe in a god that is a vague power (like the Force in George Lucas's *Star Wars* movies).

Others—such as the death-of-God theologians of the 1960s—portray the biblical God as being either figuratively or literally dead. In fact, the leading "God is dead" theologian, Thomas J. J. Altizer, went so far as to claim that the Judeo-Christian God died on the cross of Calvary, leaving it up to us as human beings to build a better world without any help from a living heavenly Father.

Some go so far as to reject the historical existence of Jesus Christ—even though such belief goes against mountains of historical evidence, both within and outside the New Testament documents.

Others believe that God is real, but that human beings can relate to Him only in this short span of life. There is no eternity, no afterlife—only today.

Still others struggle with the desire to believe in a God they cannot see, touch, hear, or feel. This is a particular problem for people who were abandoned or neglected as children. They didn't get their nurturing needs met by their parents when they were young, and they still feel abandoned and neglected by God today.

All of these conceptions are variations on the theme that God, as a personal, relational being, does not exist. The sources of all these false images of God are varied. Some come from liberal theory or New Age mysticism. Some are the ideas that come into our minds when we fail to apply ourselves to an understanding of God's Word. Some are the ideas that arise when we form our image of God on the basis of our feelings rather than the objective truths of the Bible.

Distortion 8: God is a critical parent or a condemning judge.   Many people see God as a critical parent, standing over them with a big hickory switch, just waiting for them to get out of

37

line. Others see God as a grim judge in black robes and fear that He will condemn them to a life sentence—or even an eternity—of suffering for breaking one of His laws.

Rick Hanks felt he lived out his entire childhood and adolescence under the critical glare of his father's judgment. Burned deep into Rick's psyche were the many times his father had verbally abused him, branding him a "worthless bum," a "dummy," a "filthy little heathen," plus a few labels unfit to print. As an adult, Rick felt that same critical glare—only it was God's judgment he feared.

Todd and Kirstin are in their early thirties. Todd has a good job, and Kirstin is a full-time homemaker and mother to their two children. Outwardly, they seem to be happy and contented, but inwardly, they are a very troubled couple. They are troubled by a secret.

Many years ago, when they were dating, Todd and Kirstin became sexually intimate together. Though they were widely viewed as a model Christian young couple—leaders in Young Life and other Christian activities, and very active in their church—they found themselves compulsively involved in a sexual relationship that left them feeling guilty. As adults, they looked back on the way they expressed their sexuality outside marriage, and they felt a mixture of shame and fear, especially the fear that God would no longer use them. Feeling that they had broken God's moral law, both concluded that God had put them on the shelf.

Certainly, sin has consequences. Sexual sin brings such consequences as guilt and shame, and sometimes it also leads to unwanted pregnancy, marital problems, public disgrace, and sexually transmitted diseases. But Todd and Kirstin had a distorted view of God's character. They needed to understand that while God hates sin, He loves sinners. He doesn't want to put people on the shelf; He wants to restore broken people to wholeness. That is the message of the gospel and the reason God sent His Son Jesus to die for us.

Distortion 9: God holds grudges. Some people see God as a cold and unforgiving deity who is just waiting to pay us back for our sins. They picture Him keeping a list of wrongs to be presented as evidence against us on Judgment Day. Some sins He pardons, and some He *never* forgets and *never* forgives. Commit a "really bad" sin and God will turn His back on you.

As a result of such beliefs, some people try to appease God by inflicting suffering and punishment on themselves. Carrie's approach was to punish herself, hurt herself, deny herself. Feeling that God condemned her for allowing her father to have sex with her, Carrie actually took on all the guilt, responsibility, and shame for her victimization—a common pattern among abuse victims. On a deep emotional level, Carrie believed that if she just suffered enough and deprived herself enough, she could somehow make herself acceptable to God.

Others, like Rick Hanks, try to appease God through ritualistically performing good works or through proving themselves worthy of God's love and approval. He became a driven workaholic, sometimes devoting eighty or more hours a week to his advertising business to become a success in his own eyes and God's. He felt that if he could perform well enough and achieve enough, he could somehow erase God's grudge against him.

Where did Rick get the idea that God had a grudge against him? From his father. "My dad had perfect recall," Rick bitterly told me. "He never forgot a grudge. If I wet the bed when I was five or made an embarrassing remark in front of the pastor when I was nine, my dad would still bring it up to shame me five, ten, or fifteen years later."

Though Carrie and Rick have grown in their understanding of God as a loving, merciful Father in heaven, they continue to struggle with their old, deeply ingrained images of a vengeful, grudge-bearing God. Life for Carrie and Rick is a daily effort to bring their *feelings* about God in line with their biblically based *beliefs* about God.

Distortion 10: God is not holy and perfect.   Christianity has become so secularized and institutionalized that many people today have little understanding of what holiness really means. Even among professing Christians, we frequently encounter irreverent jokes, an indulgent attitude toward sin, and a sense that God is just "one of the boys." God is gracious, loving, forgiving, and personal, but we should never forget that He is also *holy*.

Holiness, as it refers to God, means perfection and purity—an immaculate spotlessness. In God there is not the slightest hint or shadow of sin, not the faintest evil motive. How little we understand the depth of what it means to serve a holy God!

Because we have such a shallow understanding of God's holiness, many people tend to doubt God's perfection. They struggle with the biblical truth that God never makes mistakes. They struggle with the biblical truth that God is all-knowing, all-powerful, and all-present. They perceive God as forgetful or not fully aware or just plain *wrong* about some things. And when people have a diminished picture of God's holy perfection, they inevitably lower the standards of holiness and conduct for their lives.

God expects us to conform our conduct to His holiness. "Be holy, for I am holy," He says to us in His Word.[9] Does that mean God expects us to live sinless lives? Obviously not! He knows us well enough to understand that we will stumble and sin. He doesn't expect us to achieve perfection in this life. But He *does* expect us to make holiness and perfection our *goal*.

As Oswald Chambers wrote in *My Utmost for His Highest,*

> Never tolerate through sympathy with yourself or with others any practice that is not in keeping with a holy God. Holiness means unsullied walking with the feet, unsullied talking with the tongue, unsullied thinking with the mind—every detail of the life under the scrutiny of God.[10]

God Doesn't Make Mistakes

One aspect of God's holy perfection that is hard for some people to accept is that *God does not make mistakes.* That was one issue Carrie Bishop struggled with as a survivor of incest and emotional abuse. "You say God doesn't make mistakes," she told me during one of our earliest counseling sessions. Her voice shook and her eyes flashed with anger. "But what else can you call my life but one big, horrible mistake? It seems to me that God used mighty poor judgment when He allowed me to be born into a family where dear old Dad was a child abuser and dear old Mom was an emotional basket case! Face it, Dr. Stephens, I was born into the wrong family!"

I explained to Carrie that God truly doesn't make mistakes, that God didn't cause her parents to sin. All sin is against God's will. It's understandable that many people hold God responsible for everything that happens in life, both good and bad. Yet, while God could totally control our wills if He chose to, He has allowed human beings to act out their own free will—including the will to sin and hurt others. Most of the events people claim to be "God's mistakes" are actually the result of human sin and human free will.

Of course, Carrie wasn't ready to accept this explanation at the time. That's only natural, for she had gone through a lot of suffering in her life. Great pain normally takes a great amount of time to heal. Fortunately, Carrie has now reached a point where she recognizes and accepts the holy perfection of God.

"For more than thirty years, I believed that God had made a mistake and placed me in the wrong family, both as a child and as a wife," she recently told me. "I suppose it was a kind of defense mechanism to help me survive the abuse I took from my parents and later from my husband. But it was a lie, and because of that lie, I have lost years during which I could have had a right relationship with God. I'm so sorry that I ever believed that lie about God. When you write your book, Dr. Stephens, be sure and tell everyone from me that God is truly perfect. He never makes mistakes."

Carrie has been gradually building a new relationship with God—a relationship based on trust and biblical truth. No matter how you have been hurt and disappointed by life, you can make the same journey that Carrie is making. You, too, can embrace God, trust His love and wisdom, and say with Carrie, "God never makes mistakes."

In this chapter, we have examined the ten most common distortions in our image of God. In the next chapter, we are going to take an in-depth look at the various life experiences, in childhood and adulthood, that can cause our relationship with God to become distorted.

Chapter Four

Where Distortions Begin

Eric usually drove. Today, however, he had a headache so his wife, Lisa, was behind the wheel and Eric was in the passenger seat. Lisa's window was rolled down, and her chestnut brown hair floated in the warm autumn breeze. Eric and Lisa had been married only two years, and they were very happy together. Soon, Lisa's brother would be getting married too. They were on their way to the rental shop to get Eric fitted for a tux for the wedding.

As Lisa urged their white Subaru® sedan over the crest of a hill, she noted the big Lincoln® Town Car sitting in their lane. It was idling at the stoplight at the bottom of the hill. She gently applied pressure to the brakes. The Subaru® eased down the steep grade, rolling to a smooth stop about four feet behind the Lincoln®.

"What are you doing, hon?" she asked, glancing at her husband in the right-hand seat.

"Taking off this seat belt," said Eric, unbuckling the lap and shoulder restraint. "My head's killing me. I need to stretch out a bit. I'll put the belt on again when you get rolling."

The light changed from red to green. But Lisa didn't see it. She didn't get a chance. She was too busy watching the battered old pickup that was swiftly growing larger in her rearview mirror. Lisa gasped, "Oh, my! *He's not stopping!*"

Eric cranked his head toward the rear window. And that's when it happened.

A two-ton fist struck the car. Metal screamed. Lisa's spine contorted crazily as her head was wrenched backward by the initial impact, then whipsawed against the steering wheel as the Subaru® slammed into the rear of the Lincoln®. A shower of glass fragments filled the passenger compartment. The car seemed to hover two feet off the pavement for an eternity, then it settled onto its springs.

There was a distant tinkling, a nearby clank-clank, and then silence. An eerie, horrible silence. Lisa turned to the right, expecting to see her husband. But he wasn't there. Just seconds ago, he had been there, but not now—

Then she saw the gaping hole in the passenger side of the windshield. And Eric's shoe on the hood.

At that moment, Lisa was already a widow.

"I grew up feeling that I could trust God, and that He would never let anything really terrible happen to me," Lisa said about six months after the accident. "So what went wrong? Was God asleep at the switch? Or does He just not care? God promised to protect me and Eric, but He didn't! I want to know why!

"Eric is gone, and I am in constant pain since the accident. I have migraines and back pain so bad that some days I can only teach part-time. The drunk who hit us had no license, no liability insurance, and no assets. Our own insurance still leaves me with thousands of dollars in medical bills. In a split second, my life went from a beautiful dream to a nightmare. All I know is, God could have prevented the accident and He didn't. . . . And I hold God responsible."

Sometimes distortions in our image of God begin with the events of early childhood. And sometimes, as in Lisa's case, distortions can arise from the trials and tragedies of adulthood. Lisa's disillusionment with God was a direct result of her illusions about God, coupled with one of the most tragic experiences anyone could experience. She believed that God had promised never to let anything "really terrible" happen to her—yet she had lost her husband, her health, and her financial security.

God has not promised that bad things won't happen to good people. Rather, He has promised that He will see us through our suffering. It was not God's will that an irresponsible driver should plow into the back of Lisa's Subaru® at just the moment her husband unbuckled his seat belt. It was not God's will that the driver should be drunk and uninsured. Yes, God did allow the terrible accident to take place, but He allowed it to happen through the unhindered operation of human free will.

Yet, as we shall soon see, Lisa is learning that God *can* use even the worst circumstances that sinful human beings create, and He can transform them into His good.

In this chapter we will examine the *root causes* of the distortions in our image of God. Whether the hindrances in your relationship with God arise from recent circumstances (as in Lisa's case), from deep-seated childhood pain (as in the lives of Carrie Bishop and Rick Hanks), or from some other source, you are about to discover new insights into your image of God and the sources of your distortions. I believe you will find these insights to be powerful tools that will enable you to heal the distortions in your image of God.

Where Distortions Do Not Come From

To understand where distortions in our image of God come from, we will begin by ruling out sources where distortions *do not* begin.

First, *distortions never begin with the Holy Spirit*. The Holy Spirit will never say anything to us that would create a distortion in our image of God. In fact, the Holy Spirit has already communicated God's true nature—and His message is contained in the Bible. The Holy Spirit does not tell us one thing in the Scriptures and something else in our minds or hearts. A distorted image of God occurs because we fail to clearly hear what the Spirit has to say to us.

Many people state, "The Holy Spirit told me this or that," and they proceed to describe a belief totally at odds with the Bible's teachings. I have to conclude that although these people honestly *think* they are listening to the Holy Spirit, they are actually listening to their emotions, their preconceived beliefs, or their intellect.

Second, *distortions never begin with God the Father or His Son, Jesus Christ*. God is holy and does not change His nature. He does not sin, does not act unjustly, does not act unwisely. Moreover, Jesus is the full expression of the personality of God. Jesus Himself said, "He who has seen Me has seen the Father."[1] If we want to know what God is like, we must learn what Jesus is like. If we want to erase our distortions about God the Father, we must begin by studying Jesus.

Third, *distortions never begin with the Bible*. The Bible is the inspired Word of God, and it is God's revelation of Himself to us. Some people derive distorted impressions of God from their reading of the Bible, but those distorted impressions arise because of

44

human limitation, human misunderstanding, and even human willfulness—our tendency to read into the Scriptures and twist them to support our own prejudices and wishes. Distortions may begin with *our misinterpretation* of the Bible but never with the Bible itself.

Having looked at three sources where distortions in our image of God *do not* originate, let's examine situations and experiences that *do* cause distortions.

Seven Hidden Sources of Distortion

Distortions about God seem to creep into our minds and emotions without our awareness, like thieves entering a house in the dead of night. Where do these distortions come from? As I have conducted my research, studied the research of others, and counseled scores of people in my practice, I have identified seven hidden sources of these treacherous distortions that steal into our image of God: (1) the intergenerational cycle, (2) attribution, (3) parental projections, (4) self-projections, (5) object relationships, (6) personality, and (7) early religious training and experiences. Let's examine each in turn.

1. The Intergenerational Cycle

Many distortions actually have their beginnings many years or even generations before we were born. We inherit misconceptions about God from our parents, grandparents, and great-grandparents. Sometimes parents and grandparents pass down the *form* of their religion—the rules, the rituals, the legalistic formulas—without any spiritual reality.

Carrie Bishop, the woman who was incestuously abused by her father and emotionally abused by her mother, recalls that her grandmother was a religious woman who attempted to pass down the form of her religious beliefs. "My grandmother taught me the Ten Commandments," Carrie told me. "I was about nine years old at the time, and Grandma had come to stay with us a couple of weeks. She got me to recite all ten of them without a hitch, even though I didn't have a clue what 'Thou shalt not commit adultery' means. Grandma told me if I broke any of those commandments, God would be mad at me. 'He's everywhere, He sees everything, and He won't let any sin go unpunished,' she said.

"The constant fighting and abuse in my home made the little smattering of religion my mother and grandmother taught me seem so unreal and shallow. I saw the commandments my grandmother taught me being broken every single day. By the time I left home at age seventeen, God didn't mean anything to me. Going to Sunday school and saying prayers and memorizing commandments were just kid stuff.

"I didn't have any use for God until my life hit bottom. I had to go through all that misery—having all those affairs and abortions, being raped at knifepoint, getting hooked on Valium™ and booze—before I recognized my need of God. The little bit of religion I got from my grandmother and my mother—those little memorized prayers and stuff—had no power to change my life. Only a real relationship with Jesus Christ could take me out of the mess I was in."

Carrie is living proof that intergenerational distortions about God do not have to continue, generation after generation. We *can* break the cycle. We can find healing in our image of God, and we can pass a truer, more realistic image of God along to our children than the distorted image we received.

"Now I'm a mother," says Carrie. "I do a lot of things wrong with my son, Jeremy. But I do a lot more *right* things than my parents used to."

Rick Hanks is also breaking the intergenerational cycle of pain, abuse, and religious distortions that his father inflicted on him. He and his wife, Jennie, have two children, an eight-year-old son and a four-year-old daughter.

"The only way my father ever disciplined was with anger and physical pain," he recalls. "That's why I made a commitment never to discipline my children when I'm angry. I have to admit that I've failed that commitment more than once, but keeping that goal before me—never discipline in anger—has made me a better father than I otherwise would have been. If one of my kids does something that makes me mad, I try to wait till I've calmed down, then I ask God how my heavenly Father would discipline the child. I usually find some other form of discipline besides spanking—time out in the corner or on the bed or the loss of some privilege.

"Another thing my parents did was teach us kids to recite little canned prayers like, 'God is great, God is good,' and 'Now I lay me down to sleep.' They never explained anything. They just made us memorize a bunch of words. I remember being real scared by the line that said, 'If I should die before I wake, I pray the Lord my soul to take.' It gave me chills. I remember picturing God as a big black shadow that might come into my room without warning and take my soul in the middle of the night.

"Jennie and I have never taught our kids to memorize their prayers. I tell them to just talk to God, to say anything they feel like saying. So my daughter, Kerri, says, 'Thank You, God, for my roller skates and my dolls.' And Caleb says, 'Thank You, God, for this dinner, even though the peas are yucky.' I tell my kids about a God who loves and forgives. They're building a real relationship with the same loving Father I'm still learning to know."

2. Attribution

All of us make assessments about who God is based on the experiences we go through and the events we witness. It is natural that we attribute the causes of many of these experiences and events to God. If a loved one dies, we may ask, Why did God take my loved one? When a typhoon kills thousands in Bangladesh or a plane crash kills hundreds on a mountainside, we may ask, How could God cause that or allow that to happen? If we suffer a severe financial setback, we may ask, Why is God punishing me?

That's the question Nick asked me. A lean, hard-muscled health club instructor, he told me he had been angry with God ever since his father died of a heart attack when Nick was nine years old. "I never told anyone this before," he said, "but I've had a grudge against God ever since I stood at that graveside and watched my father being lowered into the ground in a box. After my dad died, I used to sit in Sunday school and church, and whenever anyone talked about the love of God, I'd think, *man, what a lot of lies!*"

Nick was twenty-eight years old when I first met him. He had been married five years earlier. "On the day Renee and I were married," he said, "I remember thinking, *At last! My life is finally coming together!* The cosmic joke was on me, man."

The night Nick and Renee returned from their honeymoon on Grand Cayman Island, before they had even unpacked their bags, Nick got an urgent phone call. His only brother had just been killed in a head-on collision.

A few months later, Nick's mother learned she had terminal cancer. Before a year had passed, she was dead.

The last straw—and the event that brought Nick to the Minirth-Meier Clinic for counseling—took place in a convenience store a few blocks from Nick and Renee's apartment. "I had gone out to pick up a few things," he said. "Sodas and a newspaper, stuff like that. I was at the counter paying for the stuff when these two guys came in with guns and held up the place. These guys didn't know that the cops had the place staked out—the store had been knocked over several times before. In a few seconds, the place was swarming with police.

"These two creeps grabbed me and the clerk. They held us hostage for about forty-five minutes. One of them jammed this big .45 under my chin, pointed right at my brain, for three-quarters of an hour. I just knew it was all over. I prayed and prayed, but I knew it wouldn't do any good. That was just the capper in a series of sick jokes God had been playing on me."

Police negotiators finally got the gunmen to give up their hostages. Nick was set free. But for a long time, he continued to be a hostage to fear, anger, and vivid nightmares. His bitterness toward God reached an all-time high. It was about two months after the episode in the convenience store when Nick came to the clinic.

"God is the Terminator, Dr. Stephens," he said as he sat in my office. "God is the Hangman. Everyone I love, God takes away. He's not fair. He's not loving. He's a cosmic practical joker with a sadistic sense of humor."

If we were in Nick's shoes, you and I might feel very much the same—at least for a time, until we were able to gain a different perspective on our trials. The fact is, the Bible depicts God as loving and good. Biblically, the evil, pain, and suffering we experience in this life are attributable not to God but to the influence of Satan in a fallen world.

What, then, should we attribute to God, according to the Bible? All that is good in our lives, from our most exhilarating joys to the simplest pleasures of a warm, sunny day.

Most of us, however, tend to attribute *both* positive and negative experiences to God, even though the Bible firmly declares that God loves us and everything He does in our lives is good. There are psychological as well as spiritual reasons why we attribute both good and bad experiences to God. By making God the One to praise in the good times and blame in the bad times, we feel that we can somehow maintain a measure of control over our world.

In times of tragedy, *why* is almost always the first word from our mouths. Believing that there is a reason for everything that happens in the world—even if it is a reason we do not understand, a reason known only to God—enhances our sense of security.

Either because of a desire to blame God for the painful experiences of our lives or because of an inadequate understanding of Scripture, some of us interpret the Bible so that it seems to make God the author of evil events. For example, some people read 1 Peter 1:6–7—which encourages Christians to view trials as a test of "the genuineness of your faith, being much more precious than gold"—then say, "You see? It says right here that God is testing me!" Of course, that's not at all what the passage says. God does not send trials to us; rather, trials are an inevitable part of life, for Christians and non-Christians alike. The point of the passage is that we should *view* and *use* our trials as tests of our faith— not to prove our faith to God (He already knows us better than we know ourselves) but to demonstrate *to ourselves* the strength and durability of our faith.

We can be confident about this: *nowhere in the Bible are we told that God inflicts pain and suffering on His people.* But when suffering comes, says the Bible, God is able to *transform* that suffering into something good, something more precious than gold. That is precisely the point of a key passage on the subject of attributing experiences to God:

> And we know that all things work together for good to those who love God, to those who are the called according to His purpose.

For whom He foreknew, He also predestined to be conformed to the image of His Son, that He might be the firstborn among many brethren.[2]

In other words, God has a purpose for all the things that happen to us, good or bad, happy or sad. And His ultimate purpose for us is that we be "conformed to the image" of Christ—that is, that our character and nature be gradually molded and shaped to resemble the character and nature of Jesus Himself.

Attribution, then, is not always a problem for our image of God. When we make healthy and positive attributions to God, we demonstrate a healthy image of God. We *should* attribute blessings to God, as in the words of the doxology: "Praise God, from whom all blessings flow." When problems or trials come into our lives, a biblical attitude holds that "God did not cause this problem or trial, but I know He can use it to refine me and make me more like His Son, Jesus."

Attribution becomes a source of distortion in our image of God when we blame God for negative events and experiences in our lives. It is a *false attribution* when we say, "God makes me afraid," because the Bible tells us God does not give us a spirit of fear.[3] It is a *false attribution* when we blame God for confusion in our lives because the Bible tells us God is not the author of confusion.[4] It is a *false attribution* when we ascribe vindictiveness or a sadistic nature to God because God is gentle, loving, and patient; the Bible tells us Satan is a roaring lion, seeking victims to devour.[5] Whenever we blame God for events not in His will and for which He is not responsible, we make a false attribution.

A paradox is at work in the world. God is sovereign and in ultimate control. However, many things that happen in the world do not happen according to His will. The key to this paradox is *human free will*.

We saw a prime example of this paradox at work in the life of Carrie Bishop. Her father sexually abused her, and her mother psychologically abused her. It was not God's will that the parents behave in such a sinful way toward their daughter. They did so because they had *free will*.

I have counseled many people who have been abused as Carrie was. Their response to that abuse usually takes one of two forms: (1) "God let that happen to me; God is responsible for my suffering"; (2) "An abusive person did that to me, and God is now using that terrible experience in my life to help me grow and rely on Him more." Here are two forms of attribution. The first blames God for the bad experience. The second credits God for taking the bad experience and transforming it into more Christlike character, as Romans 8:28–29 advises us.

In the case of sexual abuse such as Carrie experienced, we can recognize several things to be true:

- God loves all children. It is not His will for children to be hurt and abused.
- God has given parents the responsibility to love and nurture their children. It is not His will for parents to abuse their children.
- When bad things happen to children, it does not mean that God caused or willed those events or that God does not love these children.
- God promises to help us through our suffering but not to remove us from all suffering.
- God gives all people free will, and free will entails the power to sin and to violate God's will—including the power to hurt other people.
- God is ultimately in control of the world, even though He has not exercised His control to nullify the free will of those who have hurt us or to protect us from being abused and mistreated by evil people and evil circumstances. We do not understand how God can be in control and still allow bad things to happen to us. But we trust God, knowing that someday we will understand, because His ways are different from our ways, and His ways are just and righteous.

If we want to heal our image of God, we must learn to allow our attribution to be guided by God's Word. That is the lesson Lisa is continuing to learn, day by day, in the aftermath of the traffic accident that took her husband, Eric, out of her life. Today, she is at a different place than she was just six months after the accident, when she said, "All I know is, God could have prevented the accident and He didn't. . . . And I hold God responsible."

Today, Lisa says, "After the accident I spent a lot of time wrestling with God—screaming at Him, to tell you the truth. I read the

51

Bible a lot while I was in bed, twisted with back pain. One time I was so mad at God I actually threw my Bible across the room!

"But as I kept reading, I came across all the stories that I already knew but had never really thought about—Christians who were stoned, beaten, butchered; families torn apart; people put in prison for their faith. The more I thought about it, the more I realized that being a Christian is not a guarantee against tragedy. It just means we have a Friend who will take us through the tragedy and bring us safely to the other side."

Like Lisa, my friend Nick—the young man who called God the Terminator—was able to experience healing in his image of God. It was not an overnight event but a gradual process, involving months of counseling and committed, courageous effort on Nick's part.

During Nick's counseling visits, we focused a lot of attention on his feelings about the loss of his father, his mother, and his brother. We talked a lot about his attributing the losses to God. Nick came to the realization that he could never enjoy a secure and satisfied life as long as he blamed God for the tragedies, as long as he persisted in seeing God as his enemy.

"You know, Dr. Stephens," Nick said recently, "I told you how I prayed to God when those hoods shoved a gun at my throat in that convenience store."

"You said you felt God wasn't listening to you."

"Yeah. But I've been thinking. I mean, before that happened, I never would have thought I could sweat out forty-five minutes at the wrong end of a gun. But I made it. Maybe God was listening after all. Maybe I made it through that experience because He was with me. And maybe God is the reason I made it through all the other losses I've had without blowing my brains out. I thought of it, you know."

"You thought of what?"

"Suicide. But I'm okay now. Maybe I'm even learning to trust God a little bit." Nick grinned as he said that.

I think he's right.

3. Parental Projections

Brent sat in my office and described his father as unemotional, undemonstrative, and distant. "My dad never had much to say to me," he told me, "unless he got really mad." Later in our conversation, I asked Brent to describe how he pictured God. "I see God," he said, "as an old man sitting on the porch. He doesn't do anything. He doesn't say anything—unless you do something wrong and make Him mad."

"Do you notice," I asked him, "how much your description of God sounds like your description of your dad?"

He seemed startled and opened his mouth to object. Then he said, "You know, I think you're right."

Brent had the same problem that Rick Hanks and Carrie Bishop had. All three had images of God that were shaped by parental projections. Brent's image of God as distant, ineffectual, and sometimes volatile was a mirror reflection of his father's image. Rick Hanks had a father who was a saint in public and a monster in the home—and that engendered an image of God as being two-sided and phony. Carrie's abusive parents led her to see God as an abuser. Brent, Rick, and Carrie are typical of people who project the image of their parents onto their image of God.

All of us, to some degree, derive part of our image of God from our parents. In other words, we project our mental-emotional image of our parents onto God like a movie projector projects a picture onto a movie screen. If you had a warm, secure, nurturing relationship with your parents, you are more likely to have a warm, secure, nurturing relationship with God. If your relationship with your parents was bitter, painful, and stormy, your relationship with God will likely reflect that state.

Our image of God may be a projection of our father image, our mother image, the image of our preferred parent, or the image of another significant caregiver in our lives. Having counseled hundreds of people who struggle with distortions in their image of God, I am convinced that the most significant parental projection in most people's lives is that of their *father*. Other adult figures certainly have an influence on the image of God in positive and negative ways, but the father seems to hold the key to the developing mind of a child when it comes to shaping that child's image of God.

From a biblical perspective, God has placed the primary leadership responsibility for the family on the shoulders of the father. But even more than that, God has placed on fathers the responsibility to *model godly character* to their children, and to raise their children to be emotionally healthy rather than filled with anger and bitterness: "And you, fathers, do not provoke your children to wrath, but bring them up in the training and admonition of the Lord."[6]

Though the father's role in shaping children's image of God is boldy underscored in Scripture, the mother's role is significant too. The capacity for trust and security is first molded in infancy, in a mother's arms and at a mother's breast. The way a mother responds to her babies has a powerful influence on their sense of safety and inner peace—an early representation to them of God's love and nurturing care.

Popular singer Amy Grant credits her parents for shaping a positive image of God in her life. Her biographer, Bob Millard, writes that Amy's parents "lavished love and attention on their youngest daughter, instilling in her a tremendous sense of self-worth." Amy agrees. "My family made me feel so confident," she told a television interviewer.[7]

Amy's parents created a home environment, says Millard, where "a strong sense of God [was] an integral part of their family and individual lives." Amy's mother, Gloria, recalls,

> We read Bible stories to our children from the time they were a year old. We had Bible verses and Bible songs at the breakfast table, but we never had a strict situation that would make them rebel against it. What we wanted most to instill in our girls was for each of them to have a desire to know God through His Son, Jesus Christ, and to have a personal relationship with Him. All we could do was plant this desire. You can't make people do things.[8]

In my research, I found that one of the most crucial factors in a healthy image of God is the consistent experience in childhood of unconditional love and nurturing from parents or other primary caregivers. In other words, if we, like Amy Grant, had parents who were positive, affirming, and nurturing—parents who built our sense of self-worth and made us feel confident and loved—our parental projections onto God's image will tend to be accurate and consistent with who God really is. However, those of us whose parents *failed* to model God's loving and accepting nature will be much more likely to suffer a distorted image of God.

That's the bad news. But the good news is that even if we experienced unloving or ungodly parenting as children, we can still find healing in our image of God. We will explore ways to be healed in our relationship with God—and to literally be *reparented by God*—in Chapter 8.

4. Self-Projections

Most of us, to some degree, also derive part of our image of God from our self-image. Thus, a person who is very intellectually inclined will tend to see God as a vast cosmic intellect. An emotional person will probably see Him as a being filled with feelings and passions. A very demanding, perfectionist person will tend to see God as strict, critical, and judgmental. A tenderhearted person will likely see God as gracious and tolerant.

In a 1989 study, psychologist Carl Roberts found many examples of self-projection in the people he interviewed. He divided God's attributes into two categories: *nurturing* and *disciplining*. Then he conducted tests to compare people's image of God with their self-image. He found that people who pictured God as nurturing tended to describe themselves with similar adjectives: *gentle, tender, supportive, compassionate, caring, loving.* Roberts also found that women are more likely than men to perceive God as nurturing.[9]

A by-product of self-projection is that we confuse the way we feel about ourselves with the way God feels toward us. We human beings have a tendency to project our feelings about ourselves onto other people in such a way that we believe that *they feel about us the same way we feel about ourselves.* For example, if you consider yourself overweight, you may see someone looking at you and think, *That person is thinking about how fat I am!* In reality, that person may be admiring your eyes or daydreaming or reading the sign behind you.

We often make the same mistake with God. One researcher found a definite correlation between the degree to which we accept ourselves and the degree to which we see God as accepting and loving.[10] For example, a person with low self-esteem, who sees himself as shameful or bad or unworthy, will tend to believe that God also views him as shameful, bad, or unworthy. It is a dynamic I have seen scores of times in my counseling office.

We think that the way we see ourselves *must* be the way God sees us. But that is not true. If we have received Jesus Christ as our Savior and the Lord of our lives, God the Father does not see our guilt or shame. The righteousness of Jesus Christ is our covering. Even if we *feel* ashamed, God says, "I forgive you." Even if we *feel* unworthy, God says, "You are My child and a coheir of My kingdom with My Son Jesus." Even if we hate ourselves, God says, "I love you unconditionally."

With these truths as our foundation, we must begin the task of bringing our view of ourselves into alignment with the way God sees us. In partnership with our loving heavenly Father, we must begin the work of rebuilding a healthy sense of self-esteem. As our self-image heals, one more distortion in our image of God will fall away.

The person who feels confident and good about himself will tend to believe God feels the same way—not that this person will strut around popping his buttons and saying, "What a wonderful person I am!" Rather, in Christian humility, with full awareness of his sin and fallibility, he will raise his head high and say, "Praise God! I am forgiven! My sins are remembered no more!"

Clearly, restoring your self-image is a crucial step in restoring your image of God. How, then, do you go about restoring your image of yourself?

First, to restore your self-image, you must have a self. That may sound absurdly redundant, but it is really quite profound. You must have some idea of *who* you are seeking to esteem. So how do you determine who you are?

The Bible affirms that we are created in God's image. So you are a reflection of God—an imperfect reflection as a result of sin, but still there is something of God's image remaining in you. Once you have joined yourself to God through faith in Jesus Christ, you have His Spirit living in you and you can relate to God through your ability to think and feel and communicate with Him. To find the self that is worth esteeming, you must start with *who you are in Christ.*

Second, to restore your self-image, you must make a committed decision that you will *accept yourself* and *love yourself unconditionally.* Accept all your positive traits and abilities—and accept that you have negative traits and weaknesses as well. Having negative traits does not make you a bad person. Those traits simply mean you are human.

Certainly, you should seek, with God's help, to eliminate harmful habits and stubborn sins. But don't hate yourself for negative traits. Instead, love yourself unconditionally, even as you hate the sin. Love yourself so much that you want to continually purify this wonderful person God has made you to be. Your body is the dwelling place of the Holy Spirit, and you *choose* not to dishonor God or His dwelling place with self-hatred.

Learn to see yourself as God sees you: not perfect but forgiven. God created you, and He gave His Son to die for you so that you could be saved. God does not make mistakes. His unconditional love for you is the reason you can freely and unconditionally love yourself.

Third, recognize that any shame within you is *unhealthy* shame. God never intended for you to carry a load of shame. That is what forgiveness is all about: the complete annihilation of guilt, the utter obliteration of shame. Make a decision that you will take those feelings of shame, tie them up in a bundle, and shove them outside the door of yourself. Shame has no place within the temple of the Holy Spirit.

Fourth, *take inventory* of all the negative messages circulating within your thinking and your emotions. They include negative messages you received from parents, teachers, siblings, peers, or others. They even include messages you have generated within yourself—messages that decrease your self-worth and your capacity to love yourself as God intends you to. Here are examples of negative messages:

- "I'm bad. I'm shameful. I'm hopeless. I never do anything right."
- "That's just my luck. God is through with me."
- "I'll never change. I'm so stupid. No one loves me. I hate myself."
- "I never should have been born. Things will never get better. God put me in the wrong family."
- "God just wants to hurt me. Everything's against me. I'm doomed. I'm a loser. Everything's hopeless."

I've met and counseled many people who felt these feelings

and carried these messages around inside them. But I've never known even one person for whom these messages were true. Whatever negative messages *you* are listening to right now, I want you to know that *they are false messages.* Psychologists call these messages negative self-talk, and it's time for you to toss out all that false, defeatist self-talk. If you have committed your life to Jesus Christ, all of these statements apply to you. Saturate your mind and emotions with God's truth about who you *really* are in Christ and how God *really* sees you. Here are a few examples of *positive* self-talk, taken directly from God's Word (be prepared for a long list—God really thinks you're special!):

- I am the apple of my Father's eye (Ps. 17:8).
- I am loved with an everlasting love (Jer. 31:3).
- I am the salt of the earth and the light of the world (Matt. 5:13–14).
- I have everlasting life (John 6:47).
- I am set free (John 8:31–33).
- I have abundant life (John 10:10).
- I am a saint (Rom. 1:7).
- I am dead to sin (Rom. 6:2, 11).
- I am free of shame and condemnation (Rom. 8:1).
- I am a joint heir with Christ (Rom. 8:17).
- I am being changed and conformed to the image of Christ (Rom. 8:28–29; Phil. 1:6).
- I am a superconqueror through Christ (Rom. 8:37).
- I am the temple of the Holy Spirit (1 Cor. 6:19).
- I am a new creation (2 Cor. 5:17).
- I am reconciled to God (2 Cor. 5:18).
- I am holy and without blame before God (Eph. 1:4).
- I am accepted in Christ (Eph. 1:6).
- I am forgiven; all my sins are washed away (Eph. 1:7).
- I am sealed by the Holy Spirit (Eph. 1:13).
- I am alive with Christ (Eph. 2:5).
- I am God's workmanship (Eph. 2:10).
- I am strong in the Lord (Eph. 6:10).
- I have the peace of God, which surpasses understanding (Phil. 4:7).
- I can do all things through Christ (Phil. 4:13).

- I am complete in Christ (Col. 2:10).
- I am raised up with Christ and seated in the heavenly places (Col. 2:12).
- I am beloved and chosen by God (Col. 3:12; 1 Thess. 1:4).
- I have been called by God (2 Tim. 1:9).
- I am God's forever-child (1 Peter 1:23).
- I am healed by the wounds of Christ (1 Peter 2:24).
- I have overcome the world (1 John 5:4).
- I am victorious (Rev. 21:7).

Here's a practical suggestion: photocopy these positive self-talk statements and put them in your Bible, notebook, or journal. Every morning and evening, have a Bible study and prayer time—a quiet time alone with God. Read these statements aloud during your quiet time. You may also find it helpful to put these affirming statements on your bathroom mirror, your refrigerator door, or your desk blotter at work. Remind yourself often throughout the day of God's truth about you. Refer to them whenever you are tempted to be down on yourself.

Understand, of course, that these statements are *not a substitute* for your quiet time. They are simply a brief yet powerful exercise you add to your quiet time with God. Let me list four reasons Christians should have a daily quiet time with God:

1. To enjoy God's company and cultivate a warm friendship with our heavenly Father.

2. To set aside uninterrupted quality time to listen to what God has to say to us through His Word and His Holy Spirit.

3. To share with God our needs and to ask Him for His strength and help to meet the challenges of our lives.

4. To immerse our minds in God's healing truth about Himself, about ourselves, and about our relationship with Him.

I would also encourage you (perhaps as part of your daily quiet time) to look up and read the Scripture passage cited after each self-talk statement listed. Read, in God's words, what He says about you. Remember that God promises

> My word . . . shall not return to Me void,
> But it shall accomplish what I please,
> And it shall prosper in the thing for which I sent it.[11]

Our goal is to saturate our minds with God's healing truth

about His great love for us. I urge you to faithfully meet God in prayer and in His Word for at least a half hour a day (fifteen minutes in the morning, fifteen minutes in the evening). I am convinced that if you do so every day for the next thirty days, you will begin to find many of your old negative self-talk messages being replaced by the healing truth about yourself, which is found throughout God's Word, and you will have made a great start toward a lifelong habit of daily fellowship with God.

5. Object Relationships

Object relationships have far-reaching implications for our image of God. As infants, we knew our parents not as persons but as objects. Prior to about the age of two, children do not have a concept of people, parents, or God. Their world consists of objects that they "internalize." To internalize means to keep a sense or feeling of an object within oneself. An example will clarify this idea.

When a baby cries, you can pick her up, meet her needs, hold her, speak soothingly to her—and the crying will cease. During this process, the baby will perceive you as a warm and nurturing object, will absorb the sensations from you—your touch, your soothing voice, your eye communication—and will internalize these sensations as a feeling of warmth and security. You can then set the baby down in her cradle and walk away—and the baby will continue to be contented.

Why doesn't that baby immediately start to scream when you set her down? Because that baby has internalized you. She keeps the emotional sensations of your touch, your voice, and your caring within herself. If that baby were unable to internalize you as an object of caring and nurturing, she would scream twenty-four hours a day because she would never feel any peace or security. If we did not internalize our parents as objects, we could not emotionally survive the developmental stage of infancy.

In a similar way, many people have trouble internalizing God as an object of security and nurturing. They cannot emotionally trust God. They cannot sense His presence.

The basic foundations of emotional trust are laid down in the first two years of life. During those first two years, we learn to count on our primary objects (first, parents; later, God) to meet our needs. Some people, however, because of neglect, abuse, abandonment, or the loss of parents, may not have experienced a sufficient degree of internalizing of parental nurturing and love. They have grown up without the security and warmth God intended them to have. The distrust and distortion some people experience in their relationship with God can be traced to distorted object relationships with parental figures in early childhood.

So, for example, if a parent does not hold baby Johnny when he cries, John will grow up unable to feel the joy and contentment of God's internal presence. His distortion: "God is not here. He doesn't hear me when I call Him."

Or, for example, if baby Susie was separated from her parents because of death or abandonment, the adult Susan may fear God's abandonment or even feel that God abandoned her long ago. Her distortion: "I don't know if I can trust God. I don't know if He will always be there for me."

It is easy to understand how, in some cases, distortions in our image of God may be the result of problems in our object relationships. God is not tangible, not visible. If we are unable to internalize God in our minds and emotions, He will seem absent, neglectful, or nonexistent to us. We are much like the baby in the cradle: perhaps at some time in our lives, we have been held, nurtured, and soothed by God, but we failed to internalize Him. Now we do not see Him or feel Him, and we feel God is not there. It is as if He has walked away from our cradle, and we feel alone and insecure.

But God is not only nearby, He is within us if we have committed our lives to Him by faith in Jesus Christ. As with the distortions that arise from imperfect parental projections, object relationship distortions can be healed by a process of being *reparented by God*. We will explore ways of building a new Parent-child relationship with God in Chapter 8.

6. Personality

We all tend to make assessments about who God is based on the makeup of our individual personalities. Simply stated, personality consists of mind, emotion, and will. Each of us has a distinct and unique personality or psychological makeup. These examples of personality types show how personality can profoundly affect our image of God:

The obsessive-compulsive personality   This personality type is characterized by uncompromising views, perfectionism, constant doubting, drivenness, and an obsession with analysis and strict moral standards. The obsessive-compulsive person may experience recurring unpleasant thoughts and feelings of anxiety.

Obsessive-compulsive persons tend to doubt their salvation, fret over the possibility that God has abandoned them, and obsess over their salvation until they finally gain reassurance. After a while, that sense of reassurance will evaporate, and the doubting cycle will begin all over again. Such people are likely to see God as a demanding parent, expecting perfection.

The histrionic personality   In many ways, this personality type (also called the hysterical personality) is the opposite of the obsessive-compulsive type. These individuals are emotional, dramatic, extroverted, and impulsive.

The histrionic personality may experience an unstable on-again, off-again relationship with God. This relationship may be based on the individual's moment-to-moment feelings rather than on a foundation of faith and biblical promises. When a histrionic person's emotional state is bright and positive, God is a close, warm, nurturing friend. When that same person becomes angry or depressed, those feelings of anger are often turned toward God.

The paranoid personality   This personality type is characterized by an exaggerated sense of self-reference—that is, a sense that "everything that happens is directed at me." This individual will tend to interpret all remarks, actions, and events as personal threats. This person will tend to see God as untrustworthy, hostile, and threatening in a way that is directed specifically toward him. This person may be wary and skeptical in her approach to God, feeling that "God is out to get me."

The independent personality   This personality type is characterized by an excessive resentment of control by authority figures. The independent personality may tend to see God—the ultimate Authority Figure—as too controlling or intrusive.

The dependent personality   People with this type of personality exhibit a continual childlike desire to have others provide for them, make decisions for them, set their boundaries, and meet their needs. Such people tend to see God as an indulgent Father who does everything for them. If they discover that they have to take some major step in life on their own initiative, or if they are disappointed to discover that God doesn't simply hand everything to them as they demand, they will likely view God as a neglectful parent.

The borderline personality   This type of personality exhibits instability in various ares, such as behavior, mood, relationships, and self-image. This person will tend to vacillate between dependent and independent struggles with God. In the mind and emotions of the borderline individual, the image of God will seesaw between invisible/absent/neglectful and intrusive/overprotective.

The avoidant personality   This personality type avoids people, situations, and relationships. These individuals may avoid God and may also see God as an avoider. "God is like everyone else in my life," they might say. "When I need Him, He is not there."

The neurotic personality   Neurotic people experience a great deal of anxiety and the symptoms that accompany anxiety. Neurotic persons are in touch with reality but tend to reshape memories, beliefs, and experiences in ways that will reduce the level of anxiety. Thus, neurotic persons will tend to fashion whatever image of God will reduce the anxiety level or give them a sense of control over life experiences.

7. Early Religious Training and Experiences

Without question, our image of God is founded in large part on what we are taught as children in church, Sunday school, parochial school, catechism, and the home. Our early instruction can have both positive and negative effects on our relationship with God.

Kevin was a P.K.—a preacher's kid—so you would think he would have had every opportunity to build up a positive, biblically based image of God during his education and early learning. Tragically, that was not the case.

"My dad always told us, 'God's judgment is sure and swift,'" Kevin recalled during our second or third session together. "'Be sure your sins will find you out.' That was one of my dad's favorite sayings. I grew up in constant terror of a demanding, perfectionist God. I always felt like I was walking on eggshells around God— and crunching those eggshells with big clumsy galoshes.

"I continually wondered, 'Do I believe the right things? If I misinterpret the Bible in this point or that, will God take away my salvation? Will I make a mistake that will send me to hell and never even know what I did wrong?' I even pictured God *allowing* me to make mistakes because He *wanted* to punish Me!

"Ever since I was a kid, I've been afraid to read my Bible. I think it goes back to the teaching I had in church and Sunday school. The more I heard about God, the more scared I was of Him, and the less I wanted to find out about Him."

Our early spiritual training and religious experiences are basic to the development of our image of God. Religious experiences may be understood as those involving the worship of God and learning about God—attending church and Sunday school, reading the Bible, having family devotions, and so forth. Spiritual experiences may be understood as those experiences of God that are more intimate and affect the emotions—praying and meditating, feeling God's love in one's heart, having empathy for another person who is hurting and loving that person, being ministered to by someone when you are in spiritual need.

Early spiritual and religious experiences do not absolutely determine a person's image of God throughout life. Some people, even though raised in homes with very little spiritual reality or religious training, encounter influences in life that shape a strong, positive image of God in their minds and hearts. Others, though raised with good Christian parenting and teaching, encounter experiences along the road of life that create distortions in their image of God.

As a general principle, however, the more a person is exposed to healthy Christian education in childhood, the better that person is enabled and equipped to grow spiritually, to grow in a true understanding of God, and to grow in an intimate relationship with God. Positive, biblical teaching is a strong foundation upon which a child can build a healthy image of God that will endure a lifetime.

Please note that I have carefully qualified the kind of early religious and spiritual instruction I am talking about here: *positive* Christian teaching and experiences. *Negative* religious teaching and experiences can be as harmful (and often *more* harmful) than no religious teaching at all! Of all the people I have counseled, the most tragic cases have tended to be those who were exposed to rigid legalism in their early religious life, as Kevin was. People from legalistic homes tend to have the most distorted images of God and the greatest struggles with such toxic emotions as shame, anger, fear, and anxiety.

People whose image of God is shaped by legalism must go through life on a straight and narrow path without the slightest tolerance for error, failure, or human frailty. They tend to see God as an unmerciful judge and a stern taskmaster. If they do not attain moral perfection, according to the strict demands of their legalistic beliefs, they fear God's wrath and judgment. They are unable to experience the full range of God's relational personality—His mercy, love, compassion, and empathy. They live in a spiritual and emotional prison of bondage, fear, and guilt.

As I have counseled with Kevin, I have seen a gradual change in him. He is beginning to see the God of the Bible in a different light—not as a demanding perfectionist but as a patient, loving, accepting Father, full of grace and mercy. Kevin has a long way to go, and the old image of God that was drummed into him during childhood continues to haunt him from time to time. But he is now able to read his Bible, and he enjoys studying God's Word with other Christians in a home Bible study group—something he never could have done just a few years ago.

Spiritual Contamination

Left untreated, distortions in our image of God lead to a condition I call spiritual contamination—a gradual process by which the purity of the spirit is diminished by false beliefs and tainted emotions. God has made it possible for each of us to remove those impurities from our image of Him, our beliefs about Him, and our emotions toward Him. As we are encouraged in Scripture, "Let us cleanse [or purify] ourselves from all filthiness [or impurities] of the flesh and spirit, perfecting holiness" out of reverence for God.[12]

Our goal is to replace those thoughts, feelings, and behaviors that hinder our relationship with God—loneliness, depression, anxiety, worry, impatience, bitterness, isolation—with the thoughts, feelings, and behaviors guided by the Holy Spirit and listed in Galatians 5 as "the fruit of the Spirit." The following chart compares the fruit of the Spirit with the effects of spiritual contamination and shows how distortions in our image of God keep us from the spiritual vitality God intended for us.

When our bodies are overcome by disease, we become physically weak, immobilized, and dysfunctional. We experience pain. We can even die. But once the right medicine is administered, we feel better and stronger. We feel renewed and refreshed. What a great feeling to rise up from a sickbed and say, "Oh, yes! I think I'm over it!"

Spiritual contamination acts much like a physical disease. It makes us feel spiritually weak and sick. It can cause us spiritual and emotional pain and lead to doubts about God. It desensitizes us to the Holy Spirit so that we can no longer feel His presence or hear Him speaking to us. It can leave us spiritually crippled.

But it doesn't have to. Jean's story proves that it is possible, even after many years of living with a tainted spirit, to be cleansed from everything that contaminates the body and spirit.

The Fruit of Your Image of God

The Fruit of the Spirit (Galatians 5:22–23)	The Fruit of Spiritual Contamination (a Distorted Image of God)
Love	Loneliness/Isolation
Joy	Depression
Peace	Anxiety
Longsuffering (Patience/Endurance)	Worry/Impatience
Kindness	Bitterness
Goodness	Resentment
Faithfulness	Distrustfulness/Doubt
Gentleness	Uncaring/Callousness
Self-Control	Self-Centeredness/ Willfulness

A Lifetime without Tears

Jean was the woman most people in the church tried to avoid. She had a tongue like coarse sandpaper. The hard lines of her face sketched an eloquent portrait of her flinty legalistic heart. Jean had been a pillar in the church (some called her a boss) for over thirty years—about as long as her husband had been dead.

In that time, five different pastors had come and gone, and she had terrorized and intimidated each one. Jean had the power to intimidate because she had a lot of money, and she used her money to get her way.

A few years ago, something happened that precipitated a crisis in Jean's life: Rev. Robert Grayson arrived and took over as pastor of the church. Jean quickly found that Pastor Grayson could not be intimidated like his predecessors. When he didn't kowtow to her wishes regarding the new forms of music in the worship service, she hinted that her generosity had provided the organ in the sanctuary.

"And a very beautiful organ it is," Pastor Grayson replied, smiling. "Of course, it's the Lord's organ now, just as the guitar Keith Smith played last Sunday is the Lord's guitar. Both the organ and the guitar are used to make the Lord's music. I think that's a splendid arrangement, don't you?"

That infuriating man! thought Jean. *Our previous pastor would have backed down in an instant, yet Pastor Grayson doesn't even take the hint!* Jean resolved to make an appointment with Pastor Grayson and have it out. It was time he found out who the *real* power in the church was!

When she entered Pastor Grayson's office the following week, he greeted her warmly and took a seat across the coffee table from her. That caught her off guard. She was used to pastors who barricaded themselves from her by sitting behind the big walnut desk.

Pastor Grayson began by praying with her, thanking God for the years of generous service Jean had given to the church. Then he took the lead in the conversation, asking her about herself, her late husband, her faith in Christ. Nearly an hour passed, and Jean realized she had done nothing but talk about herself! No one had ever asked her about herself before. In fact, no one had ever seemed as interested in her as Pastor Grayson did. She almost forgot that her original purpose in coming was to lay down the law to Pastor Grayson!

"So it was your mother who led you to the Lord," said Pastor Grayson. "How old were you then?"

"I was six. That was almost sixty years ago. Mother got tuberculosis and died just a few years later. My father had died when I was three, so I was left to be raised by a maiden aunt. I remember sitting by Aunt Louisa at my mother's graveside as she was laid to rest. I looked at that casket and thought about my poor mother having to be shut in that box and buried under the ground, and I began to cry. Aunt Louisa leaned over and whispered, 'Jean! You stop that sniffling right this instant!' So I stopped. I don't think I've shed a single tear since."

Just then, a large shiny tear rolled down her cheek. Then another. And another. And amid the flood of tears came a flood of emotions—emotions Jean had kept pent up for most of a lifetime. Pastor Grayson found that Jean had lived with severe depression most of her life. Her aunt had raised her in the stoic belief that emotions and inner pain should be hidden, never expressed; that suffering is a virtue and joy is a sin; that only "crazy" people seek counseling or psychological help. Pastor Grayson also learned that Jean felt abandoned and punished by God.

Today, Jean knows it's okay to talk about problems with a counselor. In fact, she's learning a great deal about why she has been so obsessed with legalism and so addicted to control. Many of her emotional hurts, she now realizes, are rooted in her experiences and religious training in early childhood.

Jean still has far to go. The patterns that have been built over the course of a lifetime cannot be dispelled overnight, but they *can* be changed

Jesus came that you and I might have life more abundantly. The Bible promises that we can have peace—secure, reliable inner peace—if only we can rebuild that trust relationship with God. "You will keep him in perfect peace," said the prophet Isaiah, "whose mind is stayed on You, *because he trusts in You*."[13] Throughout the rest of this book, we will look at practical strategies for rebuilding a trust relationship with God. We will discover the sources of God's *true* image, we will explore a practical strategy for spiritual decontamination, and we will learn how to overcome the obstacles to seeing His image clearly.

We will begin in the next chapter by examining the four distinct dimensions that make up our image of God.

PART THREE

Who Does God
Say He Is?

Chapter Five

The Four-Dimensional Image

arrie Bishop was born the fifth in a family of nine children. She had one older sister and one younger sister; the rest were brothers. "I remember very little about my mother when I was growing up," she recalled, "except an impression of her as being very cold and distant. I overheard her once, talking to my aunt. 'Carrie's not the child I wanted,' she said, 'She's not pretty like her sisters.' As I look back, I realize my mother must have been very emotionally ill. My older sister actually took care of me most of the time."

When I asked Carrie to describe her relationship with her father, she backed away from me in her chair, lowered her head, and began to rock back and forth in her chair like a small child. "I have memories of him that go back to when I was no more than five," she said. "Memories of being alone with him when he was going to the bathroom. Or the two of us taking a bath together. I didn't think there was anything wrong with it when I was real little, but what does a child know?

"By the time I was six, he began having sexual intercourse with me. I don't remember much about it, except that my father hurt me and told me I had to keep it a secret. He made me feel like I had done something terribly wrong, like it was my fault. I felt dirty and contaminated. I believed God was mad at me for what I had done with my daddy.

"I remember pleading to God for help. I felt like screaming inside. But my father continued abusing me. I wondered why God didn't answer my prayer. Didn't He care about me? If He cared, why would He let this awful thing go on?

"I couldn't reach out to my mother for help. She was completely cold and uncaring toward me—except when she was angry or out of control. I remember my mother and father fighting most of the time. They would scream, hit, and throw things. Several times my mother threw hot coffee or boiling water on my father, and sometimes she would chase him through the house with a big kitchen knife, swearing, 'I'll kill you! I'll kill you!'

"Every night, even if there had been one of those horrible knock-down-drag-out fights, my mother made all of us—including my father—get down on our knees and pray. It was so weird—our whole family screaming at one another by day and praying together by night.

"Sometimes my mother made the whole family go to church. But usually she had my older sister take me and the little ones to Sunday school. My mother talked a lot about believing in God, but most of her God-talk was about how God wouldn't love us if we did this sin or how He would punish us if we did that sin. I remember being scared of God. I was almost as scared of Him as I was of my mother and father.

"I can describe my childhood with four words: *guilt, pain, fear,* and *depression.* I remember having terrible migraine headaches when I was in elementary school. I thought of them as a punishment from God. I couldn't function in school. I colored all my coloring book pages black. I didn't have any friends.

"The incest stopped sometime before my ninth birthday. My father just quit paying attention to me. At first, I thought he was rejecting me because he was mad at me. But later I discovered that he had lost interest in me when he started sexually abusing my younger sister.

"About that time my older sister left home. My mother continued to be nonexistent as a mother, so I took my older sister's place as the caretaker of the family. I did the shopping, the cooking, the cleaning, and the laundry. I cared for my younger siblings, just as my older sister had taken care of me.

"Yet I felt I was failing God and not meeting my responsibilities. I thought I was responsible for all the problems in my family. I felt powerless to stop my father from abusing my little sister. By the time I was eleven, I was trying to reconcile my spiritual beliefs with all the abuse I was undergoing. I was afraid of this impatient, controlling, unmerciful God—yet on another level I felt I needed God. I wanted Him to love me."

The Hidden Sources of Our Image of God

Carrie grew up in a family where her mother made everyone pray every night. Her older sister took her to Sunday school every Sunday, and her mother sometimes took her to church. Yet how did she view God? As a punishing, impatient, controlling force. Her view of God was affected more by the twisted, punishing, controlling example set by her dysfunctional parents than by what she was taught in Sunday school.

Our image of God is dynamic. That is, it develops over a lifetime. It changes as we grow and go through new experiences. Sometimes our personal conception of God grows closer to His true image; sometimes it regresses and grows more distorted and confused. Though God and His love for us are constant and unchanging, we may experience God in a positive way at one time and a negative way at another.

For most of us, our understanding of who God is and how we relate to Him is largely established during childhood. Those childhood impressions of God can have a powerful hold on our adult lives, strongly influencing our decisions and our emotions for decades to come. We see this dynamic at work in Carrie's life.

Carrie left home at age seventeen, repressing the painful memories of her childhood. For many years after leaving home, she never entered a church, never opened a Bible, and never as much as whispered a prayer to God. She married before she was twenty, believing that marriage would fill the emptiness in her heart. But after her marriage, something snapped inside her. A burning anger that she had long repressed suddenly flared to the surface. She became obsessed with getting even with those she felt had hurt her or abandoned her—especially her parents and God.

Yet Carrie was really set on hurting herself. She repeatedly punished herself because she saw herself as bad, dirty, and contaminated—the poisonous emotional residue of the incest her father had inflicted on her, coupled with the abandonment and capricious rage she had experienced from her mother. She also punished herself because she felt that was what God wanted for her—continual punishment and suffering because she was bad.

The man Carrie married turned out to have many of the negative traits of both her parents. He was sexually abusive and self-centered like her father, as well as neglectful and volatile like her mother. She hoped that having a baby would cause her husband to be more gentle and caring. But after baby Jeremy was born, Carrie's husband became even more emotionally distant. He stayed out with his friends at night and sometimes came home as late as three or four in the morning. Sometimes he was drunk. Sometimes he beat her.

When Carrie realized that having a baby actually increased the strain on their rocky marriage, not made things better, she threw herself into a series of extramarital affairs in a desperate attempt to fill the emptiness of her heart.

Slim, blonde, and attractive, Carrie found it easy to attract men. For a while, the fact that men wanted her sexually gave her the illusion of being loved. At the same time, she could see that her life was coming apart at the seams. Several of her adulterous affairs resulted in pregnancies. Some of these pregnancies ended in deliberate abortions, some in spontaneous miscarriages.

Carrie's private hell did not end there. Driven by shame and resentment, she continued her self-destructive roller-coaster ride in even more dangerous forms of compulsive behavior. She abused Valium™ and alcohol. She placed herself in dangerous situations in seedy parts of town and was once raped at knifepoint. At one particularly low point in her emotional life, she was so full of self-hate that she compulsively mutilated herself to assuage her guilt.

The Four-Dimensional Image

Our image of God is not two-dimensional, like a flat picture. It is not even three-dimensional, like a sculpture. It is *multidimensional*. It is built up over many years from layer upon layer of experience, teaching, influences, study, and ideas. From my research and counseling with people, I have identified four fundamental dimensions of our image of God:

1. The intellectual dimension
2. The symbolic dimension

3. The spiritual dimension
4. The emotional dimension

Let's examine each one.

1. The Intellectual Dimension

The *intellectual dimension* of our image of God is the layer we are most aware of, the layer of our consciously held beliefs. The intellectual dimension is comprised of all the things we *think* about God—all the teaching we have received, all the doctrines we believe, all the concepts we have absorbed from reading the Bible and Christian books. As biblical Christians, we think of God as holy, just, loving, sovereign, and so forth.

As we've already seen, however, the intellectual dimension of our image of God is often at odds with the other dimensions (such as the emotional dimension). And the other dimensions are frequently much more powerful and have a greater influence on our behavior and our spiritual well-being.

2. The Symbolic Dimension

The *symbolic dimension* is a layer of our image of God that few of us stop to analyze. In this dimension, we associate Him with different word pictures. Some symbols are positive and derived from God's Word. For example, the Bible encourages us to picture God the Father or His Son Jesus in various symbolic terms. Here are some examples:

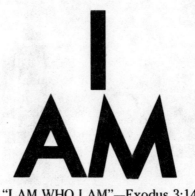

"I AM WHO I AM"—Exodus 3:14

The Creator—
Genesis 1–2; John 1:3

The Lamb of God—
John 1:29

The Savior—Luke 2:11

The Lion of Judah—Revelation 5:5

The Bread of Life—John 6:35

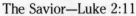

Eternal life—Romans 6:23

The Light of the World—
John 8:12

The Word of God—
John 1:1; Revelation 19:13

The Vine—John 15:5

The Provider—Genesis 22:14

King of kings—1 Timothy 6:15

The Door—John 10:9

The Morning Star—
Revelation 22:16

The Alpha and the Omega—
Revelation 1:8

THE LORD
OUR RIGHTEOUSNESS—
Jeremiah 23:6

The Prince of Peace—
Isaiah 9:6

The Good Shepherd—Psalm 23:1–4; John 10:11

Karen, a woman in her forties, is typical of many people I've encountered who unconsciously invented their own symbolic representations of God. In counseling Karen, I gave her a child's coloring book and asked her to select a picture that symbolized God as she envisioned Him and another picture that symbolized God as she would like Him to be.

For her image of God as she envisioned Him, Karen chose a picture of a panther crouched in a tree. The panther is seen from the point of view of someone on the ground. It is snarling and appears ready to leap upon—and destroy—the viewer. She used crayons to color the panther black.

For her image of God as she would like Him to be, Karen chose a picture of a little girl walking alongside a fluffy gentle lamb. I pointed out to her that the lamb is, in fact, the same symbol God uses repeatedly for Himself in the Bible. For example, the Book of Revelation calls Jesus "the Lamb who . . . will shepherd them and lead them to living fountains of waters. And God will wipe away every tear from their eyes."[1]

I've seen it happen again and again. On an emotional level, many people tend to view God in terms of very negative symbols, such as this woman's snarling black panther. But when asked to symbolically represent God as they would *like* Him to be, people almost invariably choose a symbol that God Himself uses in His Word—a lamb, a sheltering rock, a rescuer, the bread of life. In most cases, the God we would wish for is the true God of the Bible!

The healing power of warm, positive, biblical symbols for God is exemplified by Shirley. Today, she is a strong Christian woman, a devoted wife and mother. To know her and to see the depth of her faith, you would never suspect that she came from a dysfunctional family and that her father was an alcoholic. What enabled Shirley to emerge into adulthood with a strong image of God, despite the pain in her childhood?

"As a little girl, I felt such a hole in my life where my father should have been," Shirley recently told me. "His raging addiction to alcohol kept him from being the kind of father God meant him to be. So I clung to the symbol for God that you find throughout the Bible—the symbol of a loving Father. I just told myself, 'Okay, my human father is never going to be there for me. But I have a heavenly Father who is perfect, and He loves me, and He cradles me in His arms. He's my *real* father.' I've carried that image of God as my Father from my childhood to this very day.

"I think the two passages that have meant the most to me over the years are Psalm 68:5—'A father of the fatherless . . . is God in His holy habitation'—and Psalm 27:10—'When my father and my mother forsake me, then the LORD will take care of me.' I used to read those verses over and over. I ran my fingers over those verses until I wore out the pages. It was almost as if by touching those verses I could somehow touch God.

"I know some people have trouble with the symbol of God as a father. They feel estranged from God, just as they are estranged from their fathers. But for me, the symbol of the loving fatherhood of God got me through a painful childhood and kept my faith in Him intact over the years."

It is fitting, in view of Shirley's story, to add one final symbol to our list:

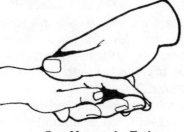

Our Heavenly Father

3. The Spiritual Dimension

The *spiritual dimension* is the degree to which we experience God via His Spirit in our innermost being. The Bible speaks of the spiritual dimension: "The Spirit Himself bears witness with our spirit that we are children of God."[2]

The spirit is the deepest domain of our being, the truest sense of our "I-ness." The spirit is supernatural, not physical or mortal. It is not limited to the mind, the body, or time and space. Every human being, Christian and non-Christian, is a spiritual being, and the spirit is the part that relates most intimately to God.

How is the personal spirit a dimension of the image of God? In these ways:

- *The conviction of the Holy Spirit.* We first come to know who God is as the Holy Spirit convicts our hearts and minds about our lost condition and our need for salvation.
- *The conscience.* We experience who God is when the Holy Spirit speaks to the conscience, convicting us of right and wrong. In this way, we begin to associate God with good and Satan with evil.

It is easy to confuse a spiritual experience of God with an emotional experience. We may feel that God's Holy Spirit is especially present with us in those times when we feel emotionally ecstatic and uplifted. But God's Word assures us that the Holy Spirit *continually* ministers to our spirits. Even when our emotions are at low ebb, even when we do not "feel saved," God's Spirit is active in the spiritual dimension of our relationship with Him—comforting, guiding, sealing us as God's adopted children for all eternity.

The Holy Spirit quietly speaks to us through the conscience; He leads us as we seek to follow Him in the choices we make; He silently comforts us and strengthens us through times of trial. Indeed, the Spirit even prays for us to the Father "with groanings which cannot be uttered."[3]

Though the spiritual dimension of our relationship with God should not be confused with the emotional dimension, they work together. We can experience the fruit of the Holy Spirit through our minds and our emotions. That's why the apostle Paul included among the fruit of the Spirit such positive emotional benefits as joy and peace. We sense the joy of the Lord or the peace of God in our hearts because the Spirit is within us, ministering to our inner being.

That brings us to what is, for most people, the most powerful and influential dimension of their image of God: the emotional dimension.

4. The Emotional Dimension

The *emotional dimension* is the realm of our feelings toward God. This layer of our image of God is built up of all the events and experiences of our lives: the way we were treated, nurtured, or wounded by our primary caregivers as children; the joys and tragedies we have experienced throughout our lives; the ways we have learned to trust—or distrust—those who are closest to us; the joys and disappointments we have experienced in our church life, from pastors and other Christian leaders, and from fellow believers.

All of these experiences summon from deep within us an emotional response—a response that, rightly or wrongly, we tend to project on our image of God. I saw the powerful impact of the emotional dimension on Carrie's faith when she said, "I realize now that my parents hurt me emotionally. I see now how their behavior damaged my spiritual life and my image of God. From my mother, I gained an impression of God as Someone who is neglectful, cold, distant, uncaring—and sometimes uncontrollably angry. From my father, I got the idea that God was Someone who might hurt you one day and toss you aside the next. That experience also made me feel that God was not available to me. For years, I asked God to free me from sexual bondage to my father, yet my prayers seemed to go unanswered.

"After my last miscarriage, I went to a doctor who happened to be a very kind Christian man. He told me I needed to get my life straightened out—that if I didn't I would probably destroy myself, one way or another. I realize now that he was like an angel from God, sent to give me a second chance in life. He gave me the name of a Bible church in my neighborhood, and I agreed to try it.

"So I went to that church. The people there were very caring, but I just didn't feel like I fit in. I didn't feel worthy to be there around all those nice Christians with their put-together lives. And the preaching and the songs reminded me of those times when my mother used to make our family go to church."

Between Carrie and God was a formidable barrier—a wall of fear and distrust that prevented her from seeing God as He truly is. That barrier was deeply anchored in the emotional dimension of her image of God. That barrier had been erected during her painful childhood. To Carrie, God's love equaled pain.

Childhood, however, is not the only time in our lives when these barriers are erected. Events in our adult experience can also strongly affect the emotional dimension of our faith and our image of God.

Keith and Ellen have been Christians for more than twenty years. Keith is an elder, and Ellen has been a leader in Bible study fellowship. They thought their faith had been tested as far as it could go when their nineteen-year-old son was accidentally killed while on training maneuvers in the Marine Corps.

Over the past eight years, Keith and Ellen had become very close to their pastor, Rev. A. B. Charles, through their social contacts and their work alongside him in the ministry of the church. He counseled and comforted them throughout their trial of grief. They viewed him as a man of godly wisdom, Christlike compassion, and unshakable integrity.

Then came the scandal that rocked not only the church but the entire community. Stories appeared in the newspaper, accusing Pastor Charles of sexual involvement with several women he had counseled in the church. At first he denied it, then he changed his story several times. Finally, he admitted having victimized the women—though he continued to minimize the seriousness of what he had done.

Keith and Ellen were heartsick as they saw the friend who had preached so forcefully about integrity and morality caught in lie after lie. They discovered that the friend who had shown them so much compassion and empathy when their son was killed had also ruthlessly exploited a number of emotionally vulnerable women in his counseling room—and had been doing so for more than ten years. Almost overnight, their respect for their pastor turned to revulsion.

"When our son died," said Keith, "it was hard on our faith, yet we got through that. But when Pastor Charles turned out to be living such a huge lie, it really dealt us a knockout blow. I mean, I would have bet my own life on that man's integrity and godliness. Yet he exploited those women as if he had the conscience of a thief!"

"It makes us wonder how God could allow such a thing to go on," added Ellen. "This man represented God to us, and we thought we knew him. Now it turns out we didn't know him at all. It makes us wonder who God really is."

Keith and Ellen are still recovering from the blow they have received to the emotional dimension of their image of God—but they are continuing to move on with their faith. They are learning to separate the image of God from the image of sinful, fallen human beings.

The emotional dimension of our image of God is intensely personal. For some people, the emotional dimension of their experience with God produces warm feelings of security and peace. For others, events may come into their lives that produce fear and anxiety toward God. For still others, these experiences may produce anger, disappointment, disillusionment, or confusion. Of the four dimensions of our image of God, the emotional dimension is almost invariably the overwhelming factor in determining the health or disorder of the relationship with God.

Four Dimensions in Agreement

These separate dimensions—the intellectual, the symbolic, the spiritual, and the emotional—combine to create our image of God. As a general principle, the more these four dimensions agree with one another, the less distortion there is in our image of God. The less these dimensions agree with one another, the more distortion we experience in our image of God, and the more dissatisfaction we experience in our relationship with God.

The exception to this principle, of course, would be the person who has a negative experience or concept of God in *all* four dimensions. Such a person would probably be an atheist, an agnostic, or a cultist (such as a New Ager or a satanist).

For Christians, however, the most common problem is a dissonance or disagreement between two more more dimensions of their image of God. To put this problem into human terms, let's examine the story of Curt Hodges.

Curt is a real estate broker, a husband, a father, a sponsor of his church's youth ministry, and a volunteer in the local Youth for Christ program. He committed his life to Jesus Christ while at a Christian summer camp when he was twelve years old. His parents divorced the following year, and Curt saw his father only three or four times a year throughout his teenage years. Despite the pain of growing up in a broken home, and despite having an intermittent relationship with his father, Curt grew in his Christian faith and attended a Christian college.

The spiritual dimension of Curt's image of God is very strong; there is no question in his mind that the Holy Spirit has been close to him throughout his Christian life. The intellectual dimension of Curt's image of God is also very strong. He has a thorough knowledge of Scripture, and his doctrine is biblical.

The symbolic dimension, however, is somewhat divided. Curt clings to the image of God as a rock and a fortress—yet he also sometimes envisions God as a man with his back turned, a man without a face. It is as though he sees God as Someone who is peripheral—or not there at all.

In the emotional dimension, Curt is even more wounded. He has a deep sense of disappointment with God. Whenever things go wrong—particularly in his ministry with young people—Curt quickly becomes angry, and his anger is usually directed at God. "God, where are You?" he asks. "Weren't You paying attention? If You want this ministry to go on, if You want these young people to know You, why don't You help out a little?"

When people like Curt come to my office for counseling, I use the chart "Dimensions of Our Image of God" to help them identify the state of their four-dimensional image of God. This chart, which appears on page 87, shows three different kinds of people:

Category 1: Those whose image of God
             is positively aligned in all
             four dimensions.

Category 2: Those whose image of God
             is divided, with positive
             and negative dimensions.

Category 3: Those whose image of God
             is negatively aligned in all
             four dimensions.

Where do you find yourself on this chart?

Dimensions of Our Image of God

	Category 1 Positively Aligned Image of God	Category 2 Divided (Positive and Negative) Image of God	Category 3 Negatively Aligned Image of God
The Intellectual Dimension	God loves me.	God is loving.	God is not available.
The Symbolic Dimension	God is light; God is love; God is my loving Father.	God is a protector, a king, a judge.	God is invisible or nonexistent; God is my enemy.
The Spiritual Dimension	I am secure in God.	I am uncertain.	I am alone and empty.
The Emotional Dimension	I feel loved, accepted, forgiven, and joyful.	I feel confused, anxious, and abandoned.	I feel angry or lonely. I am in despair.*
State of One's Image of God	**Healthy**	**Distorted**	**Severely Distorted**

*People with negatively aligned images of God tend to experience feelings of bitterness toward God or a sense of alienation and isolation from God—or they withdraw behind a shield of hardened atheism or agnosticism.

Before we discuss how you diagnosed the state of your image of God, let's look at what Curt Hodges found out. He began with the first row, "The Intellectual Dimension."

"I looked at each box in that row," he recalls. "I was about to check, 'God loves me.' Then I thought, *Why?* The only answer I could come up with was John 3:16—'God so loved the world. . . .' I knew that technically meant God loves *me*, Curt Hodges, but I had to be honest with myself. I was good at telling other people, like the kids in my YFC group, that God loves them, but I really didn't feel God loved *me*, individually and personally. So I checked the box that read, 'God is loving.' That was as much of the truth about God's love as I could intellectually agree to." Curt checked Category 2.

Examining "The Symbolic Dimension" row, Curt again hovered over the "biblically correct" answer in Category 1. But he was determined to be ruthlessly honest with himself. He knew for a fact that he did not experience God as a loving Father, even though he portrayed God that way to the young people he ministered to. He knew that his conceptual symbols for God were impersonal and remote—a protector at times but more often a king or a judge. More precisely, a king or a judge with his back turned, a king or a judge without a face. Again, Curt checked Category 2.

Examining his spiritual dimension, Curt recognized an inner tension. He felt certain that he was a Christian, and that God would receive him into heaven at the end of his life. But Curt was not sure God accepted and approved of him *now*. "Am I doing enough for God?" he wondered. "Why do I feel so much frustration in my ministry? Is God punishing me because I'm not doing something right? Is He punishing me because I have felt angry and dissatisfied with Him?" Curt had to admit he felt uncertain in his relationship with God. Again, he checked Category 2.

Looking at the emotional dimension of his image of God, Curt didn't have to think very hard. The box that read "I feel confused, anxious, and abandoned" pretty well summed up how he felt. After all, he had come for counseling because he felt guilt in knowing the Bible presented God as loving, nurturing, and caring, yet he experienced God—at the level of his *feelings*—as silent, peripheral, and absent.

Curt circled the word *Distorted* in the bottom row, indicating that was the state of his image of God. Curt knew he had work to do, and he took that as *good* news. At last he had a starting point—a distorted image of God—and a goal—to bring all the dimensions of his image of God into alignment with God's *true* image, as found in the Bible.

After completing this exercise, determine the state of your image of God by finding one column where most of your checks are. If you find distortions in your image of God, don't take it as bad news. It's always *good news* whenever we can gain understanding and insight into our problems. It gives us a place to start.

The Key Is Choice

The better we understand each of these four dimensions of our image of God, the better we will be able to heal the wounds and correct the distortions in that image. The good news for all of us who suffer from a distorted image of God is that we *can* change, we *can* grow, we *can* have a rich and fulfilling relationship with the living God of the universe, even though our image of God has been stained by a painful past.

One key to healing in each dimension of our image of God is *choice*. We all make the choice to either grow or stagnate in our understanding of ourselves and of God. Dr. Frank Minirth says, "Choices are the hinges of destiny." Our choices shape our destiny. The power to choose is vividly demonstrated in the lives of two women, Deborah and Allison. Both suffered similar tragedies, but their response to their pain has been very different.

Deborah is in her forties. Her three-year-old daughter died in a traffic accident nearly twenty years ago. "Ever since God took my baby," she says, "I have seen Him as an enemy." Deborah's feelings toward God vibrate in a narrow bandwidth between rage and fear. The focus of her life continues to be the loss of her little girl, and she deeply resents God and blames Him for her loss. She has experienced no growth in her image of God in nearly two decades.

Allison is in her mid-thirties. Her five-year-old son died of leukemia. "It's been ten years since Kyle died," she says, "and I still cry. I miss him so much. I have felt anger toward God. I have beaten my fists against a wall until they bled. But I finally had to come to a point where I realized that Kyle is with Jesus. And he's happy with Jesus. I'll always miss my little boy, but I know that God loves Kyle and everything is all right now." Allison continues to grieve, but she has made peace with God. She has grown in her image of God so that she now senses His love for her and her little boy.

The difference between Deborah and Allison is in their *choice* in responding to tragedy. A negative image of God can be fixed for life, as it seems to be in Deborah's case. But it doesn't have to be. If we make the choice to grow and change, we can experience healing in our broken image of God.

We *Can* Be Healed

In the rest of this book, we will deal with the *solutions*—the practical, workable strategies for healing the distortions that hinder our intimate relationship with our loving heavenly Father. Curt can testify that he found many of those solutions as he continued in counseling and became involved in a support group for adult children of dysfunctional families. Since he started actively working on healing his image of God, Curt has gained a deeper understanding of his anger toward an "absent" heavenly God—an anger that he now knows was actually displaced resentment toward an *earthly* father who was absent through most of his formative years. Armed with a deeper understanding of the emotional dimensions of his image of God, Curt continues to grow closer and move deeper in his relationship with God.

Another person who is experiencing healing in the emotional dimension of her image of God is my friend Carrie. "My image of God is still imperfect," she reports, "but it's mending. I continue to attend church, and week by week I'm finding it easier to worship God there. As I've grown in my knowledge of God and His Word, my spiritual understanding has blossomed. I'm still in counseling and in an incest survivors support group. I still have deep wounds.

"There are times when I confess a sin over and over, and I still feel unforgiven and dirty. In some ways, I will probably spend the rest of my life seeking a trust relationship with God—but I'm getting better, and I feel closer to Him all the time. I know that one day in eternity, I will have a perfect relationship with God—and I'll have a Father, a real, loving Father who won't hurt me but will love me forever and ever."

Finally, there is Rick Hanks, who is also learning how to be healed in the emotional dimension of his image of God. Not long ago, Rick sat in my office and talked at length about his father. "The way my dad portrayed himself to others as a good Christian man just burned me up inside," said Rick. "Here was a guy who was just not for real! Around my mother, my brothers, my sisters, and me, that man was a religious terrorist. I spent my childhood and adolescence trying to earn the love of a raging phony. And for what? For nothing! He was a saint on the outside but a *monster* on the inside!"

"What do you think your father's two-sidedness did to your image of God?" I asked him. I could see a light go on in his eyes as he thought back to the way he had viewed God most of his life.

"You know, I think I understand something now. I remember I used to think God was two-sided, just like my dad. I never consciously related my image of my dad to my image of God, but I see the connection now. I used to get mad sometimes when I'd read in the Bible or hear people talk about God being loving and merciful. I remember thinking, *That's not how God is at all. God is a punisher. Better be careful around God, boy, or He'll really let you have it!* I'm beginning to see it all more clearly. My dad was the phony and the punisher, not God."

The distortions in our image of God can be corrected. There is hope for healing. There is a pathway to a closer, richer relationship with God than you may have ever dreamed possible. In the next chapter, we will take another step toward that goal as we uncover God's *true* image.

Chapter Six

God's *True* Image

I t's time to use your imagination. I'm going to describe a scene to you. As you read, try to picture it vividly in your mind. Not the impressions you receive, the emotions you feel. Try to put yourself completely into this scenario.

Imagine with me . . .

It is Sunday morning. You enter the sanctuary of your church and take a seat toward the back. You don't want to be noticed. You don't want to talk to anyone. You just want to be left alone while you listen to the music and the sermon.

After a couple of hymns are sung, the pastor steps up to the pulpit. You expect him to begin his sermon. Instead, you hear the pastor speak two words . . .

Your name!

You are so startled you practically jump out of the pew! You can't believe you heard him correctly. But he is looking right at you! He says your name again! All around you, people turn and crane their necks to see you.

You rise hesitantly to your feet.

"Yes," the pastor continues benignly, "I would like you to come up this morning and give your testimony."

You stammer and wring your hands. "But I . . . I . . ."

"Oh, I know it's short notice, but all I want you to do is honestly tell these people about your personal experience with God."

You step out into the aisle and make your way to the front of the church. The pastor leads you to the microphone, but before turning the mike over to you, he adds, "My friends, I present to you a person who really knows God on a heart-to-heart basis. This person will now share with you what it means to walk every day with Jesus Christ." Then he hands you the microphone.

Now . . . what did you feel?

What emotions did this word picture evoke within you? Fear? Guilt? Horror? Anxiety? Dread? Shame?

If you experienced any of these negative emotions, you almost certainly struggle with a distorted image of God. And you are not alone. Oh, there might be a few who could actually take up that pastor's challenge confidently and unhesitatingly. But I'm convinced that many of us would find it a shattering experience.

What would you do in such a situation?

Would you stand before the congregation and honestly share your feelings about God? Would you be tempted to bend the truth or edit certain thoughts and feelings that might be too shameful or painful? Could you stand before that congregation and say without doubt or hesitation, "I can guarantee to you that God delivers what He promises"? or would you simply stand silent before the congregation—silent because you really have no idea who God is?

Who is this God we pray to, worship, sing hymns about? How can we truly love God, as the Bible says we should, with all our hearts, souls, minds, and strength[1] when He cannot be seen, heard, felt, or embraced? Is it truly possible to know God just as intimately as we can know a friend?

Most important of all, what is God's *true* image? Who *is* God?

Pulling Out the Truth

"How do you *feel* about God, Rick?" I asked during our second session together. Rick Hanks was still claiming that his relationship with God had never been better. I suspected otherwise but did not say so. When I asked Rick this question, I was careful to put extra emphasis on the word *feel*.

"Well . . ." Rick hesitated a long time. His brow furrowed, and he seemed to grope for words. "Well, He's my Lord."

"That's fine," I said, "but I was asking you, how do you really *feel* about God? What *emotions* do you have when you think about God?"

"You mean like love or something?"

"Yes."

"Well, yeah. I . . . you know . . . I love God."

"You don't sound too sure."

"Of course I'm sure," he said, sounding a little irritated. *"I love God!"*

"Okay. Fine," I said. "So tell me what you love about Him."

"Huh? What do you mean?"

"What is it about God that makes you love Him?"

"I don't see what you're getting at, Dr. Stephens."

"Okay," I said, "let me give you an example." I pointed to a framed picture of my wife, which hung on the paneled wall of my office. "When I fell in love with my wife," I continued, "the first thing I was attracted to was that she was very pretty. I was attracted by her eyes, her hair, her face. Then I got to know her better, and I fell in love with her kindness, her devotion, her courage—the beauty of her spirit. These are a few of the attributes or traits of my wife that made me want to love her."

"But I don't see what that has to do with loving God."

"Well, God has attributes and traits too," I replied. "What are the attributes and traits of God that make you want to love Him?"

Rick shook his head. "Loving God and loving people are two different things."

"You mean," I said, "because God is invisible?"

Rick looked confused and a little wary—as if he thought I was setting a trap for him. "Well, yeah," he ventured hesitantly, "I guess so. I mean, you can't love God like you love a person, can you?"

I shrugged. "Can't you?"

He looked away and thought a moment.

"Rick," I went on, "you say you feel love for God. Certainly, you must have some *reasons* for loving God. There must be *something* about God that makes you *want* to love Him."

Without meeting my eye, he said, "All I know is, I was taught to love God. You're *supposed* to love God."

"Why?"

Silence.

"Why, Rick? Why are you supposed to love God?"

He leveled his gaze at mine. His mouth was drawn into a tight, grim line. His eyes were hard. "You're supposed to love God," he said, "because God'll punish you if you don't."

I sat back in my chair and sighed. Now we were getting somewhere. "Good. That was honest, Rick," I said. "Now, tell me. How do you really *feel* about God?"

This time there was no hesitation, no looking away. "I feel scared," he said. "I think something awful could happen any moment. I try to live my life to please God, but I'm always scared I'm going to do something wrong and make Him mad. Then He's *really* gonna lower the boom on me."

"Did you ever talk to God about how you feel?"

Rick looked at me as if I was crazy, as if I had just suggested we both go out and paint the entire state of Texas hot pink. His mouth opened and sounds tried to come out, but he clearly didn't know what to say. The idea of actually taking honest feelings to God— feelings of fear or doubt or anger—was a new thought to him.

"You know, Rick," I continued, "when you have a set of beliefs and attitudes about somebody but never honestly share how you feel, you consign yourself and that person to an unsatisfying relationship. That's true whether it is a relationship with people or with God."

"I don't know how to tell God things like that," said Rick. "Fact is, I hardly know how to talk to God at all."

"I think the first step, Rick, is to admit those feelings to yourself. You need to bring all those feelings out in the open and acknowledge them, not pretend they don't exist." I reached into my drawer and pulled out a clipboard, a couple of printed sheets of paper, and a pen. "Right now, I have a couple of exercises I'd like you to fill out. They don't take long, and I think you'll be surprised how much you'll learn from them."

He took the materials out into the second floor lobby of the clinic, and he began to write.

And he began to *discover*.

Who Do You Say God Is?

Right now, we're going to do a couple of quick exercises, adapted from the same exercises I gave to Rick Hanks. I think you will find them revealing and helpful. Here is the first exercise.

Complete the sentences below as honestly as you can. For your own sake, I urge you to hold nothing back. This exercise will help you express feelings you may have never told another person before. You will be amazed at just how healing it can be to put your feelings into words for the first time.

1. When I pray to God or imagine God, I picture Him in my mind as _____.

2. What I love most about God is _____
_____.

3. What I fear or dislike most about God is _____
_____.

4. I often feel God cannot love me because _____
_____.

5. For God to love and accept me, I would probably have to __
_____.

Before we close this exercise, let me ask you this: What do you think is God's primary goal for your life? The answer becomes evident when we personalize John 3:17 so that it reads, "For God did not send Jesus into the world to condemn me, but that I might be saved instead."

Think about what that means! God has no desire whatsoever to hurt you or condemn you. He sent His Son Jesus into the world so that you would be saved! In light of that truth, please complete the following sentences:

6. This verse presents God in a way that is very different from the way I have pictured Him and felt about Him. In the past, I have tended to feel that God was _____
_____
_____
_____.

7. But this verse is telling me that God_____
_____
_____
_____.

God's Attributes

The next exercise is a list of attributes that might be applied to God. Attributes are traits or character qualities that you feel would describe God, according to your experience. Remember, this is not a checklist to determine if you are "theologically correct" or "doctrinally orthodox." This is a checklist to help you better understand your *emotions* and *experience* of God, so please try to reach deep within your feelings as you mark your answers.

For each line, place a check by *one* letter. Choose only the attribute that best describes God as you genuinely feel about Him and experience Him. Following the checklist, I will show you how to interpret your answers.

1. I most often feel that God is
   ☐ A. condemning ☐ B. objective ☐ C. forgiving and merciful

2. In my experience, I have found God to be
   ☐ A. neutral ☐ B. fair and just ☐ C. partial and biased

3. I most often feel that God is
   ☐ A. involved ☐ B. asleep ☐ C. observant

4. Throughout my life, I have tended to experience God as
   ☐ A. demanding ☐ B. considerate ☐ C. loving

5. I tend to view God as
   ☐ A. omnipotent and perfect ☐ B. capable and consistent ☐ C. limited and fallible

6. I most often relate to God as a
   ☐ A. higher power ☐ B. friend ☐ C. father

7. I most often feel that God is
   ☐ A. insensitive ☐ B. available ☐ C. nurturing

8. I most often feel that God is a
   ☐ A. role model   ☐ B. deliverer   ☐ C. disciplinarian

9. In my experience, I have found God to be
   ☐ A. unreliable   ☐ B. trustworthy   ☐ C. responsible

10. I tend to view God as
    ☐ A. real   ☐ B. believable   ☐ C. imaginary

11. I tend to feel that God is
    ☐ A. understanding   ☐ B. empathetic   ☐ C. aloof and
        and   and   distant
        approachable   touchable

12. I generally see God as
    ☐ A. a dictator   ☐ B. Lord   ☐ C. an authority

Interpreting the Results

On the checklist, each multiple-choice answer is assigned a point value between 1 and 3. Below is a key that lists the point values for each answer. Please don't think of this as a test that you are being graded on, as if you were in school. There is no grade, no pass or fail. This is a diagnostic tool. The purpose of the checklist of God's attributes is to evaluate your image of God.

1. A = 1	B = 2	C = 3
2. A = 2	B = 3	C = 1
3. A = 3	B = 1	C = 2
4. A = 1	B = 2	C = 3
5. A = 3	B = 2	C = 1
6. A = 1	B = 2	C = 3
7. A = 1	B = 2	C = 3
8. A = 2	B = 3	C = 1
9. A = 1	B = 3	C = 2
10. A = 3	B = 2	C = 1
11. A = 2	B = 3	C = 1
12. A = 1	B = 3	C = 2

After you have totaled your answers, check below to see how to interpret your total.

If You Scored from 12 to 21

A score in this range probably means that you are experiencing God in a negative way, as a person who is nonloving and even threatening. The attributes you selected tend to be unfavorable, which would indicate that distortions are likely in your image of God and your relationship with God.

If You Scored from 22 to 29

A score in this range probably means that you hold a safe and neutral position on who God really is. You may be avoiding intimacy with God by riding the fence. That is especially true if you tended to select several attributes with a point value of 2.

If your answers tended to be a fairly even mix of 1s, 2s, and 3s, you likely feel ambivalent or uncertain in your experience with God. Perhaps you hesitate to admit to all of the negative feelings you have toward God—feelings you hold now or have experienced in the past. Another possible interpretation is that you may hesitate to admit or accept the concept of a perfect and holy God.

If You Scored 30 or Above

A score in this range means that you selected attributes representing a biblical Christian concept of a perfect, loving, holy God.

Did you have a difficult time with the checklist? Don't worry. Most people do!

Choosing just one attribute that most consistently describes your view of some aspect of God's character can be frustrating. All of us vacillate. At times, we may feel God is understanding, even empathetic like a close friend. At other times, we may feel that God has removed Himself from us; when we pray, we pray to an empty sky.

Most of us maintain positive *and* negative views of God at different times. If forced to choose between a negative or a positive attribute—as you were forced to when you did this checklist—

many people will choose a neutral one because people tend to feel guilty admitting a negative perception of God.

Trying to separate our feelings from our beliefs is difficult. We may want to check the attribute that describes God as forgiving because we know the Bible says He is a forgiving God. At the very same time, we may want to check the attribute that describes God as condemning because in the depths of our emotional experience we feel judged and criticized by God.

You may have noticed this tension and frustration within yourself as you did the checklist. If so, you have encountered—at the level of your feelings—one of the key principles of this book. That key principle is this:

> A healthy image of God results when
> our *feelings* about God are the most consistent with our
> *beliefs* about God.

Of course, this principle assumes that our beliefs about God are based on the Bible and thus grounded in the truth. In my research, I have had several hundred Christians do the very same exercises you have done in this book. The results tend to show that most Christians have biblical *beliefs* about God, but they experience *feelings* toward God that are at odds with those *beliefs*.

In doing the checklist of God's attributes, you may have felt anxious or tense as you wavered between two inconsistent answers (say, between "demanding" and "loving"). The tension you felt is a measure of the conflict between what you *think* and what you *feel* about God—and it is an indicator of distortion in your image of God.

A Two-Way Relationship

"I know God will provide for me, but . . ."
"I know God is with me, but . . ."
"I know God is loving, but . . ."
"I know God understands what I'm going through, but . . ."

Throughout one of our early conversations together, Carrie Bishop kept telling me all the things she knew about God, yet each time she followed it with a *but*. Deep down, Carrie didn't really *feel* the things she knew about God.

So I had Carrie do a couple of written exercises. In fact, they were much like the exercises you just did in the preceding pages. Carrie's responses indicated that she had compartmentalized God. She had all the attributes of God she liked in one compartment, and all the attributes she didn't like in the other compartment. She could easily recite the attributes she liked right on cue. She tended to repress and deny the attributes she didn't like, but they were there all the same—and they were distorting her relationship with God.

"I know you really believe that God is loving and understanding and all that," I said, "but I wonder if *all* parts of you believe that. Is there a part of you, somewhere deep within you, that distrusts God? Is there a part of you that doesn't feel God is truly loving? Do you feel anxious when I ask that question?"

At that moment, all the baling wire that Carrie had used to hold her fragmented image of God together suddenly came unbound. "I knew He was an understanding God," she said, "but I didn't feel He understood *me!*" As she spoke, she spread her hands in a pleading gesture, as if to say, *Please understand what I'm trying to say because I don't even understand it myself!*

"Carrie," I said, "I'd like you to read something." I took a few sheets from a folder and handed them to her.

It was a letter from God!

Since Carrie had gained further insight from doing the written exercises, I wanted her to read another letter from God—similar to the "Open Letter from God" at the beginning of this book. Though I don't claim that this letter is directly inspired by God, it is based on Scripture. In this letter, God told Carrie about His *true* image.

Now I want to share that same letter with you. I want you to hear God describe Himself in His own words. Here is a letter from God to you.

A Letter from the Heart of God

My dear child,

At the beginning of this book, I wrote a letter to you. I told you that I love you, I miss you, and I truly want the best for you. I said, "Let Me show you the tenderness of this Father's heart."

Maybe you weren't quite ready to receive those words when you first picked up this book. Maybe you weren't quite ready to trust Me then. I understand. And I accept you right where you are. Please don't feel you need to dress up your feelings for Me or hide anything from Me. I know what you've been through, and I truly understand.

You may still have areas of mistrust and misgiving toward Me. I want you to have complete freedom to express to Me whatever you feel. Please don't be afraid that I might be offended or angry with you. All I really care about right now is that you find healing, and that our relationship be restored. For that to happen, you need to get to know Me better. You need to know who I really am. So I'm going to tell you about Myself.

Everything I'm about to tell you is in the Bible, sprinkled here and there throughout the Old and New Testaments. But I just wanted to bring all of these different facets of Myself together in one place, here in this letter, so that you can see this mosaic of Me assembled into a vivid picture. If you read these words with an open heart, you just may begin to see Me as you've never seen Me before.

WHO AM I?

I am the I AM.

I know, that statement probably sounds nonsensical to you. But let me explain. A long time ago, I told a sheepherder named Moses to go to his people Israel, who were captives in Egypt, and to tell them that I was going to deliver them from their captivity. Moses asked Me, "When they say to me, 'What is His name?' what shall I say?" And I told him, "I AM WHO I AM."

That means, first of all, I am not just one among many gods but the one true God; there is no one else besides Me. I am not to be compared with any other so-called god.

Second, "I AM WHO I AM" means that I am beyond all explanations and all human understanding. I created a universe so vast that a beam of light can travel for a hundred billion years and not reach the end of it, and so complex that no physicist can fully understand all its laws. I cannot be explained to human understanding. I simply am who I am.

Third, "I AM WHO I AM" means that I am personal; I am an I—not an it. Some people like to say that God is a force or a feeling or an idea or nature or energy. But let's get all of that nonsense out of the way. I am not a thing. I am a Person with thoughts and feelings and purposes. Don't ever let anyone tell you that I am impersonal or indifferent or remote. I am the original Person after which the personality of every human being was patterned. Your personality is a reflection of My own. I am real; I am close to you; I am involved in your life. Everything you feel, I feel with you.

There's something else you should know about who I am.

I am God the Father.

I am also God the Son, Jesus Christ.

I am also the Holy Spirit.

I am not three gods. I am one God. I am the Creator of the universe. I am the Voice who spoke to Moses from a burning bush. I carved the Ten Commandments with My finger in tablets of stone. I am the Baby in the manger in Bethlehem. I am the One who said, "Let the little children come unto Me." I am the Carpenter who was nailed to a tree. I am the Spirit who dwells within every believer.

I am your Creator, your Father, your Savior, your Lord, and your Friend.

WHAT AM I LIKE?

I am like a lamb. I am gentle and warm and soft. Hug Me. Love Me. Be comforted by Me.

I am like a lion. I am strong and great and powerful. But don't be afraid. Think of yourself as one of My cubs, and think of Me as your Protector. When you hear My roar, take courage. You have a powerful defender at your side.

103

I am the Bread of Life. Come to Me, and you will never be hungry.

I am the Vine. Cling to Me; you will be My branch, and you will have a fruitful life.

I am the Light of the World. Follow Me, and you will never be in darkness.

I am the Good Shepherd. I have given My life for you. What more can I do to prove My love for you?

I am the Door. Enter through Me, and you will find salvation and peace and rest and a cool green pasture.

I am your Father. Remember what My servant Paul wrote: "God has sent forth the Spirit of His Son into your hearts, crying out, 'Abba, Father!'"² Do you know what that word Abba *means? It's a word used by Jewish children in Paul's time as a term of affection for their fathers. In English, that word would be* Daddy. *That's how I want you to think of Me—not as some remote mystery in the sky but as your Daddy. I want you to trust Me and come to Me just as a little toddler trustingly approaches his daddy.*

Perhaps I am the Father you wish you had. Or the Father you never had. Whatever fatherhood should be, I am. Feel My arms around you. Strong arms, yet gentle. I would never hurt you. My arms are safe and protective.

Hear My voice. Deep, yet sweet. Soothing. Reassuring. Listen to the words I say: I love you, My child. I will never leave you. We will always be together, you and I. Always. Even when time has ended, you and I will go on forever and ever. You are precious and beautiful in My sight. I love you so much.

If only you knew. If only I could make you understand.

Someday, you will *understand. That's a promise.*

I wish I could show you the place I have prepared for you, the place where we will spend eternity together. I wish I could give you a tour of the many rooms, the many mansions, I have prepared for My children in eternity. I wish I could show you just a handful of the beautiful worlds that you and I will visit together.

Someday, I will take you to a city where there is never any night. No sun or moon is needed there because I am the Light of that city. A river, clear as crystal, runs through that city.

Someday, you can dip your feet in its cool stream or drink from it if you like. You will see colors in that city more pure and vibrant than anything you've ever imagined. And many more wonders await you. I can hardly wait to show it all to you.

Until that day, you and I have to be content with a relationship in which you can't see Me and I can't always reach you. I'm always here, I'm always speaking quietly to your heart, but sometimes—because of your pain or your distrust or your willfulness or your weariness or your busy, distraction-filled day—I just can't seem to get through.

But I'll keep trying. Will you try too?

THE GARDEN AND THE GREEN PASTURES

A beautiful song describes the relationship that I want to have with you. Perhaps you have heard this song many times before but have never really stopped to imagine the scene and feel the feelings that this song evokes. So let Me speak the lines to your heart right now. The song is called "In the Garden." As you read the lines, please walk with Me through that garden and listen for the sound of My voice . . .

> *I come to the garden alone,*
> *While the dew is still on the roses;*
> *And the voice I hear,*
> *Falling on my ear;*
> *The Son of God discloses.*
>
> *And He walks with me, and He talks with me,*
> *And He tells me I am His own.*
> *And the joy we share as we tarry there*
> *None other has ever known.*
>
> *He speaks, and the sound of His voice*
> *Is so sweet the birds hush their singing,*
> *and the melody that He gave to me*
> *Within my heart is ringing.*[3]

That is the relationship I long to have with you. Not someday. Today. *I want to walk beside you in that beautiful, quiet garden and inhale the fragrance of the roses with you. I want to talk with you, laugh with you, listen to your joys and hurts and fears, and embrace you with My arms. For now, I will have to* meet you in the garden of your prayers, but someday, we'll meet face-to-face in a garden that is perfumed with the scent of roses. We'll walk arm in arm, and we'll talk friend to friend.

Until then, let Me be your Shepherd. I promise, you will have everything you need. I will take you to the lushest, sweetest, greenest pastures you've ever known. I will be your guide to the clearest, most peaceful waters you've ever seen. I will restore your soul. I will show you the paths of righteousness.

Don't be afraid. I will protect you, come what may. I will guide you and comfort you. I will feed you and provide for you, even when you feel hemmed in by troubles and enemies.

I will lavish the fragrant perfumed oil of My love on you. The cup of your life will not be able to contain all the goodness and mercy and blessing I will pour out on you, both in this life and in the life to come.

This *is who I really am.* This *is My true image.*

Why are you so surprised?

Ah, but you are delighted *too! I am glad. I must tell you, dear child, I am delighted with* you *also! Yes, I truly am.*

If you ever feel sad or distrustful or fearful, please come back and read this letter again. And come to Me in prayer, and let's talk it over together. Don't forget to read the Bible I've given you. With each new day you meet Me in My Word, I promise to give you some new insight or comfort. Until we talk again,

Blessings today and always,

Your loving heavenly Father

A Father's Heart

As Carrie finished reading, she looked up at me with tears shining in her eyes, and she said, "Is this true?"

"Yes," I said. "That is who God truly is. That is what your heavenly Father's heart is really like. That is how He truly loves you."

The letter she read—and you have just read—is nothing more than a few bits and pieces of Scripture tied together in a slightly different package, in somewhat different words. I firmly believe it's a message God wants all of His children to hear, and that's why He has placed this message in His Word. That's the true image of Himself that He has given us in His Word. That is His heart, His desire, His goal, for you and for me.

He truly loves you, delights in you, and wants to have a vibrant, dynamic, two-way relationship with you. Now that we have a clearer sense of who God truly is, we are to take an important step. In the next chapter, we will examine the principles for purifying our image of God and keeping it pure. We are about to explore the process of spiritual decontamination.

Chapter Seven

Spiritual Decontamination

In her mind, Allison was beating her fists against God.

She leaned against the wall of her son's bedroom, pounding her fists against that wall. With each blow, she cried, "Why? Why? Why?" When she had finally spent her strength, her fists were aching. One knuckle was bleeding.

She slumped to the floor, put her back against the wall, and wept for an hour, surrounded by the toys and books and games that had been her son Kyle's whole world for five short years. Now Kyle was gone, his life stolen from him by leukemia, a senseless killer-disease.

"I never felt so alone and so hurt in my life," said Allison. "There was a time when I thought nothing was harder than being a single parent. I was wrong. The hardest thing of all was watching my little boy die. I was so furious with God! There are so many awful people in this world, people who steal and kill other people. Why would God want to take my innocent little boy?"

Putting God on the Witness Stand

Though Allison had been a Christian most of her life, she spent almost the entire first year after Kyle's death completely consumed with anger against God. "I couldn't help myself," she explained. "I couldn't turn off my hatred for a God who would allow something like that to happen. Many times I went into Kyle's room and beat my fists against that wall. I think, in some ways, that wall represented my image of God—solid, unyielding, and silent. I wanted God to explain Himself, to say He was sorry for what He did to Kyle.

"After a while, I got tired of facing that wall and beating my fists bloody on something that couldn't feel pain. One day, I was cleaning the living room and found some of Kyle's toys behind the sofa—some marbles and a couple of those cheap little toys you get in those Happy Meals® at McDonald's—and I just started to cry and miss Kyle so much. And I got angry with God again. So I went into Kyle's room to beat on that wall. I had cleaned out all the toys and furniture from his room, and I had given everything to Salvation Army. The room was bare to the walls, but it was still the place I went to scream at God.

"I raised both fists—but instead of hitting the wall, I just started to pray. It wasn't a very respectful prayer, but it was honest. I said, 'God, You know I'm so mad at You right now! You let my little boy die, and that was the worst thing anyone has ever done to me. I don't see how You can be a loving, just God and still let something like that happen! I don't see how I can ever forgive You. But I can't go on being mad at You forever. Somehow, You and I have to make peace. I can't live without a God anymore.'

"I walked out of Kyle's room, feeling absolutely wretched. A part of me wanted to hold on to my hatred against God, and another part of me knew I was killing myself with all the anger and bitterness. I went to my own room, flung myself on my bed, and had a good cry. Then I picked up my Bible. I didn't *want* to read my Bible, but I had been demanding that God explain Himself, and I knew that if I honestly expected God to speak to me, I would have to go to the place where He has already spoken—the Bible.

"I felt like a prosecutor putting God on the witness stand as a defendant in a murder trial. I was going to cross-examine Him and sweat the truth out of Him. And I knew right where to turn in the Bible to get His testimony: Job chapters 24 to 42, where Job asks the same kinds of questions I had, and where God answers Job out of the whirlwind.

"I almost screamed, 'Yes! Yes!' when I read about Job telling God off: 'I cry out to You, but You do not answer me; I stand up, and You regard me. But You have become cruel to me; with the strength of Your hand You oppose me.' And I read the words that God spoke to Job out of the whirlwind—words like, 'Where were you when I laid the foundations of the earth?' and 'Would you indeed annul My judgment? Would you condemn Me that you may be justified?'[1]

"I was so hurt and so spent, and the answer God gave Job was really no answer at all. God just told Job, 'I'm so far beyond your comprehension that you'll never understand My purposes.' And I was mad at God for giving such a lousy answer. Then I thought, *But what if that's the only answer there is?*"

"At Least We're Talking"

Allison said she sat on her bed, trying to focus her thoughts. "I was more miserable than the most hardened atheist because I believed right down to my bones that God was real and that He had the power to do anything—including the power to heal my little boy of his leukemia. For some reason, He didn't use that power to save Kyle. As I sat there on my bed, I was as full of bitterness and self-pity as I've ever been in my whole life.

"But as angry as I was with God, one thing stuck in my mind from the Book of Job. Near the end of the book, after He had listened to all of Job's angry questions, God said to Job's three friends, who had given Job a lot of pious-sounding advice, 'You have not spoken of Me what is right, as My servant Job has.'[2] God had just told Job, 'Who are you to criticize My judgments?' Then He turned around and affirmed Job, saying, 'Job spoke of Me what is right.' And I felt God affirming *me,* telling me it was okay to ask hard questions of Him while I was hurting. I felt God saying to me, 'Allison, I know how much you've been hurt. And I accept you and your feelings. We're going to get through this thing together.'

"I just put my Bible down and cried. I think that was when I really hit bottom. I felt like everything was drained out of me— even my hatred toward God. I knew He loved me. I felt He was patiently waiting for me to love Him again. I still pictured God as a wall, silent and impenetrable. But for the first time since Kyle died, I felt that wall might actually have feelings.

"I said to Him, 'Okay, God, I don't understand You. And I don't know if I can really trust You. And to tell You the truth, I'm not expecting a lot out of this relationship, but if You give me nothing more than what You've already given me, I'll follow You anyway. I don't have anywhere else to go but to You. So even if I have to limp across the finish line, I will finish my course with You.'

"It's hard to explain what happened next, but it was as if that hard, silent wall suddenly exploded into a thousand pieces. I won't say that I never felt anger toward God after that. But I can say I never went into Kyle's room and pounded my fists against that wall again. That was the day I made a commitment to surrender my life and my feelings to God. It hasn't been easy. I still scream at God sometimes, but now I do all my screaming during my daily prayer time. I'll admit my relationship with God is kind of rocky at times, but it *is* a relationship. It's real. Sometimes I talk and He listens; sometimes He talks and I listen. At least we're talking. I feel much closer to God today than I've ever been before."

The Stages of Spiritual Decontamination

What Allison has described is a process I call spiritual decontamination. Like most people with serious distortions in their image of God, Allison has experienced tragic, painful circumstances that have *contaminated* her emotions and her relationship with God. I want to be very careful and very precise in explaining what I mean when I talk about spiritual contamination and decontamination.

The apostle Paul counseled us to "cleanse ourselves from all filthiness of the flesh and spirit."[3] Or as another translation puts it, "Let us purify ourselves from everything that contaminates body and spirit."[4] I believe the primary thrust of that verse refers to the contamination of sin. The emotional contamination that Allison experienced had nothing to do with sin. It had to do with pain and grief and displaced emotions, which were caused not by anyone's sin but by the tragic death of her only son.

Although I believe this verse is primarily focused on the contamination of body and spirit resulting from sin, I believe the truth of this verse can also be applied to the contamination of the spirit resulting from toxic emotions, tainted beliefs, and poisonous memories since our minds and emotions are of the flesh and not of the spirit. I believe God genuinely wants all of His children to purify themselves from *anything* that would interfere with a pure trust relationship with Him—including emotional and mental contaminants such as shame, bitterness, fear, anxiety, and false beliefs about God.

111

The good news is that we *can* "purify ourselves from everything that contaminates body and spirit," including those emotional and spiritual contaminants that have been inflicted on us by dysfunctional family members, painful life experiences, or other sources. Let me sketch a word picture of what the spiritual decontamination process is like.

Imagine a rocky windswept Alaskan shoreline—a place where clear, cold Pacific waters daily cleanse the pebble-strewn beaches and the tidal pools. The shoreline is aswarm with life. Sea otters play in the surf, and various species of aquatic birds nest among the large rocks along the beach. Many varieties of fish play beneath the sparkling surface of the waves. It is one of the cleanest, most beautiful environments in the world. It is a place called Prince William Sound, and the date is March 24, 1989.

On this day, a couple of miles offshore an oil tanker wallows off course in shallow seas. Suddenly, the ship's hull strikes the rocky ocean bottom and ruptures. Thick black crude oil pours out of the breach in the hull and spreads toward the coastline. The churning seas whip the oil slick into a gooey emulsion called mousse, which coats everything it touches—rocks, pebbles, sand, birds, fish, and otters. It is filthy. It stinks. Worse of all, it kills.

The shoreline is contaminated, and the contaminants destroy life along the beautiful Alaskan shoreline. To preserve the life of the shore, miles of rocky beaches must be *de*contaminated. They must be scrubbed, cleansed, and purified. Every inch of contaminated shoreline must be washed with steam or high-pressure water. Every oil-drenched bird or otter must be carefully scrubbed by hand.

Today, as I write these words, the decontamination of Prince William Sound in Alaska is nearly complete. Yes, some scars of the oil tanker disaster remain, but the shore life and marine life that were once threatened by thick black crude oil have now returned pretty much to normal. The environment has survived, although the cleanup process has not been easy or inexpensive.

The spiritual decontamination process is similar to the process of decontaminating an oil-stained shoreline. To preserve our spiritual life, we must bring our feelings and our memories into the open and hose them clean. We must carefully scrub the stink of shame and the poison of pain out of our inner being. The process may be costly in terms of the time spent and the effort it takes to face the truth about ourselves and our hurts. And even after we have undergone a thorough process of spiritual and emotional cleansing, some scars may remain.

But the poison and the stench will be gone. Life will return. We will feel pure and cleansed inside, and we will be able to taste the sweetness of the abundant life God wants for us.

I invite you to join me in working through the process of spiritual decontamination. From my research and my experience in counseling people with distortions in their image of God, I have identified a four-stage process for removing the contaminants of painful emotions, tainted beliefs, and shattering life experiences from your image of God and your experience with God. In the story at the beginning of this chapter, Allison described three of the stages. Here are the four stages of spiritual decontamination:

1. Reach a spiritual low (hit bottom).
2. Surrender the old image, accept the new.
3. Trust God.
4. Take continuing inventory of your image of God.

Let's look at each stage in turn.

Stage 1: Reach a Spiritual Low (Hit Bottom)

No law says that a person *has to* go through Stage 1. Not everyone needs to hit bottom before reaching the point of letting go of distorted beliefs and feelings about God. Some people are able to decontaminate their image of God *without* going through a painful spiritual low.

Unfortunately, for whatever reasons, a great many people must start at Stage 1. For them, the process of becoming healed of a distorted image of God is much like the process of being delivered from alcoholism or drug addiction: healing must often be preceded by a painful "bottoming out" experience. Many people seem to be unable to make major changes in their thinking and behavior *without* being stretched to the emotional and spiritual breaking point.

I hope you don't reach such a low point in your life before you are ready to ask God to decontaminate your spirit, mind, and emotions. But if you must hit bottom at some point in your life, or if you are at that low point right now, I want you to know that God stands ready to receive your honest feelings and to bathe you in His love and mercy.

If you have not yet had to go through the dark tunnel of a spiritual low, I would urge you to reach out to God *right now,* asking Him to begin His healing work in your spirit, mind, and emotions. If you truly desire to experience healing in your image of God, He will meet you where you are, and He will draw you to Himself. You have God's word on it: "Draw near to God and He will draw near to you."[5]

Stage 2: Surrender the Old Image, Accept the New

We see this stage very clearly in Allison's story. She finally had to release her old image of God—the image of Him as an enemy, the One who had taken her child's life. "A part of me wanted to hold on to my hatred against God," she said, "and another part of me knew I was killing myself with all the anger and bitterness. . . . I said to Him, 'Okay, God, I don't understand You. . . . [But] I'll follow You anyway. I don't have anywhere else to go but to You. So even if I have to limp across the finish line, I will finish my course with You.'"

Allison made a conscious choice—a choice that was in direct conflict with the anger and bitterness she felt—to turn her back on the old image and embrace the new image, the image of God she found in the Bible. I hope you made that same decision as you were reading God's description of Himself in the previous chapter.

Stage 3: Trust God

There's an old story that packs a lot of truth in its punch line. A mountain climber fell over the edge of a cliff. He managed to save himself at the last moment by grabbing a spindly branch that grew out of the side of the precipice. Looking down, he saw it was a sheer two-hundred-foot drop to the jagged rocks below. Hanging by that slender branch, he prayed, "God, if You just save me from this predicament, I'll do anything You ask!"

In reply, God said, "Anything?"

"Yes! Yes!" shouted the climber. "Just don't let me fall! I'll do anything You say!"

"Okay, I'll save you," replied God. "Just let go of the branch."

Allison was in a predicament much like that of the mountain climber—and she *did* let go of her branch. In her case, the branch was her need to understand God. "I wanted God to talk, to explain Himself," she said at one point. But later she was able to pray, "Okay, God, I don't understand You. And I don't know if I can really trust You. . . . [But] I'll follow You anyway." You can see a subtle but powerful transformation taking place in Allison's life as she speaks those words. Notice that even as she says, "I don't know if I can really trust You," she has *already begun* to trust God. She has already committed herself to following Him. A tiny glimmer of healing has already taken place as she begins to pray.

Very often, trust begins not with a feeling but with a choice and an action. Though we feel distrustful, we *choose* to trust and we *act* on our decision to trust—and the feelings come later.

Part of Allison's decision to trust God involved *surrender*. She surrendered her need to have God and His ways explained to her, and she surrendered her need to control the circumstances of her life. Unfortunately (though understandably), Allison had to reach a level of absolute dissatisfaction and pain in her relationship with God—she had to hit bottom—before she was willing to open His Word and listen to His voice again. Once she did, her image of God as a blank and silent wall was shattered, and God became God again.

I want to underscore this fact. If you want to have a restored and undistorted image of God, you must take these *absolutely necessary steps*:

- Give up the need to understand God and His ways.
- Give up the need for total control of your life.

Once you are able to do these things, you have begun to trust God.

Stage 4: Take Continuing Inventory of Your Image of God

Today, Allison continues to seek healing in her experience with God. She continues to find new pieces to the God-puzzle, and she is edging closer and closer to a trust relationship with Him as each day passes. One thing Allison does to maintain her progress toward a purified, restored image of God is to take a continuing inventory of her mental and emotional image of God.

I have developed a simple procedure people can use to take inventory of their image of God on an ongoing basis. This exercise will identify the experiences, influences, and choices in your life that have distorted your image of God. You'll have a chance to fill in this inventory on page 119. But first, let me explain how it works.

In column 1, "Distortions in My Image of God," list any of the following:

- Negative feelings toward God
- Negative thoughts or beliefs about God.
- Negative pictures or symbols you hold in your mind about God.

In column 2, "Origins of My Distortions," record any life experiences and choices that might have caused or shaped those distortions in your image of God. Ask yourself, what has taken place in my life that might explain the way I feel toward God? Remember, the distortions may have been fostered by any combination of the following influences:

- Negative experiences in infancy and childhood
- Parents who portrayed a distorted image of God's nature
- Your personality makeup
- Hurtful experiences in later life that you have falsely attributed to God
- Religious or spiritual abuse, or serious errors in your religious training
- Misunderstanding of the Bible
- Contamination of your thinking and emotions by the influences of society

In column 3, "God's True Image," write a brief description of God's *true* image as you know it to be from your study of the Bible and from His letter to you in Chapter 6. Focus on the contrasts between your false, emotion-based image of God, as recorded in column 1, and the truth that God has revealed about Himself in

His Word. For example, you may *feel* that God has rejected you, so in column 1 you write, "I feel that God has disowned me." However, you *know* that the Bible reveals God to be loving, accepting, and forgiving, so you write in column 3, "God loves me. God will never turn me away."

The Image of God Inventory

I DISTORTIONS IN MY IMAGE OF GOD	I am afraid God wants to hurt me. I feel God is cold, unavailable, and easily angered. I picture God as a critical judge.
II ORIGINS OF MY DISTORTIONS	My father used to hurt me and sexually abuse me. My mother was cold, distant, and volatile. My mother was a harsh, demanding perfectionist.
III GOD'S TRUE IMAGE	God is love. God is close, available, and patient. God is merciful.
IV MY NEW IMAGE OF GOD OR EXPERIENCE WITH GOD	I feel warm and secure. I feel God's loving arms around me. I picture God as the loving father of the prodigal son: His arms reach out to welcome me home.

In column 4, "My New Image of God or Experience with God," write about the new, healed image of God and relationship with God *now being formed in your mind and heart* as a result of trading your old distortions for God's truth. You don't need to have warm feelings toward God as you fill out this column. For now, just affirm the image of God you *want* to have, based on God's true image as revealed in the Bible. Accept that column 4 may not be your present image of God, but it is your goal—and it is a goal you will reach as you allow God to saturate your mind and emotions with the truth about Himself from His Word.

Carrie Bishop, whose story we have followed through previous chapters, did "The Image of God Inventory" early in her counseling process at the Minirth-Meier Clinic. Looking at what she wrote may help you do your inventory.

You will recall that Carrie was sexually abused by her father and emotionally abused by her cold, distant mother. What Carrie recorded during the time when she was *just beginning* to experience healing in her image of God is on page 117.

Now, it's your turn.

I realize you may be tempted to skip these exercises, thinking it's enough to read the chapter and scoop up the information. However, the distortions about God most likely reside in the *emotional dimension* of your being—not the intellectual dimension. That's why reading—a primary intellectual rather than emotional exercise—is not sufficient to bring about healing. If you want to begin to be healed of the distortions in your image of God, you must work through the exercises.

On page 119 is an "Image of God Inventory" for you to pray over, reflect on, and fill out. If you find this exercise difficult, if you experience feelings of anxiety or sadness or anger, be patient with yourself and *please persevere.* You must face these issues and feelings squarely. Remember that God will be with you; rely on Him for strength, comfort, and insight.

My prayer is that God will give you an extra measure of grace and understanding of your innermost self and of His loving and nurturing character as you take this step deeper into your feelings and, I trust, a step closer to God.

Take Your Anger to God

What did you learn about your image of God from this exercise? I'll tell you what many people discover: they feel anger toward God. In column 2, "Origins of My Distortions," most people record painful events or situations in their lives, and it is quite common for them to look back on those events and situations and say, "Why did God allow that to happen to me?"

The Image of God Inventory

I DISTORTIONS IN MY IMAGE OF GOD	
II ORIGINS OF MY DISTORTIONS	
III GOD'S TRUE IMAGE	
IV MY NEW IMAGE OF GOD OR EXPERIENCE WITH GOD	

Is that the way you felt?

If not, do you have no anger toward God? Or are you not really in touch with the way you feel toward God?

Many Christians have difficulty admitting that they feel anger toward God. The anger is there, it is real, it is hurting their relationship with God, yet they refuse to acknowledge it, even to themselves. If you want to find healing in your image of God, *you must resolve any anger toward God.*

The anger you feel toward God may actually be displaced anger, which you originally directed at your parents or someone else who hurt you. At some point in your life, you began to blame God for the pain in your life. Part of the function of "The Image of God Inventory" is to enable you to more clearly see the true sources of your pain and anger so that you can direct those feelings where they belong instead of toward God.

So how do you resolve your anger toward God?

First, ask God to open your understanding, penetrate any denial, and reveal any anger or bitterness in your heart. Ask God to disclose the *true* source of your anger. Remember, the power of denial is strong. Our subconscious minds often try to hide from the truth contained in painful memories. So, instead of being angry with the person or the event that truly hurt us in the past, we often redirect and misdirect our anger toward God. Yet God, through His Holy Spirit, has the power to break down the walls of our denial and reveal the true sources of our anger to us—if we *want* Him to and if we *ask* Him to.

Second, to resolve your anger toward God, you must be honest. Understand that it's okay to tell God you are angry. Job did, the psalmist did, and so did many prophets in the Bible. Allison, too, was very honest with God about her anger—and I sincerely believe that her honesty was a major part of her healing process.

You may want to turn away when you hear her cry out in prayer, "God, You know I'm so mad at You right now! You let my little boy die, and that was the worst thing anyone has ever done to me." The words are too disturbing, the feelings too stark, and perhaps her anger is too much like your anger, which you insist on repressing and denying. But the fact is, her prayer is much like prayers recorded in the Bible, such as this one:

> Awake! Why do You sleep, O Lord?
> Arise! Do not cast us off forever.
> Why do You hide Your face,
> And forget our affliction and our oppression?
> For our soul is bowed down to the dust;
> Our body clings to the ground.
> Arise for our help,
> And redeem us for Your mercies' sake.[6]

Read the Psalms and the writings of Isaiah, Jeremiah, Ezekiel, Hosea, and Habakkuk, and you will hear God's people asking Him honest, even angry questions. The relationship between these prophets and their God was often stormy, often loud and argumentative—but it was a *relationship*.

Third, in your anger, remember that God is always for you, never against you. He is a perfect, holy, loving Father, and He would never do anything to you out of selfishness, spitefulness, or sin. It is precisely because He loves you so completely and unconditionally that He invites you to bring your honest feelings, pain, and even anger to Him. He welcomes you and your true feelings because He is your loving Father, and He wants to heal you.

You cannot be close to Someone you hate and blame and distrust. You must resolve those feelings, and to resolve them, you must admit they are there. Once you bring those feelings out in the open, as Job did, as Allison did, you and God can talk about those feelings together in prayer. And to solve the problem, you must name the problem: "God, I am angry with You. I need to talk to You about it." It was okay for Job to say that; it's okay for you to say it too.

Right now, as you are reading these words, you may be thinking to yourself, *No! I could never say that to God! He would be angry with me! No, no, no, I must never admit that I feel angry with God!*

If that is what you are thinking, let me ask you something. Which is worse: to be angry with God, or to be dishonest with Him and with yourself? If anger and blame are in your heart right now, doesn't He already know it? How can you expect to hide something like that from God? God is just waiting for you to admit your feelings to yourself, so the two of you can talk honestly together in prayer and resolve your problems together.

If you are a parent, you must know how it feels to discover that your child has broken a vase or a lamp. You hear a crash, you come into the room, and you see the wreckage on the floor. You look around the room, knowing full well that the object didn't jump off the shelf of its own volition. Then you spot your child, hiding behind a chair. You pull your child out of that hiding place and demand an explanation.

But *why* do you want that child to tell you what happened? It's *obvious* what happened. You already *know* what happened. You are not demanding information you don't already have. You want that child to recognize a truth about herself. You want your child to learn from the experience.

It's the same way with God. He knows our feelings. He knows

that we are angry. He knows that we are hiding from Him. He's just waiting for us to admit the truth *to ourselves,* to come out of hiding, to restore the trust relationship between us and God.

"One bold message in the Book of Job," writes Philip Yancey in *Disappointment with God,*

> is that you can say anything to God. Throw at him your grief, your anger, your doubt, your bitterness, your betrayal, your disappointment—he can absorb them all. As often as not, spiritual giants of the Bible are shown *contending* with God. They prefer to go away limping, like Jacob, rather than to shut God out. In this respect, the Bible prefigures a tenet of modern psychology: you can't really deny your feelings or make them disappear, so you might as well express them. God can deal with every human response save one. He cannot abide the response I fall back on instinctively: an attempt to ignore him or treat him as though he does not exist. That response never once occurred to Job.[7]

Unfinished Business

As you did "The Image of God Inventory," you may have learned a truth about yourself that many people discover. Perhaps you uncovered some unfinished business from the past that needs to be resolved. By unfinished business, I mean those negative or painful experiences of the past that rise up and contaminate your emotions and your spirit in the present. These contaminated experiences keep you from experiencing the abundant, fruitful life God intended for you. Unfinished business may include *past* feelings (anger, resentment, anxiety), *past* memories (rejection, incest, rape, abuse), or *past* attitudes (I'm worthless; I'm bad") that keep you from responding to life *right now* in a positive and healthy way.

Many of us believe that time heals all wounds. That's not necessarily true. Many old feelings, memories, and attitudes stay with us for years, even for life, and continue to wound us again and again. Many psychologists, psychiatrists, and neuroscientists believe that the mind contains a complete and perfect memory of every event that happens to us. If that is true, these perfectly recorded memories are stored at a level beneath our conscious awareness. We cannot consciously choose to recall each of these memories, yet they can still reach up and affect our moods, our attitudes, and our behavior—often without even being aware of their influence. These memories may even affect the way we relate to God.

Rick Hanks tells about an experience that shows the effect unfinished business can assert over our lives. Rick and his wife, Jennie, are members of a Koinonia Group in their church. These groups of eight to twelve people meet together in homes to study the Bible together, share their issues and problems, and pray for one another on a weekly basis. Week by week as they have been meeting together, Rick has become increasingly aware of feelings of annoyance toward Fred, an older man in the group. Rick's annoyance came to a full rolling boil during one particular meeting. It began as Rick's wife, Jennie, was sharing about her childhood.

"I grew up in a dysfunctional home," she told the group. "You'd have a pretty good idea what my family was like if you saw the movie with Donald Sutherland and Timothy Hutton. Honey, what was that movie called?"

Rick's brow furrowed. "Oh, I know the one you mean. I can't remember the title."

The others in the group looked back blankly.

"Anyway," Jennie continued, "the mother in that movie—she was played by Mary Tyler Moore—was a very cold, alienated woman who repressed and denied her emotions. If you brought up a subject or some feelings she was uncomfortable with, this woman would just look at you, almost like she was looking right through you, and then she would change the subject. My mother was exactly like that—"

"Ordinary People," Rick said. "The movie was called *Ordinary People."*

"That's right," said Jennie. "I saw that movie three times. Cried my eyes out each time. That family was so much like the family I grew up in."

"Wasn't that movie rated R?"

The question came from Fred, who sat frowning across the circle from Rick and Jennie. Rick noticed that his arms were folded across his chest and his head was cocked at an arrogant angle. Fred was a widower in his early sixties, with a hard-chiseled face and iron gray hair and mustache. Only last week, as they were driving home from a Koinonia Group meeting, Rick had remarked to Jennie, "Something about Fred sure rubs my fur the wrong way." But Rick had *never* been as annoyed with Fred as he was at the moment—the moment when Fred interrupted his wife's sharing with an off-the-wall question about a movie rating.

"What difference does it make what the movie was rated, Fred?" asked Rick. Everyone in the room could feel the tension in the room ratchet upward one notch.

"Well, I just don't think Christians should be watching R-rated movies, that's all," Fred declared in a cocksure tone that grated like fingernails on the blackboard of Rick's soul. "I should think that would be pretty obvious to most Christians."

"Actually, Fred," Jennie began, trying to strike a conciliatory note, "I don't really know what the movie was rated. The point is that—"

"You listen to me, Fred," Rick interrupted, and he was actually shouting and coming up out of his chair. He jabbed his index finger in Fred's direction as if it were a gun. "What kind of question is that to ask? What kind of thickheaded idiot would interrupt someone sharing about her pain and her family issues just to ask some stupid, judgmental question about a movie rating? Who cares if it was rated X, Y, or Z? It wasn't a porno movie, for crying out loud! It was a story about a family with a lot of problems, and—"

Rick stopped talking and looked around the room. Everyone looked embarrassed—and no one more than Fred. "Gee, I . . . I'm sorry, Rick," said Fred. "I didn't mean to start a ruckus. I just—"

Rick slumped into his chair. "Ohmigosh," he said, looking completely miserable. "I'm so sorry! Fred, Jennie, everybody, please forgive me. I don't know what made me explode like that! I just—" Looking across the room at Fred, it suddenly hit him. "Fred, could I tell you something about me?"

Fred nodded slowly.

"When I was a kid," said Rick, "there was this rule in our family: no going to the movies. Nothing, not even Disney movies. I always thought that was a stupid rule. I mean, the preacher and his family could go to the movies, but the Hanks family couldn't. My dad said it was something to do with the Bible and staying separate from the world or something, but I always figured it was just because he was cheap.

"One Saturday afternoon, I sneaked out to the matinee with my friend Billy. It was a John Wayne movie. I didn't enjoy it at all, I felt so guilty and scared I was gonna get caught. Fact is, I *did* get caught. Some friend of my dad's saw me coming out of the theater and mentioned it to my dad. I fetched a pretty good beating for that! Then my dad locked me in the cellar for the night. He said, 'You like those dark movie-houses so much, boy-howdy, let's see how you like it in the cellar for a while!' I was about thirteen, and that was the first and last time I was in a movie theater until I left home."

There was a faraway look in Rick's eyes as he told his story. After he finished, he seemed to return to the group. He turned his eyes on Fred. "You know, Fred," he added, "I only now realized how much you remind me of my dad. You even look a little like him. Then when you asked that question about the movie rating, something in me felt like a little kid, being bullied by my dad again."

"Rick," Fred said apologetically, "I'm really sorry if I said anything to—"

"No, no," said Rick. "It wasn't you. This was unfinished business between me and my dad. You just sort of got caught in the line of fire. Fred, I don't want to belittle your convictions about movies or anything else. You keep your convictions, and I'll just keep dealing with my old man's ghost until I get the stuff he did to me out of my system."

Though Rick continues to make progress in dealing with the ghosts of the past, he still occasionally stumbles over a bit of unfinished business in his life. Unfinished business can contaminate our relationships with other people, as it contaminated the relationship between Rick and Fred. It can also contaminate our relationship with God.

Rick had struggled for weeks with negative feelings toward Fred, not realizing that when he looked at Fred and listened to Fred talk, a deeply buried part of him was actually seeing and hearing his father. Many of us have the same struggle with God that Rick had with Fred. Our goal is to root out and expose those areas of unfinished business with the past so that we can decontaminate all of our relationships in the here and now. We want to deal with God and with other people in terms of what is real *now*, not in terms of misplaced feelings of a dimly remembered past.

Three Strategies for Finishing Unfinished Business

The question I'm sure is uppermost in your mind is, How do I achieve emotional closure in those areas of unfinished business in my life? Let me suggest three specific strategies to finish your unfinished business and further the spiritual decontamination process in your life.

First, make a conscious, determined effort to *get in touch with your feelings*. That phrase may sound like so much jargon and psychobabble, but all it means is that you should try to really understand and admit your feelings to yourself.

When feelings such as anger, shame, fear, or anxiety arise in your relationship with God and others, you should ask yourself, Why am I feeling this way? Where does this feeling come from? Why am I feeling emotions that are so out of proportion to what is happening in my life right now?

That's what Rick Hanks did. In the middle of his tirade, while he was in the very act of chewing Fred out for his question about the movie rating, he realized that his anger was totally out of proportion to what Fred had done. Rick stopped, looked at Fred, and thought to himself, *What is it about Fred that set me off?* And that's when the memory came to him about his father beating him and locking him in the cellar for going to the movies.

The mind is an amazing device, always working below the surface of our awareness, making connections, searching out information, feelings, meaning, and memories. If we pause and let the mind do its work and make those connections, sometimes the answer we seek will bubble to the surface, just as it did for Rick Hanks.

Another way you can tune in to your feelings is to recognize those times when you feel as if you are two people at the same time—one person who is angry and out of control, and another person who is amazed and horrified by the out-of-control person's behavior. "It was so embarrassing," Rick said later, looking back on the shouting incident with Fred. "I remember while I was letting Fred have it with both barrels, I felt like a part of me was standing off to the side watching this crazy man launching into a fit of rage . . . and that crazy man was *me!* It was almost as if the rational part of me wanted to clamp a hand over the mouth of the raging part of me, but the rational part of me just stood there."

Most people can remember an experience such as the one Rick describes. The raging, out-of-control part of you is reacting *not* to a provocation in the here and now but to some unfinished business of the past. The angry part of you is screaming at an abusive parent, a harsh teacher, or some other "ghost" from the past, which represents pain, unfairness, mistreatment, or domination. The present provocation may not be that serious at all; it has simply struck a submerged but very sore nerve in your soul.

Again, the warning signs that you are reacting to unfinished business include the following:

- Any emotion that is out of proportion to the problem or provocation
- A sense of being two people—one rational and one out of control—during times of extreme frustration, stress, or emotional upheaval

Sensitivity to these early warning signs can help you be more aware of the true sources of your emotions, especially those emotions rooted in unfinished business of the past. With this new awareness, you will be able to find ways to close the books on the past so that your unfinished business can at last be finished.

The second strategy to deal with unfinished business is to *keep a journal.* Call it a spiritual journal or just plain Dear Diary. Record those times when strong feelings, memories, and insights regarding your past crop up and affect your present life and behavior.

A journal is a good place to write down your "Image of God Inventory." I would suggest you pick one regular time a month to assess the state of your image of God. After keeping this journal for a few months, reread what you have recorded. The changes that you experience over a period of months and years may be so small and gradual that you will not even notice them until you read over what you have written.

But as you reread your journal and your old inventories, you will discover that significant areas of your feelings and your memories have begun to heal. Old issues that used to hurt you and drive your unhealthy behavior will be closed, over, and done. A daily journal can be a powerful ally in your spiritual decontamination process.

The third and final strategy to finish unfinished business is to *pray for insight and healing* as you give that unfinished business over to God. As you pray, imagine that you are placing the bundle of hurt and bad memories—whatever your unfinished business may be—in God's hands. Then imagine the relief you feel as He takes the bundle of toxic emotions and casts it far out into the depths of the deepest sea.

Don't expect to pray one prayer—"God, take away all my unfinished business"—and it will all be gone. Playwright Eugene O'Neill expressed a profound truth when he wrote, "Man is born broken; he lives by mending. The grace of God is the glue." The healing of your brokenness, the finishing of your unfinished business, is not something that happens as a single once-and-for-all event. Rather, it is a task to which you devote your entire life. As long as you live and grow, you will continue to uncover areas of unfinished business that must be dealt with, by God's grace and with His help. As you bring each bit of unfinished business to God, singly and specifically, He will take it out of your hands and heal it.

That is how you live. That is how you grow. That is how you mend.

Decontaminating the Bitter Heart

As I close this chapter, I want to offer a final word on the subject of spiritual decontamination—a word of warning. Many emotions threaten our spiritual and emotional well-being: anger, anxiety, fear, distrust, self-hate. But I believe the deadliest emotion of all is bitterness.

In Proverbs, we are told, "The heart knows its own bitterness."[8] Not the mind, the intellectual part of our being. *The heart*, the part that is submerged, hidden from view, the seat of our emotions. In our minds, we may deny that there is bitterness within,

128

but the heart knows its own bitterness. If we fail to decontaminate our spirits, if we fail to resolve our anger and distrust toward God, those toxic emotions can settle in our hearts and become a poisonous sludge of bitterness. That bitterness, if it is not cleaned out of our hearts, will gradually poison our spirits so that we are unable to receive God's love.

Many years ago, novelist Stephen Crane wrote a few poetic lines that paint a stark and vivid picture of the effect of bitterness and resentment on your life and mine:

> In the desert
> I saw a creature, naked, bestial,
> Who, squatting upon the ground,
> Held his heart in his hands,
> And ate of it.
>
> I said, "Is it good, friend?"
> "It is bitter—bitter," he answered;
> "But I like it
> Because it is bitter
> And because it is my heart."

That is what the poisonous emotion of bitterness is like.

As a counselor, I've seen many people whose hearts had become so full of the toxic sludge of bitterness that they actually seemed to like it, to revel in it, to smack their lips on the bitter taste of resentment and self-pity and the lust for revenge. If you suggest to them that they need to release their bitterness and learn to forgive, they snarl at you. Like the creature in the poem who squats in the desert, devouring his bitter heart, these people are figuratively eating their hearts out and dying by degrees. Bitterness has become their lover, their drug, their addiction, their reason for living—even though it has contaminated their spirits and their relationship with God.

It is easy to see why the Word of God warns us so strongly to "let all bitterness . . . be put away" from us[9] and not to allow "any root of bitterness" to spring up like a poisonous weed within us.[10] If you truly desire to experience spiritual decontamination, yet find yourself unable to forgive the hurts that have been done to you or unable to stop blaming God for the way your life has turned out, you need help. I encourage you to talk to your pastor or to a professional Christian counselor. Get the help you need.

Don't spend another day squatting in the desert, feeding on bitterness, eating your heart out.

God is calling you out of the desert and into a life of abundant joy. Please listen to His call and follow His voice.

Learning to Trust

It had been a hard week for Carrie Bishop. The car broke down, and the mechanic handed her a $600 repair estimate. The pest control man found termites under the house. Jeremy fell while running the hurdles at school—and that meant a trip to the emergency room and a dozen stitches. That was just the beginning of the long list of problems Carrie shared with her friend Annie over a lunch of sub sandwiches and diet colas.

"You sound so stressed out," said Annie. "I can hear it in your voice."

"I just don't know why God is throwing all these problems at me at once," said Carrie with a deep sigh.

"Well, I think I know exactly what you need," said Annie. "I have an extra ticket to the David Meece concert this Saturday, and I think God has that ticket reserved for you."

When Saturday night came, Carrie and Annie were in Row 10, center aisle, as David Meece performed his set. It was a touching performance; he played and sang and shared about his life. As she listened, Carrie felt the weight of the past week's problems and pressures lifting from her shoulders. At times she laughed, and at other times she felt herself choking back tears.

Near the end of the concert, the theater lights went down very low. A spotlight lanced the darkness and radiated around Meece, seated at a grand piano, as he softly, sweetly sang a song called "Learning to Trust." For Carrie, it was as if Meece was expressing the deepest feelings of her heart. He sang,

> There's a father in your sweetest dreams
> Who's always there to meet your needs
> He never ever lets you down
> There's a mother in your heart of hearts
> Who always plays the perfect part
> She never lets you hit the ground.

This is the need of children
These are their tender dreams
And oh how it hurts when they don't come
   true

   That's why I'm learning to trust in You
   In everything I do
   I'm learning to trust in You
   'Cause I know in my heart that You're true
   I'm learning to trust in You—
   But sometimes it's so hard to do

Father, little children must grow up
And to grow we've got to learn to trust
And to trust we've got to cling to You
And when You tell me You will hold me close
It's the very thing I need the most,
But it's the hardest thing to do

I've got this pain inside me
It speaks to me loud and clear.
When there's so much to gain there's always
   so much to lose

   That's why I'm learning to trust in You
   In everything I do
   I'm learning to trust in You
   'Cause I know in my heart that You're true
   I'm learning to trust in You—
   But sometimes it's so hard to do

Keep calling me drawing me closer
Don't let me hold back
Whatever it takes I must break through
The heart of the child is broken
But his time has come
Whatever he lost I'll find in You[11]

Repeat chorus:

During the applause that followed the song, Annie looked at Carrie and saw the tears on her face. She put her arm around Carrie and gave her a hug. "What's wrong?" she asked.

Carrie brushed the tears away with her fingertips. "That's me," she said. "That song is my story."

131

That night when Carrie got home, she checked on Jeremy, who was already asleep in bed. Then she went to her room and knelt beside her bed. "Dear God," she said, "all my life, I've been feeling hurt and angry and fearful. It's because of bad things that happened to me a long time ago. It's because of so many dreams that never came true. And I just realized tonight that I have been directing all that hurt and anger toward You. I don't want to do that anymore. Thank You for speaking to me through that song tonight. Help me to learn to trust You."

That night, Carrie took a major step in her process of spiritual decontamination as the Holy Spirit used a song to open her eyes to her unresolved feelings toward God. Today, Carrie continues to grow and mend in her relationship with God. She is learning to trust her loving heavenly Father.

In the next chapter, we will explore practical steps to experiencing the fatherhood of God in a warm and positive way. Even if you feel cheated out of your childhood, and robbed of the joy and contentment that should have been yours as a child, you are about to learn how to be *reparented* by your loving heavenly Father.

Chapter Eight

Reparented by God

Where is my childhood, Dr. Stephens?"

The mascara was running from Carrie's eyes as she asked that question. I reached across the table and handed her a tissue. She took it and held it absently in her hands and let the mascara run.

"I mean, don't I get to be a child at all?" she asked. Her eyes were lifted toward the ceiling, Godward it seemed. "I had to be my father's sex partner when I was no more than five. By the time the sexual abuse stopped, I had to take my sister's place as caretaker of the family. I never had a real daddy. I never had a real mommy. I had to *be* the mother in the family from the time I was nine years old. It's not fair, Dr. Stephens. It's just not fair."

Carrie was exactly right. It wasn't fair.

I've known a lot of people like Carrie—people who have been robbed of their childhoods, robbed of the nurturing, joy, and innocence that should have been theirs in the formative years, and robbed of their image of God. Their question is always the same, and the question is a fair one: "Where is my childhood?"

Rick Hanks looks back on his days growing up in a white clapboard farmhouse in Texas. "The place I lived in looked like one of those Norman Rockwell paintings," he recalls. "People saw my dad as a pillar of the church and of the community. Everyone thought the Hanks family was such a happy clan. If they only knew what really went on! If the houses hadn't been so far apart, people would have heard the hollering and the whippings. They would have heard kids crying in the cellar—that was one of my dad's favorite punishments. They would have heard him shouting like a revival preacher one minute and swearing like a sailor the next.

"I used to think all kids were scared to death of their old man. It wasn't until I was in my twenties or so that I really began to realize how *weird* my family system was! I decided that when I became a parent, I was *never* gonna lock my kids in the cellar or beat them till their backsides bled—but I thought I was inventing some new kind of parenthood. I thought all the fear and screaming and pain and stuff I had as a child was *normal!* Now that I see how warped my childhood was, I feel like I didn't really have any childhood at all."

Rod is missing a large and crucial piece of his childhood. He has virtually no memories of his father or any sense of who his father truly was. "As long as I can remember," Rod says, "my father worked at least three jobs. None of them paid very well I guess because we were always fairly poor. If my dad got a vacation or a layoff, he'd find some kind of fill-in work. Maybe he worked so hard because he had a lot of bills to pay. Or maybe he worked so hard because he loved his family and wanted us to have as many things as possible. Or maybe he worked so hard to get away from his family. I'll never know. He died of a heart attack the year I graduated from high school." Rod feels abandoned and robbed of a father.

Retrieving Your Lost Childhood

For good or ill, our earliest understanding of God is mediated through our parents. These fallible, sin-prone human beings we call Mom and Dad first represent God to us. The tragic fact of life for many of us is that our parents have done an imperfect—or even an outright *atrocious*—job of representing to us the perfect fatherhood of God.

Many of us have been raised without receiving the mental, emotional, physical, and spiritual nurturing we need to grow into whole, happy, secure individuals. Like those individuals whose stories I recounted at the beginning of this chapter, you may feel that your childhood has been stolen from you, and your adulthood has been detoured along a path of pain and dysfunctionalism. You never got what you needed from your parents, you never learned to trust them, and as a result, you never learned to trust your heavenly parent, God the Father. As a result, you fear the prospect of living out the rest of your life with an empty heart, a discontented mind, a wounded spirit, and damaged emotions.

If I am describing the state of your heart right now, I want you to know that there is hope. I'm not going to give you platitudes or a motivational pep talk or some vague, warm-fuzzy sermon to think about. In this chapter, I am going to give you a practical step-by-step strategy for being *reparented by God*. If you feel you have been robbed of the security, happiness, and growth God intended you to experience in childhood, I have good news for you. God has made it possible to experience all the nurturing and joy of childhood—*right now*. He wants to become the loving, giving Parent you never had—*right now*. You can learn to open your life to God so that you can receive His acceptance, unconditional love, and caring in your life—beginning *right now*.

Get ready. We're about to explore a four-step process for retrieving your lost childhood.

Reparented by God: A Four-Step Process

Here is the process Rick, Carrie, and hundreds of others have followed to find a new Parent-child relationship with God.

Step 1: Make a conscious decision to separate any negative experiences in your past—particularly experiences with your parents—from your image of God. Recognize that God is God—living, loving, holy, perfect, nurturing, and trustworthy. In the past, you may have projected your image of your parents onto your image of God. But from now on, you will choose to replace the distorted image your parents placed in your mind with the truth that God has communicated to you in His Word.

To remove the emotional residue of those negative experiences from your image of God, you may have some hard work to do: the work of *forgiveness*. If your parents or other primary caregivers hurt you, it's time to forgive them. Easier said than done? Of course it is.

But perhaps genuine forgiveness is easier than you think.

When I say the word *forgiveness,* what is your response?

"Oh, no! I can't forgive my father! After the way he abused me, I can't stand to be in the same room with him anymore! How can I tell him I forgive him? It would be like excusing what he did!" Or

"I can't forgive my parents because they're both dead! How can I forgive them if I can't even say to them, 'I forgive you'?" Or "I don't want to forgive my mother. I don't like her, and I can't stand to be around her! She is so manipulative that instead of saying, 'I forgive you,' she'll have me feeling guilty and saying, 'Please forgive me!'"

All of these responses are common, yet all make the same mistake: they confuse *forgiveness* with *reconciliation*. Please understand some facts about forgiveness.

To forgive someone, you don't have to reconcile or be friends with that person. Certainly, God encourages us to seek reconciliation whenever and wherever possible. But reconciliation isn't always possible. That is why the Bible tells us, "If it is possible, as much as depends on you, live peaceably with all men."[1] Reconciliation depends on two people doing the right thing; forgiveness requires only one person—*you*.

To forgive someone, you don't have to say, "I forgive you." If the person who hurt you is abusive or destructive or slams the door in your face, you may have to forgive silently within your heart. If you truly forgive, you will probably *want* to express your forgiveness to that person, but the person may not give you the chance. Oftentimes, people simply do not want your forgiveness and will not accept your forgiving words.

To forgive someone, you don't have to like that person. You don't have to excuse what that person did. It may not be humanly possible to forget what that person did.

Forgiveness is saying, in the depths of your heart, "I will not allow this person to control my emotions and behavior any longer. I will not waste any more of my time thinking hateful thoughts about this person. I will not contemplate revenge against this person. I will not bring up his sin again. I will not judge him. This person will have to answer to God for his sin someday, but he no longer has to answer to me."

There are spiritual and psychological reasons to forgive. The spiritual reason is that we desire to obey God, and He has told us to forgive others just as He has forgiven us: "Be kind to one another, tenderhearted, forgiving one another, just as God in Christ also forgave you."[2] When we forgive people who have hurt us, we restore to them their God-given worth and value—not because they deserve it but because God has already done the same for us.

The psychological reason to forgive others is to free ourselves from the bondage, the pain, and the victimization that other people have inflicted on us. When we forgive, we make a choice to no longer allow other people's sin to dictate how we feel or what we do. Forgiveness gives us the freedom to truly live our lives as God intended.

Once you have forgiven the hurts of the past, you will find it much easier to make an all-important emotional and psychological distinction—the distinction between *people* who have hurt you and *God,* who wants only to heal you, never to hurt you.

You may find that you forgive one day, and the next day all the old feelings of pain and hatred return. Many people need a little extra help to truly forgive the hurts of the past. If you are one of those people, I encourage you to find a counselor, a pastor, or a Christian therapist who can help you ventilate your painful emotions in a confidential atmosphere while providing you with the insight and prayer support to enable you to attain closure in those areas that have been causing your pain.

Step 2: Make a conscious decision to start over with God. God has given you a clean slate. Every hurt and sin of the past has been wiped away by the sacrifice of Jesus Christ upon the cross. That includes the hurts and sins others have committed against you as well as those you have committed against others. Because of Jesus, every day is a brand-new day.

Think of the experiences of the past as having a positive purpose in your life. You didn't go through those experiences simply to feel hurt or shame. You went through those experiences to become wiser.

Learn from the past—but don't relive it. Live only in today.

As you make the choice to start over today with God, remember to accept Him for who He truly is: your heavenly Father—a parent who is perfectly loving, forgiving, accepting, and nurturing. He is pleased with you. He is proud of you. He wants nothing but the best for you.

Step 3: In prayer, invite God to be your Father of choice. You didn't choose your birth parents. You didn't choose your step-parents, foster parents, or other primary caregivers. But God is a Father you can choose. He is a Father you can invite into your life. He does not crash into your life like a steamroller. He does not demand that you have a relationship with Him. Rather, He knocks at the door of your life, and He politely, lovingly, gently asks for admittance to your heart. You can bar the door, or you can open the door. The choice is entirely yours.

Step 4: As you approach your heavenly Father, come as a child. Jesus said that to enter the kingdom of heaven, we must humble ourselves and become as little children.[3] What did Jesus mean? He meant that we approach God humbly, trustingly, obediently, lovingly.

Our prideful human tendency is to try to relate to God as one adult to another. But we cannot relate to God adult to adult. His ways are not our ways. We are not His equal. We can come to Him only as little children come to their father.

Adults want to understand, compartmentalize, dissect, and rationalize God. Adults tend to intellectualize their relationship with God. But God does not invite us to intellectualize Him. Instead, He invites us to *know Him!*—not know *about* Him but know Him personally and intimately.

Most people read the Bible to find out *about* God. But Jesus suggested that it is infinitely more important to *know God* than to know *about* God. The Pharisees and scribes of Jesus' day made it their business to know the Scriptures backward and forward, to know all there is to know *about* God. The problem, said Jesus, was that they didn't *know God* in a personal way. They missed the most essential truth about God because they approached Him as adults, as attorneys and learned scribes and philosophers rather than as children.

If we want to be reparented by a loving heavenly Father, we must come to Him as humble, trusting children.

Nurturing the Child Within

Carla was born in a missionary hospital in the Belgian Congo—which is now the country of Zaire, in the heart of Africa. "I have these early memories of living in this little white house at a mission station in this beautiful green country with my mother and father and a housekeeper," she recalls. "The memories are vague but happy. My mother taught me at home until I was eight, and then I was sent away to missionary school—a boarding school about two hundred miles from where my parents lived.

"I felt so scared and abandoned when my parents left me at that school. I remember thinking, *I can't believe this! I can't believe my parents would really send me away like this!* My mother had schooled me at home before. Why couldn't she just continue home-schooling me? Why did they send me away? I actually began to wonder if my parents loved me or not."

As Carla remembers them, the instructors at the boarding school were very strict and unfeeling. "It may not be fair to judge the teachers at the school by the way I felt back then," she says. "I'm sure my perceptions of the people who ran the school were colored by my insecurity and resentment. But I remember distinctly feeling I was all alone, surrounded by monsters. Even God seemed distant, cold, and alien to me there."

During school breaks and stateside furloughs, Carla had the chance to catch up and get reacquainted with her parents. She carries many warm and happy memories of those times, yet they were like the punctuation, and the times of loneliness and abandonment at boarding school were like the sentence. To this day, Carla struggles with the fear of abandonment by her friends, her family, and God.

However, she has made enormous progress in recognizing the closeness, caring, and nurturing of her loving heavenly Father. "I really have begun to experience God," she says, "not just as a being in the sky I pray to, but as a Father—the close, available Father I didn't have as a child. Don't get me wrong. I love my birth parents very much. I realize now that they made sacrifices to serve God as they saw fit. The memories of feeling abandoned still hurt, of course, but now I understand how much it hurt them to be separated from me. I couldn't understand it when I was eight years old, but they really loved me. It tore their hearts out to send me to a boarding school. They just didn't see any other way."

What has helped Carla the most in being reparented by God?

"It sounds silly and paradoxical," she replies, "but the thing that has helped me grow and mature the most has been the rediscovery of my own childlikeness. When I was a child, I never got a chance to work through my insecurities and fears. So as an adult in my late thirties, I've had to become a child all over again."

Each of us has an emotional part that needs love, nurture, and security from childhood into adulthood. This same part of us experiences fear of living in the adult world—fear of being rejected, fear of being hurt, fear of recalling shameful or frightening memories. No matter how nurturing our parents are, this childlike part of us must, at sometime, be reparented by God. The whole point of becoming aware of this childlike part of ourselves and of issues we never resolved in our childhood is not to become self-centered or self-absorbed. Rather, the point is to discover ways to internalize and experience God's presence at a deeper and more meaningful level.

Why is it important to resolve childhood issues to experience a rich relationship with God? Because our relationship with God began in childhood! These issues are often the key to becoming emotionally and spiritually liberated adults.

In addition to the four-step process I outlined above, some people may need to take additional steps toward emotional healing and experiencing the fatherhood of God. Consider these suggestions for reparenting the child within you:

1. Sing children's songs about the love of God—songs such as "Jesus Loves Me" and "Jesus Loves the Little Ones Like Me, Me, Me." Listen carefully to the words of these songs. Let the simple truth of the words saturate deep into your inner being.

2. Learn to release your emotions with childlike freedom, especially when you talk to God. As you pray, if you feel like singing, *sing*. If you feel like laughing out loud, *laugh*. If you feel like crying, *cry*. If you have children or are around children very much, you know that children have few, if any, inhibitions when it comes to expressing emotion. Learn to become like a child in the presence of your heavenly Father. Singing, laughing, and crying can be the purest, sincerest, most honest prayers you ever pray.

3. Reconnect with childlike sources of joy, play, comfort, and security. Some people find it helpful to hold a teddy bear or some other plush toy while talking to God. Others find it healing to

engage in play with modeling clay, crayons, or colored pens, using these tools of childlike creativity to fashion pictures and symbols of God's nature and His love. The child within you yearns to recover what has been lost. If you've felt robbed of your childhood, it is never too late to rediscover the joys and comforts of childhood.

4. Find a biblically based Christian counselor and support group to help you work through your inner child issues. You may need another person or an intimate community of caring to resolve the hurts you suffered in childhood. A Christian counselor or support group can help you by listening to you, affirming and accepting you, and mirroring you to yourself so you can gain deeper insight into your issues. Many churches offer Christian support groups for incest survivors, adult children of dysfunctional families, adult children of alcoholics, substance abusers, codependents, and others whose lives have been negatively affected by inner child issues.

5. Keep a journal. In the previous chapter, I suggested a journal as a tool to help you bring emotional closure to unfinished business. A journal can also be a way of releasing pain and anger within the safe confines of a confidential personal record. It can also be a place where you can record your joys, successes, and progress in healing your image of God.

Many parents record the physical growth of their children by marking a growth chart on the child's bedroom wall. Your journal can be your spiritual and emotional growth chart, marking each step of your progress as you gradually meet those needs that have gone unmet since childhood, as you gradually heal the hurts of your inner child.

Childhood Lost, Childhood Found

"Where is my childhood?" said Carrie, her eyes bright and alive with joy. "It's right here, Dr. Stephens." She patted the place over her heart. "I've got a heavenly Father—a heavenly Daddy really—and He has given me my childhood back. I can slip into my 'child self' and go to Him whenever I need to."

This conversation took place nearly a year after Carrie sat in my office with her mascara running, grieving for a childhood she never had. During that year, she took advantage of literally scores of ways to discover God's loving fatherhood in her life—and to rediscover her childhood.

"I've been able to see the true parenthood of God," she said, "by spending more time with my son. Jeremy and I talk a lot together, and that helps me rediscover the world through his eyes. We do things together. I love Jeremy so much more than he could possibly realize, and that makes me understand that God must feel the same way toward me. God must really wish He could get it through my thick head how much He really loves me.

"I think the hardest thing I've ever done was to decide to forgive my parents for the way they hurt me. I've hated them so much, and that hatred has ruled my emotions and controlled my behavior for all these years. I've had to release that—not for their sakes but for mine. And it's working. I still can tap into the old fears and bitterness about my abusive father and my cold-hearted mother. But I choose not to. I choose to breathe the fresh air of forgiveness. Living with bitterness is like breathing smog.

"I have very little contact with my birth parents anymore. I don't feel God expects me to because they still continue to emotionally abuse me in various ways. I believe God expects me to be *responsibly* connected to them. By that, I mean I have boundaries now, and I don't allow myself to be around my parents if they do not honor my boundaries or if they treat me abusively. I haven't disowned my parents, but I feel I have actually been adopted by a *new* Father, a real Father, a Father who loves me. He chose me and I chose Him. That's what counts.

"Lately, I've really felt God's presence when I pray. I call Him Daddy. I sing. I cry. I get angry. I laugh. I just bring whatever I'm feeling out in the open and lay it before God. And then I listen for Him to speak to me, half expecting to hear Him *scold* me! But He never scolds. He comforts."

Rick Hanks has had a similar experience. "One of the most healing experiences for me," he says, "has been the process of parenting my kids. I pray with them, and I sing with them those simple children's songs about Jesus and His love. When I look into my kids' faces and see the trust and the sense of security in their eyes, I get a sense that, yeah, this is how it's supposed to be! I sang all those same songs when I was a kid, but now they mean something to me. Now I know it's really true. Yes, Jesus *does* love me. The Bible tells me so.

"I was looking back over my journal the other day. It brought back to me how I used to feel, how I used to see God. I was amazed at how angry I used to be with God. The difference between then and now was like night and day. If I didn't have this journal, I wouldn't have seen all the progress I've been making.

"There are still bits and pieces of my father's image in my image of God. I can see that intellectually, though it's hard to change that emotionally. But I am getting healed, bit by bit. I think I've finally reached a place where God has become more of a father to me than my original father was. I look at the passages in the Bible about the love and grace of God the Father and I'm bowled over. I think, *Wow! So that's what a father is* supposed *to be!*"

Yes, God is all that a father is supposed to be. He can become your Father too—your Father of choice. He has chosen you and loved you since before the world began. Now He invites you to choose Him and love Him in return. I urge you to let this Father of all fathers love you as you were meant to be loved.

In the next chapter, we will look at the obstacles that keep us from enjoying that wonderful relationship God intended for us— and we will explore strategies for surmounting those obstacles.

◦§ **PART FOUR** ◦§

Knowing God
Intimately

Chapter Nine

Obstacles to Knowing God Intimately

L arry was in the last semester of his master's program at seminary, and he was looking forward to graduation in the next couple of months. Though he had a part-time job as a counselor to parolees, he was hoping to land a full-time position in Christian counseling. He was also eager to begin work on his doctorate. He had complete confidence that God was leading him step-by-step into a counseling ministry. His relationship with God was very positive, and he wanted nothing more than to devote the rest of his life to full-time Christian service.

Shortly before graduation, life threw Larry a curve. Not simply a curve, a hardball.

First, Larry's wife, Donna, became seriously ill. It would be a long time before Donna would get better. Because of her illness, she was asked to leave the job she enjoyed. Both of them worked, but mostly Donna's earnings kept them afloat while Larry was in seminary.

A few weeks after Donna was hospitalized, Larry lost his job. He had planned to quit that job as soon as he landed a counseling position on a church staff. After sending out over a hundred resumes, Larry had not landed a job. Meanwhile, Donna's illness grew worse, and the medical bills were mounting. So did all their other bills. Within a couple of months, their meager savings were eaten up. Larry and Donna were so broke that they lived on ten dollars a week for groceries.

"I Can't Recommend You"

During that time, Larry got a phone call that devastated him emotionally and spiritually. It was a call from their minister.

"Larry," he said, "I regret having to make this call. But you have

147

a right to know. If anyone calls me for a reference regarding your fitness for a ministry of Christian counseling and pastoral care, I will have to say that I can't recommend you."

Larry was stunned. "But . . . but why?"

"I have been going over the record of your giving to the church, and I was surprised and disappointed to see how much it has fallen off lately. I'm sure you will agree that a giving spirit is an absolute requisite for the ministry."

"But certainly you know that my wife has been sick! We've both lost our jobs! I didn't want to cut back on our giving, but how can we give what we don't have?"

"Larry, I know you've got problems. I know Donna has been sick and you've been under financial stress. But people in the ministry are required to live by faith, Larry. If you were truly qualified to be in ministry, you would give out of faith that God will provide for you and Donna. No, I'm very sorry, but my mind is made up. I simply can't recommend you for the ministry."

Larry hung up the phone and sat down, staring at the wreckage of his life in stunned amazement. He had never imagined that on top of all the hurt and struggle of the past few months, he would now find himself sabotaged by his own minister! Talk about kicking a man when he's down.

When he told Donna about the call, she was incredulous. "Larry, what are we going to do?" she asked. "Why is God allowing this to happen to us? Is He just going to let us drown? Is He angry with us? Is it something that we did? Has God decided not to use us anymore?"

"I don't know, Donna," Larry replied bleakly. "I just don't know. Maybe the minister is right. Maybe I just don't have enough faith to be in the ministry."

"How much faith is 'enough' faith, Larry?" Donna demanded, halfway between tears and anger. "What does God want from us? I don't want any more pain! I don't want any more worry! I thought we were at the breaking point before, Larry, but now we've gone past that point. It has to end, Larry. At some point God just has to take pity on us and turn off the pain!"

Larry and Donna had reached a dark and frightening juncture in their lives. Their trust relationship with God had been dealt a crippling blow. But they had not yet hit bottom. They were about to discover that things could still get worse.

"How Can I Trust You?"

A couple of weeks passed. Larry's fear and depression deepened. Donna's health continued to languish. Larry wondered if he would have to watch his young wife waste away to nothing. As his worries mounted, Larry's image of God began to undergo some changes. His *feelings* toward God changed. His *intellectual* image of God changed. His *spiritual* relationship with God changed. Larry continued attending church during that time, though all the joy he once found in Sunday morning worship seemed to have dried up and blown away. Because of Donna's health, she attended church only on an intermittent basis, and the minister's comment further crippled her ability to trust God.

During that time, friends were scarce, and the aura of loneliness that hovered over their lives was deep. The semester was winding down toward graduation, but Larry no longer looked forward to the end of school with hope and anticipation. He was just going through the motions, going to class, then coming home. He had already started feeling discouraged about finding a Christian counseling position.

One day, Larry came home from school feeling depressed, which was unusual for him. He went into the bedroom and looked down at his wife, who appeared to be sleeping. She was very weak, and she slept a lot. Larry didn't want to wake her, so he quietly sat down in a chair and put his head in his hands. But Donna wasn't asleep. Through half-closed eyes, she saw him sitting dejectedly. "What's the matter, Larry?" she asked wanly.

"Did I wake you up? I'm sorry."

"I was awake. Tell me what's wrong."

"I've just reached the breaking point, Donna," he replied. "I don't feel like reading my Bible anymore. When I pray, I don't feel anyone's listening. I used to ask myself what God wanted me to learn through all this hurt. The thought that really scares me now is, maybe I'm not supposed to learn anything. Maybe God has just turned His back on me, and that's all there is to it. I gave three years of my life to go to seminary so I could serve Him, and now He's just going to throw me away. Donna, I've never been so scared in my whole life . . . and I've never been so angry with God, either."

Donna was silent for several long seconds—so long, in fact, that Larry thought for a moment that she had fallen asleep. Then, in a tired whisper, she said, "God will come through, Larry. No matter what happens, no matter how things turn out, we'll make it."

As usual, Donna's gift of encouragement was there like a safety net to keep Larry from tumbling into a pit of despair. Larry leaned over, kissed Donna's forehead, and squeezed her hand. He didn't really believe everything would be all right. But he knew he had to *try* to believe—if only for Donna's sake.

In the next few days, Larry forced himself to send out another batch of resumes, and each one met with rejection. Financially, they had scraped bottom. Larry knew he had to get a job—*any* job—as soon as possible. Poring over the "Help Wanted" section of the newspaper, he found a low-paying job as a security guard at a warehouse. The following week, he found another part-time job as a security guard. Then, with two days left to fill, he took a third job.

Night after night throughout the summer, Larry sat on the warehouse roof with his walkie-talkie and his big four-cell flashlight. There was nothing to do but watch the parking lot and think. The more he thought, the more depressed he became. It was during those long, monotonous summer nights that Larry finally hit a spiritual and emotional bottom.

"God," he prayed, pacing along the edge of the rooftop under a black midnight sky, "I've spent years preparing myself to help people solve their spiritual problems. Instead, I'm here on top of this warehouse feeling about as useful as old coffee grounds. I trusted You, God. I believed You were leading me. But, God, I've got to be honest with You. I feel like You've let me down. How can I trust You after all we've been going through?" Larry continued to work the security jobs through the summer.

Fall arrived, and the cool wind brought in a breath of fresh air. Larry found a counseling job, and Donna's condition improved to the point that she felt strong enough to look for work. Larry could hardly believe the turnaround in his circumstances. Donna was going to make it—and so was he!

At the same time, he felt guilty for the anger and doubt he had experienced while walking his rounds on that warehouse roof. Finally, he could see that God had never turned His back on them. Rather, God had carried him and Donna through the past six months of stormy trials. Though the pain of their circumstances had clouded their image of God, He was there all along.

Today, Larry's faith and his image of God are restored—and Larry has learned some valuable lessons about his ability to endure trial and uncertainty, and about God's reality during trying times. His faith has gone through a process of being hardened like tempered steel.

It's not easy for us to find God and experience intimacy with Him during times of trial. I know that from personal, painful experience because the Larry in that story is me. My wife, Donna, and I have been through times when we felt God had hidden Himself from our sight. But now we can see how God has brought us safely through our trials.

I wanted you to know that the principles I share in this book are derived not from theories or academic research but from the Word of God and real-life experiences—my experiences and those of the many people I have counseled at the Minirth-Meier Clinic. When people tell me about the struggles they are going through with their emotional pain and spiritual confusion, I can't sit unmoved and write out some psychological or spiritual prescription: "Read two verses and call me in the morning." No, their pain strikes a responsive chord in my spirit.

I *know* it is sometimes hard to find God. I *know* how much it hurts to feel that God has abandoned you, that He has moved away, that He no longer cares.

But God has *not* hidden Himself from you. He can be found—even through an obscuring haze of emotional hurt; broken memories, physical suffering, financial distress, abuse, grief, and other trying circumstances. God's goal for your life is that you would experience a genuine, intimate relationship with Him.

In this chapter, we will explore ways to develop a rich and rewarding intimacy with God—a relationship that can stand even against the storms and trials of life.

Four Obstacles

Why does it seem that God is so hard to know? If God truly wants us to know Him and trust Him, as the Bible says He does, why are there such enormous barriers to intimacy between us and God? Is it God's problem or ours?

I can confidently state that God does not make Himself hard to know. He has revealed everything we need to know about Him in His Word. The problem is not with God, His nature, or His revelation of Himself in the Bible. The problem is within us, within our fallen humanity. Despite the clear revelation of God in His Word, we find it difficult to intimately know Him because of the following obstacles:

Obstacle 1: Each of us has different expectations of God.

Some people have very high expectations of God, and some have low expectations. All Christians want to feel that God is caring and actively involved in our lives. Some Christians, however, have an overwhelming emotional need to see God acting directly, visibly, and dramatically on their behalf on a daily basis. From their image of God, these people derive their sense of security in an uncertain world. If major aspects of their lives are out of control (they suffer a financial setback, a serious illness, or an accident; they are victimized by crime or some other disaster) they become very anxious and afraid. They feel either that they have let God down or that God has let them down. Such people have very high expectations of God.

Now, there is nothing wrong with having expectations of God per se. Throughout the Bible, God gives us many promises, and basing our expectations of God on His promises is perfectly healthy. Problems arise, however, when our expectations of God *exceed* His promises—that is, when our expectations become unreasonable.

What unreasonable expectations do we often place on God? We expect God to answer our prayers on *our* terms in the time frame of *our* choosing. We expect God to perform dramatic miracles to solve our problems and to prop up our sagging faith. We expect God to protect us from all hurt, misfortunes, and disappointment. We expect God to rescue us from the consequences of our sin and folly. We expect God to keep us emotionally charged up and exhilarated. If these expectations are not met, many of us get angry with God.

Now, what about people with *low* expectations of God? Can low expectations lead to distortions in the image of God? Absolutely. A person with low expectations of God tends to be self-sufficient, and being excessively self-sufficient is a serious obstacle to knowing God. At the extreme end of the spectrum of self-sufficiency is the completely self-contained person who says, "I have no need of God, His love, or His authority over my life."

But even persons who do not take self-sufficiency to such extremes can experience distortion in their relationship with God. They tend to be self-willed and turn to God only in crises. They tend to chafe under God's authority and resent any hint of being "controlled" by God or others. They tend to exhibit pride. They want to steer the course of their own lives, and they become angry if they think God is interfering.

A certain degree of self-sufficiency can be healthy—*if* a person can relate to God, look to Him for insight, strength, and wisdom, while still taking full responsibility for their choices.

Our needs and expectations strongly influence how we experience God. If we have many needs and high expectations, we may feel God is not available when problems arise. We'll think, *God is asleep on the job.*

But if we have few needs and low expectations, we would laugh at the person with multiple needs and high expectations. "God is not asleep!" we might say. "He's just waiting for you to do something about your own problems. Just take responsibility for yourself and get on with your life."

Self-sufficient people who have few needs and low expectations often have difficulty committing their lives to Jesus Christ, even when they believe the gospel is true. We see this principle in the story of a self-sufficient, self-willed young man named Brad.

Brad is a sales engineer for a computer firm in Santa Clara, California. Jack, Brad's boss at the computer company, is a strong Christian. Jack has made a point of befriending Brad, and he and his wife have had Brad over for dinner and conversation numerous times. Jack has not pressured Brad. He had simply shared his convictions from time to time in the natural course of their friendship.

"You know, I really respect your beliefs," said Brad on one occasion. "In fact, I think the faith that you and your wife have is something really special. I'd like to have a faith like that myself. This may surprise you, but I believe God is real, and I believe Jesus died for my sins. It makes sense. But I'm not ready to become a Christian yet."

"Oh?" said Jack. "Why is that?"

"Because I like my life-style," said Brad. "I like the movies I watch. I like to party. I like to drink. I don't want to be tied down to one woman. I like to date around—and when I say 'date,' I don't mean just dinner and a movie and a handshake at the door. If I became a Christian, I'd have to change my life-style to suit God. I don't want God controlling my life and killing my fun."

Jack attempted to show Brad that God is a loving Father, not a controlling tyrant, and that any changes Jesus brought about in his life-style would be for the better. But Brad was too self-sufficient and self-willed to be persuaded. That conversation took place several years ago, and Jack and Brad have had many conversations about spiritual things since then. To this day, Brad refuses to accept the grace and love of a God he persists in viewing as too controlling.

Each of us should consciously examine our needs and expectations of God. Do we demand too much of God? Are we too self-willed and self-sufficient for our spiritual good?

To overcome the obstacle of either too-high or too-low expectations of God, we start with God's Word. If our expectations are unrealistically high, our goal is to replace those unrealistic expectations with a biblical understanding of God and His promises to us. If our expectations are too low, our goal is to invite God to come into our lives in a dynamic way, to truly be our Lord, to replace our self-sufficiency with His all-sufficiency.

Whether our expectations are too low or too high, we can realign them according to the promises in God's Word. Those promises are the basis of a healthy set of expectations toward God: we can expect Him to love us, forgive us, support us, encourage us, walk alongside us, speak to us, listen to us, discipline or teach us in love, remain unchangeable and reliable, never leave us or forsake us, and provide all the things we truly need for a life of contentment and peace.

Obstacle 2: We often base our beliefs about God on our feelings rather than objective truth.   Our search for God is primarily emotional rather than intellectual. We all want a God who will fill the God-shaped void in our hearts, at the feelings level of our being.

The first thing we must understand about feelings is that they are always real, but they are not always true. Feelings have no concept of objective reality. Feelings do not know what is real or not real. Feelings do not distinguish between what is true and what is not true.

Our rational minds, the thinking level of our being, can comprehend objective reality. Our minds can discern what is true from what is not true.

We have all experienced this contradiction between our feelings and our rational minds. Watch a scary movie, and your rational mind will say, "It's only a movie." At the very same moment, your feelings will cause your heart to pound with fear. Your feelings do not know that it's "only a movie."

In the same way, our rational minds may read the Bible and say, "God is good; God is love," while our feelings—which may have been damaged by painful circumstances, abuse, or shame— may say, "I am afraid of God; I don't like God."

At this point, we need to understand where our feelings come from. Psychological researchers have established that our feelings are not simply a product of what happens to us but a product of *how we perceive and interpret* what happens to us.

For example, if you come home late from work and your spouse says, "Where have you been?" you are going to have an emotional reaction. But your emotional reaction will be based not on the *event* of being questioned by your spouse but on *your perception and interpretation* of that event.

If you interpret your spouse's question to be a display of anger, and if you believe that this person is trying to act like your parent, you will probably experience emotions of anger and defensiveness. You will feel criticized, attacked, and misunderstood.

But if you interpret your spouse's question to be a genuine demonstration of concern and love, and if you believe that this person was really worried that something might have happened to you, you will probably experience positive emotions. At a feelings level, you will sense that you have been cared for, wanted, and loved.

Now, let's relate this example directly to feelings toward God. Let's say you are walking down the street and you are panhandled by a young man on the street corner. "I haven't had a meal since day before yesterday," he says. You have a few extra dollars in your pocket. You *could* give those dollars to the man on the street corner. Instead, you say, "Sorry, I can't help you." He smiles back and says, "I understand. Have a good day." You walk on.

How do you think God feels about what you have just done?

If you believe it is a sin not to help someone in need, and *if* you believe that the person was truly needy, and *if* you walked past him merely because you planned to spend those dollars on yourself, you probably feel guilty, ashamed, and unworthy in God's sight. You may feel God is disappointed in you. You may even see Him as angry or disgusted with you, like a critical parent. You might hear God saying to you, "Why didn't you help that man? How can you be so stingy?"

If, however, you believe that giving money to the man on the street corner would merely enable an alcohol or drug habit rather than really help him, and *if* you believe that God is merciful and will accept you whether you help the man or not, you will probably feel at peace with yourself and with God. You may ask God to give you wisdom the next time you encounter a street person so that you can do something more effective, such as directing him to a mission where he can get help or taking him into a cafe and buying him a meal. But you do not feel that God is judging you. You do not feel ashamed or unworthy.

Here are two ways of looking at the very same circumstances. It is not the circumstances themselves but our *thoughts* or *beliefs* about those circumstances that determine how we feel God views us. Our feelings about that event are real, and they affect our self-image and our image of God, but those feelings are *not* necessarily true. If we allow ourselves to base our experience of God on our negative feelings, our relationship with God can become seriously, needlessly distorted—and a vicious cycle can set in. It is like a self-fulfilling prophecy. We falsely believe God has isolated Himself from us, so we proceed to isolate ourselves from His love. If we want to experience true intimacy with God, we must learn to separate our subjective feelings and emotions from the objective, revealed truth of God's Word.

Obstacle 3: Many of us have an idealized concept of God. If you could design your own god, what would he be like? These days, it seems, everyone has a private fantasy god or an idealized god.

Some would like a god that is a remote warm light—an impersonal but agreeable force for love and niceness. They don't want this god to intrude on their freedom. Rather, they want this god to be there to receive them into some vague and dreamy afterlife after their death. But this is not the God of the Bible.

Others would like a cosmic Santa Claus kind of god—a cheerful, indulgent giver of gifts who asks nothing in return. They would like this god to take care of them, to excuse all their sins, to keep them out of all problems and difficulties. But this is not the God of the Bible.

Still others try to envision a god as the collective human spirit, the sum total of all that is good within the human race. Such people blithely ignore the question of sin and have no idea what to do with all that is evil within the human race. But this is not the God of the Bible.

Who, then, is the God of the Bible?

According to the Bible, God is loving and nurturing. He always does what is best for us (even though we don't always agree with His judgment). He is all-powerful. He is all-knowing. He is personal, and He cares about each of us individually as His children. He is waiting to receive us in heaven to be with Him throughout eternity. He is the God of truth, and everything He says to us in the Bible, both Old and New Testament, is true.

That is the God of the Bible. That is objective truth.

These days, many people place a low premium on objective truth. You often hear people say, "You have your truth, and I have my truth." People want to have total freedom to invent any reality and any god they choose. That sounds nice, but the universe doesn't work that way. If your truth and my truth are not *the* truth, they are *lies*, period.

Anyone who chooses to make up a god, based on subjective feelings and fantasies, commits a mistake of eternal proportions. It is the spiritual equivalent of walking into an airplane propeller with your eyes closed. We don't have to invent a fantasy faith based on a fantasy god. The true God has already revealed Himself to us. His *true* image is found in the Bible.

Obstacle 4: Each of us interprets Scripture differently.

The same Bible passage—and even the same *word*—may mean different things to different people. And this is no small matter. The way we interpret Scripture has everything to do with the way we experience God. Some people base their entire experience of God on a handful of selected verses.

For example, I've known some people who use James 1:2 as a "handle" for understanding God. Their entire conception of God is based on this verse: "Count it all joy when you fall into various trials." Based on a distorted view of this one verse, these people have concluded that God delights in their suffering. To them, God is a cosmic sadist, and the way to find favor with Him is to be miserable.

These people have a diminished understanding of who God is. This verse—especially when you place it in the context of the entire Word of God—does not say that God takes pleasure in our pain. It says that when trials come our way, and we demonstrate a capacity to grow through those trials, God is pleased that we are demonstrating Christlike character. A verse like James 1:2 cannot be separated from other verses, such as John 10:10, where Jesus said "I have come that they may have life, and that they may have it more abundantly." And this verse cannot be separated from all the other verses telling of God's desire that our "joy may be full."[1]

You cannot build a reliable image of God on the foundation of a few scattered verses, any more than you can build a strong house on the foundation of a few scattered stones. Every individual verse must be seen as a buttressing and interlocking with the entire structure of God's Word. Whether you are constructing a house or an image of God, you must start with a solid foundation.

Where Do We Turn?

Many factors interfere with our ability to accurately, intimately know God. These obstacles are part of our humanness, part of our frailty, part of our condition as sinners and as broken people in need of God's mending grace. Given these obstacles, what hope do we have for restoring our broken image of God? Where do we turn for an accurate representation of who God really is?

Should we turn to Scholars and Scientists? No, many of them are philosophical in their approach to God and many do not believe in God. Should we turn to theologians? You can, but there are those who are unsure themselves about God's image.

Where, then, should we turn? To the church?

That is where my friend Carrie Bishop turned when her doctor told her she needed to get her life straightened out. It was a good church full of caring people, a place where the full Word of God was diligently preached. Though it was hard at first for Carrie to sit through a worship service, she now worships in that church regularly. Through the support and fellowship of the church, Carrie has been strengthened in her pursuit to know God. Carrie has also learned through her church friends to rely on God, and not the people in the church for her image of God.

Having said all that, I must underscore the fact that the church itself is *not* the final authority on the truth about God. Many excellent pastors and churches, by their love and their faithfulness to God's truth, diligently attempt to mirror God's image to a broken world. Unfortunately, many other churches and pastors have distorted God's image so that it is virtually unrecognizable.

Some churches are lifeless institutions where the Word of God is not accurately represented, Jesus is not proclaimed, and God is no longer worshiped in spirit and in truth. Other churches cling to orthodox dogmas but have become cold and unloving; individuals cannot find the grace and mercy of a forgiving God in these legalistic churches. Other churches are merely places where people go to be entertained by dynamic preaching and powerful music—what the Bible calls "sounding brass or a clanging cymbal,"[2] a lot of sound but no true worship and no genuine love. Other churches are run as businesses: the pastor is the CEO, the elders are the board of directors, and the primary goal is to operate in the black.

Churches, like individual Christians, may or may not reflect God's image accurately. The church is not an objective standard or an absolute authority on the true state of God's image.

Where, then, can we turn for insight into an intimate, personal connection to the true and living God? There are only three sources:

1. The Holy Bible
2. Jesus Christ
3. The Holy Spirit

Let's take a closer look at each one.

Source 1: The Holy Bible

Very often in Christian circles, we talk about the importance of Bible study and prayer, and it rolls off us like water off a duck's back. "Yeah, yeah, yeah, Bible study and prayer, that's so basic, everybody knows that," we say with a wave of the hand. "But what's the *real* secret to the Christian life?"

If you're one of those people who wants to know the secret, let me tell you: *the secret is that there is no secret!* It's right out in the open. Talk to God. Listen to God. Study His Word.

"But I've tried prayer," people tell me. "I've tried Bible study. I can't get into it. It doesn't work for me. The Bible has always been used as a weapon against me, so it is difficult for me to feel safe and secure reading it."

Have you *really* tried it? Have you spent just fifteen minutes every morning for thirty days straight? Have you *truly* given the discipline of daily devotions a fair shake? I've never met a person who said yes to those questions who still claimed life was unchanged.

Something miraculous takes place when we give ourselves to a deep, honest, personal, two-way relationship with God on a daily basis. It may not take place the first day or the first week. But if we persevere in prayer, if we do not only talk but *listen* for God's voice, if we read His Word as though we are hearing God speak to us for the first time, our spirits, our emotions, our image of God, and our experience with God *will be changed,* guaranteed. God will cease to be merely an idea that we learn about in church once a week; He will become the Father we have longed for all our lives. He will become the source of our comfort, our nurture, our security, and our sense of being loved.

(To get started on your devotional journey, see the "Thirty-Day Image of God Restoration Program," which begins on page 195. It is a basic interactive Bible study and prayer devotional, specifically designed to help you find deeper intimacy with God and greater wholeness in your image of God.)

Through the Bible, God tells us all we need to know about Himself and His relationship with us. The Bible reveals God the Father through the life of Christ and the revelation of the Holy Spirit. Once we accept the Bible to be the divinely inspired and infallible Word of God, we begin the process of restoring our image of God.

The Bible doesn't just contain information about God. It is filled with stories, images, and symbols through which we can *experience* the truth about God at an *emotional* level. Remember, most of us have been wounded at the feelings level, and that is where most of the distortions in our image of God have taken place. God wants to reveal Himself not only to the intellect but to the innermost being. That is why He has constructed His love letter to us— the Bible—in such a way that it gives us information and touches our emotions.

As we immerse our minds and our emotions in the vivid images and powerful truths of God's Word, we will experience spiritual and emotional healing. God's truth will saturate us, washing away the smudges and debris from our image of Him, replacing our distortions with the clarity of His true image.

Let me suggest a four-step plan for studying God's Word and seeking the truth about His image:

1. Pray, asking the Holy Spirit to clear away your old distorted notions of God, and to give you the wisdom and insight to understand the truth of His Word.
2. Read the Bible as if you are hearing each sentence for the very first time. Listen carefully for fresh truths *from* God *about* God.

3. After reading, meditate. Ask God to speak to you. Listen to what He is saying. Pray over the words you have read, then reread them.

4. Compare Scripture with Scripture. Use a chain reference (study helps that many Bibles include in the margins or at the bottom of the page) to compare the passage you have just read with other passages on the same theme.

Ask questions: How does my understanding of this verse match up with what the rest of the Bible says? Have I distorted the meaning of this verse by taking it out of context? This verse says, "Be angry, and do not sin."[3] Does it mean that the way to keep from sinning is to be ticked off all the time? Or could it be that I've missed the real thrust of this passage?

These are the kinds of questions we should ask ourselves whenever we encounter verses that seem to perplex us or seem to conflict with what God says elsewhere in His Word. It is risky to base our beliefs about God on a careless or incomplete understanding of His Word.

Angela risked her life because of a distorted image of God and an incomplete understanding of Scripture. "My husband, Ted, physically abused me for the first three years of our marriage," she said. "He would fly into a rage and beat me, then afterward he would cry and tell me how sorry he was and beg me to forgive him. We'd pray together, and then things would be calm for a few weeks, sometimes even months. Then it would happen again."

Angela and Ted were fairly new Christians, and Angela was very confused about how she should respond to her husband's anger and violence. She loved Ted, but she was also afraid of him.

Though Angela read her Bible every day, she didn't always understand what she read. As Ted's violence grew steadily worse, she turned to a Christian friend, Kathy, for counsel. "Sometimes Ted gets really mad," she said. "I don't know how God wants me to respond when he gets angry like that." Angela failed to mention that when Ted got mad, he sometimes beat her until she was bruised and bleeding!

Kathy shared with Angela a passage that read "Wives, submit to your own husbands, as to the Lord. For the husband is head of the wife, as also Christ is the head of the church."[4] Angela's brow furrowed as she read those words, and she touched her hand to her cheek, as if remembering some painful wound she had received there. "I . . . I guess I'll just have to do a better job of submitting to my husband," she said after a few moments of reflection.

So Angela tried to do what the passage said. Yet it seemed that the more submissive she tried to be, the more enraged Ted became. "It was weird," said Angela, "like he was hitting me to get me to fight back. When I didn't, he became even more violent."

One Saturday night, Ted gave Angela a particularly brutal working over. It ended, as usual, with Angela lying moaning on the couch and Ted being full of remorse. "Angela, honey, I'm so sorry," he said tearfully. "Please forgive me. I promise I'll never do it again."

Angela could hardly answer. "Hospital" was all she could say through her swollen lips.

"No," said Ted, horrified that his brutality would be discovered if he took his wife to the emergency room. "No, you'll be okay, honey. Just rest. You'll feel fine in the morning."

Sunday morning, Ted went to church. When people asked about Angela, he told them she wasn't feeling good, but she'd be okay. Marianne, the pastor's wife, thought she detected something wrong in Ted's manner—an edge of nervousness, and even guilt, when he talked about Angela. Monday morning, she stopped by Angela's home after Ted left for work. As soon as Angela opened the door, Marianne gasped in horror. Then, ignoring Angela's slurred protests, Marianne bundled her into the car and rushed her to the hospital where she was treated for a broken jaw and facial cuts and contusions.

"Marianne talked me into making an assault complaint against Ted," Angela recalled. "The point was not to hurt Ted but to make him see the seriousness of what he had done. For his emotional and spiritual good, Ted needed to experience the consequences of his sin and take responsibility for his behavior. The court gave Ted probation, and the church quietly disciplined him. There was no public humiliation or anything. Ted was called in to meet with the pastor and two elders of the church, and he was placed in an accountable relationship with those men. He had to agree to undergo counseling at the Minirth-Meier Clinic and meet with the pastor and the two elders once a week.

"Ted was angry and defensive at first. He blamed Marianne for interfering. He blamed me for making the complaint. He was mad at the pastor and the whole church. It took weeks to break down his denial, but eventually, he could see how much he had hurt me and how much he needed help.

"Ted has learned to manage his anger, and I have learned a little bit more about how to interpret the Bible. My friend Kathy meant well when she shared that passage about wives being submissive, but now I know that passage was never intended to cover a situation where a husband is committing assault against his wife. Ted was ignoring the verses that tell husbands to love and care for their wives.

"I did the right thing by confronting Ted with his sin. Galatians 6:1 says that those who are caught in a pattern of habitual sin, as Ted was, must be confronted and restored, not simply allowed to go their merry way, hurting themselves and others.

"You can't understand all there is to know about God or the Christian life from just a handful of verses. God is so much bigger than that. Life is so much more complicated than that. I'm glad Marianne helped me see that before something much worse happened."

Source 2: Jesus Christ

The second source God has given us to enable us to know Him on an intimate basis is His Son, Jesus Christ. Through Jesus, God has identified with us—with our pain, grief, and even death. And through Jesus Christ, we can relate to God, face-to-face. The Bible declares Jesus to be *not* half man and half God but *fully* human and *fully* God. Jesus claimed to be God and to be one with the Father since before creation.[5] And Jesus stated that to know Him was to know God the Father. "If you had known Me," He said, "you would have known My Father also; and from now on you know Him and have seen Him."[6]

Imagine for just a moment that you lived in Palestine two thousand years ago. Imagine that you were able to walk alongside

Jesus, to hear the sound of His voice, to look into His eyes as you asked Him questions about God and about life. Out of all those who have lived throughout human history, those who were able to actually see and hear and touch Jesus were privileged to have met *God in the flesh.*

And yet, I believe that we Christians at the end of the twentieth century have an even greater privilege. We cannot see or hear or touch Jesus, but we have something that people of two thousand years ago didn't have: we have the New Testament.

In the New Testament, we have a concise, complete account of Jesus' birth, His life, His death, His resurrection, and His message to us. As we study that account and immerse our minds and emotions in that message, we come to know Jesus Christ in a way that people of the first century A.D. never could. The God-inspired New Testament tells us all we need to know about the character of Jesus. And because Jesus said, "He who has seen Me has seen the Father," that same New Testament record tells us all we need to know about the character of God the Father as well.

The presence of Jesus with us today is just as real and dynamic as it was for His disciples so many years ago. The difference between now and then is that His presence in those days was physical. His presence today is spiritual. As J. I. Packer observes in *Knowing God,*

> Jesus' way of speaking to us now is not by uttering fresh words, but rather by applying to our consciences those words of His that are recorded in the Gospels, together with the rest of the biblical testimony to Himself. But knowing Jesus Christ still remains as definite a relation of personal discipleship as it was for the twelve when He was on earth. The Jesus who walks through the gospel story walks with Christians now, and knowing Him involves going with Him, now as then.[7]

Source 3: The Holy Spirit

Through the Holy Spirit, God ministers to us in the intimacy of our human spirits. Through the Holy Spirit, we come to know God on a personal and deeply intimate basis. "But the Helper, the Holy Spirit," said Jesus, "whom the Father will send in My name, He will teach you all things, and bring to your remembrance all things that I said to you."[8]

The Holy Spirit speaks to us as we study the Bible, opening the eyes of our understanding so that we can see the nature and character of God in its pages. The Holy Spirit also speaks directly to our spirits and our emotions as we meditate, pray, and commune with God.

The Bible, Jesus Himself, and the Holy Spirit agree on the *true* image of God. The Holy Spirit never contradicts the words of Scripture or the words of Jesus. Any ideas we have about God that we *think* come from the Holy Spirit should be tested against the Word of God and the message of Jesus to see if they are truly of God.

"I Can Almost Smell the Butterscotch!"

"I loved that sweet old man," said Rick Hanks during a recent conversation. He was reminiscing about the pastor of the church he was raised in back in Sweetwater, Texas. "He was white-haired, and he had these sad, soulful eyes like a hound. His ears stuck out like two open doors on a pickup truck. But he was the gentlest, kindest man I ever knew.

"He always kept a pocketful of butterscotch candies wrapped in cellophane, and when he'd greet us kids at the door after Sunday preaching, he'd shake hands with me, as solemn as can be. But when I took my hand away from his, there was one of those yellow candies, right in the palm of my hand. And I'd look up at the preacher, and he'd give me a wink.

"Sometimes I thought of that kind old preacher as being like Jesus. I could really picture Jesus sitting there on a hill under the olive trees, calling the little kids to come gather round. And then He'd wink at them, reach into the pocket of His robe, and pull out a big handful of butterscotch candies.

"The God I learned about at home was another matter altogether. Dad was always drilling into us kids how God expected us to be perfect, how He always punished sin, and all those awful things that happened to people He took a disliking to. Of course I didn't realize it until I'd been in counseling, but I really identified God with my abusive father. And that's where I learned to hate God.

"When I heard the word *God,* I used to get a picture out of the

Old Testament—you know, thunder on Mount Sinai, a pillar of cloud in the daytime, a pillar of fire in the night. I could see God just the way my father described Him, a judge in a black robe, sitting on a throne, damning wailing sinners to hell. I couldn't match up my image of God with my image of Jesus.

"For years I've had an image of the Holy Spirit as being faceless, blank, and bland. Now that I can look back and see things more clearly, I realize my image of the Holy Spirit was probably shaped by my mom.

"When my dad would abuse us verbally or with his fist or his belt, my mom would just get a sort of blank look on her face. She'd mentally check out of the situation. She knew my dad was being mean and unfair, but she never did anything, even when we begged her. We'd say, 'Momma, don't let Daddy beat us,' but she stayed neutral. After the beating and the hollering were all over, my dad would stomp out of the house and slam the door. Then my mom would say to us kids, 'That's just the way your daddy is. You just have to learn to get used to him.' She must have said that about a thousand times, but I never did get used to him.

"So that's been my image of God. Or rather, my images, plural. A kind, gentle Jesus. An abusive, volatile heavenly Father. A neutral, ineffectual Holy Spirit. I'm still working on getting my image of God in focus—not three gods but a single, unified *God*. I've made a lot of progress."

I asked Rick what helped him the most in bringing his image of God into focus.

"Prayer and the Word," he replied without hesitation. "I used to hide from the Father, just like I hid from my earthly father to stay out of the way of his anger and his fists. But now I force myself to come into God's presence in prayer on a daily basis, whether I feel like it or not. Lately, I don't feel as much like hiding. I feel God loves me and accepts me.

"When I was a kid, all I knew about the Bible was what my dad told me, and all of that was pretty distorted information. Now I read the Bible for myself, and I'm forming a lot of new impressions. It's like a whole different Book from the one my dad preached out of. I've been meditating on those symbols of God you showed me, Dr. Stephens. It helps me to see God as the Good Shepherd or the Prince of Peace. Images of God as a source of peace and serenity mean the most to me since my old image of God was one of violence and fear.

"As a result of my new understanding of the Bible, I can see much more clearly the identification between the Father, the Son, and the Holy Spirit. I'm beginning to sense—not just intellectually but here in my gut—that I'm not dealing with three different gods but with three expressions of a single personality."

Our time was almost up, but Rick seemed to have one more thing he wanted to tell me. He paused and grinned with a hint of embarrassment.

"What is it?" I asked. "What do you want to say?"

"Well, this is going to sound silly . . ."

"No, go ahead. What's on your mind?"

"Well, I get up early before the rest of the family, and I pray and read the Word in my big leather chair in the den. Lately, I've had mornings with the Lord that have been really good. I've honestly felt God talking to me, encouraging me, loving me. And on those mornings when I'm talking to God and feeling Him talking to me, I swear I can almost smell the butterscotch!"

My friend Rick Hanks has learned—and continues to learn on a day-by-day basis—where to turn to discover God's *true* image. His old distorted image of God, which was placed there by a violent and unloving father, is gradually being replaced by the truth of God's Word.

In the next chapter, we will look at how we can encourage an accurate image of God and an intimate relationship with God in our children.

Chapter Ten

Giving Your Children a Hug from God

A couple took their three-year-old son to church to be dedicated. During the dedication service, the pastor told the boy that *dedication* means that his mommy and daddy are promising to raise him to know Jesus and to have God living in his heart. The boy listened with wide-eyed attention.

The next morning the boy bounced down to breakfast with an excited expression on his face and his hand tucked under his pajama shirt. "God is in my heart!" he announced. "I can feel Him bumping around in there!"[1]

This story, told by comedian Dick Van Dyke in his book *Faith, Hope and Hilarity,* illustrates the challenge and the joys of teaching our children about God—who He is, how we can know Him, how we can have Him living inside our hearts. Van Dyke—the veteran star of Broadway, TV, and films such as *Mary Poppins*—is also a father of four and a former Sunday school teacher, so he has given a lot of thought to the question, "How can parents help shape a healthy image of God in their children?"

"Have you ever tried to tell a child about God?" he writes.

> Grown-ups take it for granted that God is all-powerful, all-wise, all-perfect, all this and all that, but to children this is pretty exciting stuff. This God, whoever He is, must be the biggest hero of them all: smarter, braver, and stronger than any of those guys in the comic strips and on TV. He's probably flying round up there in Heaven with a cape and a big "G" on His chest, as He zaps all the villainous evildoers. As one boy explained to his smaller buddies, "God is greater than Superman, Batman, and The Lone Ranger put together."[2]

In his book, Van Dyke collected stories from parents and Sunday school teachers across the country. Several of these stories amusingly illustrate the powerful influence of fathers in shaping their children's image of God. "A four-year-old," writes Van Dyke, "was sure he knew exactly what God looks like: 'Just like my Daddy, only lots bigger.'"[3]

How do you explain to a child what God—this invisible, omnipresent, all-seeing Being—is like? One mother tried to explain God to her three-year-old daughter, with entertaining results. "God is everywhere," said the mother. "You can't see God, but He can see you."

The little girl's face came alight. "Let's guess where He's hiding!"[4]

Other snippets of kid theology from Van Dyke's book range from the fanciful ("God has a big fat tummy, and we're in it") to the frightening ("God is a giant who is on a mountain and hits people with a stick if they are bad").[5] These words underscore the responsibility that is ours as Christian parents, charged with the awesome task of raising our children in the nurture and admonition of the Lord.

Children Running on Empty

The Minirth-Meier Clinic book *Love Is a Choice* contains a diagram we often use at the clinic to illustrate the love relationship God planned to exist between parents and their children. We call it the "Love Tank" diagram,[6] and it looks like this:

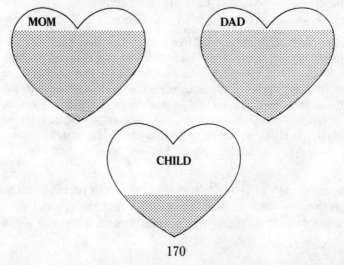

All of us have a reservoir of love, which is graphically represented as a heart-shaped love tank. Imagine having a love tank deep within yourself and a fuel gauge showing how much love is stored there. When we are born, that tank is empty, and the gauge reads "E." God's plan is for our parents to pour love into our love tanks out of the reservoir of their love tanks. As we grow, our inner love tanks fill, little by little. By the time we reach adulthood, our love tanks should be full enough that we can fill the tanks of our children.

In functional families, each generation pours love into the love tanks of the next generation, and that generation passes its love to the next, and on and on in a beautifully cascading cycle of love. Children grow up secure in the love they have received from their parents, and secure in the love of God. (These heart-shaped tanks are shown less than completely full because being imperfect human beings, we can never have perfectly full tanks; the only love tank that is ever 100 percent full is God's.)

In dysfunctional families, children do not receive the filling of their emotional love tanks as God intended. They may receive neglect instead of nurturing; unpredictable outbursts of rage instead of steady, firm, loving discipline; absence instead of involvement and availability; coldness and criticism instead of acceptance and affirmation.

How do we fill the love tanks of our children? What are our specific acts and behaviors that fill up their inner reservoirs with the sense of love and security God intended them to have? We give our children our time and attention. We give them our availability. We give them our affirmation, affection, and forgiveness. We give them all the gifts God has given us through His Son Jesus Christ.

Children deprived of these ingredients grow up with an undersupply of love and security. They may attempt to fill the gnawing emptiness in their love tanks with any number of false love-substitutes: drug abuse, alcohol abuse, or food abuse; sexual promiscuity; workaholism; religious legalism; or some other compulsive behavior. Adolescents or young adults with an aching emptiness in their love tanks are also easy prey for cults and the occult. Their image of God is distorted, and the New Age and other false religious systems are quick to exploit their need for security and belonging that has never been met in childhood.

The Child's View of God chart shows the contrast between the child with a well-filled love tank and the child with an empty love tank—and how each child tends to perceive God.

A CHILD'S VIEW OF GOD

Child with a Well-filled Love Tank	Child with an Empty Love Tank
Present and available	Absent and unreal
Loving and caring	Neglectful and unconcerned
Holy, just, and fair	Unjust, unfair, and biased
Stable and reliable	Touchy, unpredictable, and untrustworthy
Kind and merciful	Uncaring and vindictive
Gracious	Demanding
Generous, the Giver of good gifts	Malicious, the One who stomps out enjoyment
Affirming	Impossible to please

As you compare and contrast the traits, consider which set you tend to display toward your children. Which column most represents your character and your parenting style? In what areas do you need to improve to better exemplify a healthy example of Christian character and the image of God?

When Jesus was on the earth, He invited the little children to come to Him. He embraced them and spoke lovingly to them. When Jesus hugged them, they were getting—in a very direct sense—a hug from God. Jesus no longer walks the earth as a flesh-and-blood man. God is spirit, and children cannot go to a spirit for a warm flesh-and-blood hug and a gentle word of affirmation. The affection and the unconditional love of God are real, but they are mediated through human parents. It is our job as parents to give our children a hug from God every day.

If we are neglectful, impatient, explosive, condemning, and/or legalistic, we will build our children's image out of these same raw materials. It won't matter very much what we *tell* our children about God or what they learn about Him in Sunday school or church. We will have already imprinted our distortions of God's character in their minds and emotions by our sinful and dysfunctional behavior.

Our goal as Christian parents is to fill the love tanks of our children, day by day, cupful by cupful. As their inner reservoirs of love and security rise to the brim of their hearts, their relationship with God will grow strong, reliable, and secure.

America's Saddest Home Videos

Here is a story that took place a short time before Carrie Bishop came to me for counseling. In fact, the incident was one factor that caused Carrie to see that she needed help in dealing with her emotional and spiritual issues.

Carrie stood in the bleachers of the junior high gymnasium, a camcorder whirring away in her hands, her right eye glued to the eyepiece, the camera lens focused on the hardwood court below. Her thirteen-year-old son Jeremy had just been fouled by a player on the opposing team, so he was taking his place in the center of the key. As she peered at the black-and-white image of her son in the viewfinder, Carrie grinned tensely. "Okay, Jer, this is it!" she called hoarsely. "It's a one and one, Jer! Don't miss the first one!"

Jeremy ran one hand through his brown hair as he placed the toes of his shoes against the charity strip. He bounced the ball twice on the floor. He could hear his mother shouting his name, urging him to make the shot. He eyed the hoop. It seemed like it was a million miles away. His stomach felt constricted, as if it were tied in a knot. His hands shook as they clutched the ball. He sucked in a deep breath, held it, and launched the shot.

The ball sailed in a high parabola. From the stands, Carrie's camcorder followed its flight. The ball thudded against the backboard, a little left of center, and fell onto the rim of the hoop. It rolled once around the rim. It dropped.

But not through the net. No point. And no second shot.

Carrie took the camcorder away from her face, which had become a contorted mask of fury. "Jeremy!" she bellowed. "Jeremy Mark Bishop, what is the matter with you!"

On the court, Jeremy turned, white-faced, and saw his mother stalking down the bleachers, oblivious to the shocked faces of parents and students who watched the game. Jeremy knew what was coming, and he also knew he could do nothing to stop it. But the ball was back in play, and he had to bear down and get back in the game.

So Jeremy played. Legs pumping, lungs straining, a lump of shame in his throat bigger than any basketball, Jeremy moved up and down the court with his teammates. At the same time, his mother stormed up and down the sidelines, screaming, "Jeremy, that was so *stupid!* That was the easiest point you ever could have made! How could you blow an easy shot like that?"

After the game, Carrie drove her son home. Jeremy spent the first couple of miles looking out the passenger-side window. Finally, he spoke. "How could you do that, Mom?"

"Do what?"

"Holler at me like that," he answered. Both anger and tears seemed to be fighting for control of his face. "In front of the guys and the coach and everybody. That was so awful."

"Jer, I was just trying to encourage you to do better, that's all!" Carrie said defensively. "You're my kid and I love you. I just want you to do your best." She reached out and put her hand on her son's arm, but he shook it off angrily.

"Don't touch me!" he growled.

Not another word was said for the rest of the drive home.

The next day was Carrie's day off from work. After she drove Jeremy to school, she came home, rewound the videotape she had taken of Jeremy's game, and began to watch. She came to the place where Jeremy missed the shot from the free throw line—but the tape didn't stop there. She had forgotten to press the red button on the camcorder. There, on the TV screen, was jerky video footage of her shoes, the bleachers, the gym floor. The pictures might have been funny, like something from that TV show with Bob Saget, but the soundtrack was not funny at all.

Horrified, Carrie heard her voice: "Jeremy Mark Bishop, what is the matter with you! That was so *stupid!* How could you blow an easy shot like that?"

She stopped the tape, dropped her head in her hands, and began to weep. "Jeremy, Jeremy, what am I doing to you?" she cried.

There *Is* Hope

As we've seen in previous chapters, Carrie was raised with a near-empty love tank. Her father was sexually abusive and her mother was emotionally abusive. One way Carrie learned to compensate for the imperfections of her childhood was to become a ruthless perfectionist. She maintained the perfect image, kept her house perfectly clean, dressed her son in the perfect clothes, and demanded complete perfection in everything he did, from his grades in school to his sports activities.

Today, Carrie realizes that one reason she has been so driven to live through the achievements of her son is that she has long felt her life was worthless. In an attempt to build a "perfect" life for her son, she was destroying him emotionally.

Several months after that incident, during one of Carrie's early visits to my office, I could plainly see the fear in Carrie's eyes as she asked, "How do I fill my son's love tank when my own is completely dry?"

Perhaps you can identify with Carrie's fear. Perhaps you, too, feel trapped in the cycle of intergenerational pain. You have grown up with a distorted image of God, now you see yourself inflicting similar pain on your children, and you feel helpless to stop yourself.

That's how Carrie felt, but after she watched the videotape and heard the hurtful things she yelled at her son, she cried out to God for help. And God showed her what to do.

That afternoon, Carrie picked up her son from school as usual. He sat sullen and silent all the way home. When they got to the door, Carrie opened it and let Jeremy enter first. From the front door, he could see into the dining room. Taped to the dining room wall was a big hand-painted sign that read:

JEREMY, I'M
SO SORRY, PLEASE
FORGIVE ME.
I LOVE YOU SO
MUCH,
MOM

On the table was a plate of Jeremy's favorite thing in the whole world: oatmeal cookies with chocolate chips and M & M's.®

"I made them myself," said Carrie, "with extra M & M's.®'" And she began to cry. "Oh, Jer, I'm so sorry—"

The hug her son gave her told her everything was all right. Carrie had created a memory to last a lifetime in the heart of her young son—the memory of a parent who says, "I'm sorry."

There *is* hope. Carrie's story proves that you are not doomed to repeat the patterns inflicted on you by your parents. The fact that you are reading this book shows you are aware that you need to deal with your image of God issues. Here are some steps you can take:

1. Get the help you need.   If you are dealing with emotional and spiritual issues arising from your family-of-origin, please take the step of seeking the help appropriate to your need—a Christian counselor, psychologist, or psychiatrist; your pastor; a support group or a recovery group. If you don't know where to turn for help, your pastor can refer you to the help you need.

If you are abusing your children—physically, sexually, or emotionally—you must get help *immediately*. Don't wait. Don't try to "get better" on your own. If you truly love your children, don't hesitate for another second to get the help you urgently need.

2. Communicate honestly with your children.   As human beings, parents make mistakes. Even the best parents will yell, discipline inappropriately, say hurtful things, or act thoughtlessly from time to time. When you do, you have a duty as a Christian parent to honestly admit your mistakes to your kids. You may be reluctant to humble yourself before your children and say, "I was wrong. Please forgive me." But if you fail to admit the wrongs you do to your children, they will grow up feeling that *they* are to blame for your inappropriate behavior.

When you communicate honestly with your children, admitting your wrongs and asking their forgiveness, you break that cycle of intergenerational pain. You tell your children, in effect, "I just did something I'm sorry for. That is not the example I want to set for you. That is not the kind of person I want to be. That is not the kind of person God is." Honest communication—including confession of your faults—helps to erase the distortions of your sins and mistakes from your children's image of God.

3. Spend time with your children, talking, praying, and singing about God's love. This is good therapy not only for your children but also for *you.* As Jesus said on more than one occasion, the path to spiritual wholeness lies in becoming as little children.[7] So cultivate a childlike faith within your heart. Sit down with your children and sing songs about God's love: "Jesus Loves Me," "Jesus Loves the Little Children," "Jesus Loves the Little Ones Like Me, Me, Me."

Tell your children stories about God's love. Either paraphase the stories of the Bible, or get one or two children's Bible story-books. Read, pray, and sing with your children at a special time each day—say, at breakfast or at bedtime. Don't make it a deep time of solemn religious instruction; make it *fun!* You will find that the time you spend building a healthy image of a loving God in your children's hearts will also bring healing in your image of God.

Ten Steps to Building a Healthy Image of God in Your Children

As Christian parents, we want to raise our children to have a positive image of God. Scripture charges us with the solemn responsibility to raise our children in the training and admonition of the Lord, not to provoke them to wrath and leave them with an emotional residue of bitterness and anger.[8] Here are some specific things you can do to build an emotional foundation in your children that leads to a healthy image of God:

1. Create a home environment where feelings—including feelings of anger—can be appropriately expressed. Children and parents should be continually learning to express anger and other emotions in ways that do not hurt other people. When children are allowed to explode in uncontrollable anger, they become baby tyrants, controlling the mood of the entire family. In a similar way, unpredictable and disproportionate flare-ups of *parental* anger can terrorize a family and shake children's sense of security.

When children become angry, they are likely to scream, hit, kick, or otherwise act in an inappropriate way (to put it mildly!). As a parent, your tendency is to try to change their behavior—to stop the screaming, the hitting, and the kicking. Unfortunately, many parents also have a tendency to suppress or minimize the very real feelings that prompted the inappropriate behavior.

One way you can fulfill the biblical admonition to "not provoke your children to wrath" is to make a genuine effort to understand their feelings. "What are you angry about?" you might ask. "I'm not going to allow you to yell and hit people, but I do want to understand why you are angry. It's okay for you to tell me you feel angry. But I want you to express your anger in a way that doesn't hurt yourself or other people."

When children are unhappy or afraid, you cannot turn off those feelings by denying them. If you say to children, "Don't feel unhappy," or "You have no reason to be afraid," all you do is make them feel ashamed of their feelings. Instead, you should encourage your children to talk about their feelings, honestly and openly.

2. Be an open, approachable parent. Make a conscious effort to be the kind of parent children can approach with any issue, any problem, any feeling—and always feel *safe*. There should be no off-limits topics and no out-of-bounds issues.

That doesn't mean you never discipline or say tough things to your children. But even tough things can be said in a firm, gentle way, surrounded by unconditional love. No matter how tough the issue, your kids should never feel unsafe or wary around you, as if they have to tiptoe on eggshells in your presence.

3. Forgive and receive forgiveness. Never hold a sin over children's heads. Once the matter is dealt with, forgive it and forget it. Don't remind the children of a sin you forgave a week ago or a year ago. If you do, you didn't really forgive.

When you do something that hurts your children, admit what you did, tell them you are sorry, and ask them to forgive you. As you build the concept of God's forgiving grace into the minds and hearts of your children, they will grow to healthy adulthood, able to forgive and to receive forgiveness as God intended, free of the poisonous emotion of shame.

4. Never use God as a threat. Telling children that God will hurt or kill them if they sin can distort their view of God for life. I've counseled many people who were threatened in this way when they were children. Now, in their thirties, forties, and beyond, they see God as an enemy, ready to punish them any moment. Always portray God as loving and forgiving. If you use God as a threat against children, you slander the character of God.

5. Respect your children's emotional boundaries. The most extreme forms of violating children's emotional boundaries include sexual and physical abuse. Children who are abused learn to see the victim role as normal, and they grow up expecting to be abused by other people and by God Himself.

But there are also subtler forms of violating children's emotional boundaries. Some parents dominate their children emotionally. They make their decisions for them, choose (or pass judgment on) their friends, rescue them from every difficulty, manipulate their feelings, and cling to them when they approach the stage of maturity where they should be let go.

As a Christian parent, you naturally want to be involved in your children's lives. You want the best for them. You want to give them your time, show you are interested in their lives, and demonstrate an appropriate level of affection. But to raise healthy kids with a healthy image of God, you must also give them the right to be themselves, think their thoughts, feel their feelings, and develop as individuals separate and distinct from you. If you live through your children or smother their personhood with your control, they will grow up with areas of severe distortion in their emotions and in their relationship with God.

6. Help children make healthy attributions to God. Sometimes your children approach you with tough questions: "Why does God allow people to steal and hurt other people?" or "Why does He allow so many people to starve in other countries?" Or a child may say, "I don't like God! He could have kept Grandma well, but He let her die!"

These are normal questions and feelings. Whenever children ask these questions or express these feelings, you have an opportunity to help them build a more realistic and reliable image of God. You should be unshockable and accept what they are feeling without condemning or scolding them. After listening to the children express their feelings, you should explain God's character as best you can in a way that is appropriate to their level of understanding.

For example, to the child who blames God for world hunger, you can say, "I know you are feeling that God is unfair to allow people to die of hunger. But you know, the Bible says that God loves the whole world and does not want anyone to suffer and perish. If you look closely at the situation in a country like Ethiopia or Cambodia, you find out that it is not God but sinful people who have caused all that suffering. Some sinful people want to have power so they can lord it over everyone else, and that causes wars and hunger and a lot of suffering.

"The only way God could stop these things from happening would be to take away our human free will, and He chooses not to do that. We cannot understand everything that God does or allows, but we know that God wants us to choose, in our own free will, to follow Him and to help other people. Instead of being angry with God for allowing people to go hungry, why don't you start setting aside some of your allowance each week so you can give it to help hungry people find food and find Jesus?"

7. Build warm memories. Some of the richest, most lasting memories of our lives are built during childhood. A child's thinking is more emotional than cognitive, and a child's memory is triggered by strong emotions. In other words, a child's memory is much more strongly affected by *feelings* than by *facts*. Every day, your children experience emotions—feelings of love, joy, and security, or feelings of pain, sadness, and shame—and they will carry those feelings in the inner being for a *lifetime*. If you want to care for children spiritually, you must nurture them emotionally.

The best times to build a child's image of God are those times when emotions are warm and pleasant, when there is a sense of excitement, discovery, and fun. You can use those golden moments to plant an idea, a feeling, a rich sense of God's pervasive presence and love toward us.

During a visit to Disneyland, a brief comment can transform a fun experience into something meaningful in the lives of children: "If you think this is fun, imagine what heaven must be like!" A vacation in the mountains or at the seashore can be used as an object lesson in God's wisdom and creative power. A beautiful sunset or a rainbow can be described as a gift of God's love to us.

Any spare moment in the day can be an opportunity for you and your children to pray together, simply and briefly: "Thank You, God, for the gift of this day. We're really enjoying our time together. Amen." Keep prayers short and personal—not poetic, lengthy, or religious sounding. Pause and give thanks to God for that special report card or that letter from Grandpa. Or take a moment in the middle of the day to pray together for a special need: "Please help Evan not to be afraid of visiting the dentist," or "Please help Molly find her missing library book."

Make time to be a friend to your children. Read stories to them. Sing with them. Play with them. Put your grown-up fingers in the modeling clay or the finger paints. Make drawings alongside your children, using their crayons and colored markers. Show them that you enjoy their company, and while you're at it, tell your children how Jesus enjoyed playing with children. These activities are beautiful opportunities not for teaching deep theological lessons but for making your love relationship with God a natural part of your fun times, your happy moments, your daily life.

8. Become involved in your children's spiritual education. Church, Sunday school, and vacation Bible school are important influences on your children's image of God. Dick Van Dyke writes,

> Many parents got their kids interested in the Bible at home only to have a dull [Sunday school] class turn them off again. A mother in Los Angeles told me what happened after she read some Bible stories to her children one day. Her four-year-old girl said, "Isn't God wonderful? I just love Him." Her brother, age six, said "Wait until you go to Sunday school. You'll hate God."

Van Dyke knows that bringing the Bible alive for kids, week after week, can strain even the talents of the star of *Mary Poppins!* He taught twelve- and thirteen-year-olds in the Dutch Reformed Presbyterian Church of Long Island, New York. "Teaching Sunday school is one of the most important jobs there is, because it's training for life itself," he observes.

> The first lesson I learned as a Sunday school teacher had more to do with show business than theology: get their attention and keep them interested while you're doing your act. . . . I found the kids seemed to get more out of a lesson if we dramatized it. I'd bring along a tape recorder and some scripts, and the kids would play the roles of such biblical characters as Jacob and Esau.[9]

Involve yourself in your children's spiritual education at church. Make sure the Christian education experience is stimulating, lively, and engaging for their active minds. Then reinforce their spiritual education at home.

Explain the meaning of Bible stories to them in terms they can understand and relate to. Help your children identify with the person in the story. If a child is a preschooler or grade-schooler, select stories featuring children and young people. Be alert to any misconceptions your children might gain from the stories they hear at Sunday school or at home. Some well-meaning teachers and parents have done a lot of harm to their children's image of Jesus by reading from the King James Version and not explaining what those Shakespearean-era words mean. For example, what do these words of Jesus—as translated in 1611—say to children of the "Sesame Street" generation: "Suffer the little children . . ."?

9. Discipline with love and consistency. A major source of spiritual distrust is parents who display conditional love, who punish their children out of anger, and who practice discipline that varies according to their internal tension barometer. Inconsistent and unloving discipline causes children to live in fear, never knowing what will set Mom or Dad off, never sure if their next step will earn them a rap in the mouth, a harsh rebuke, or no response at all. Those who felt wary around their parents in childhood tend to feel wary around God in adulthood. They expect God to have the same erratic temper as their parents, and they are continually fearful of God's unexpected anger and retaliation.

Consistency in affirming and reinforcing children is crucial. Love should always be offered freely and unconditionally, even in the face of tough discussions, bad behavior, and bad report cards. Children must know where the boundary lines are, which consequences follow which actions. Parents can't always be 100 percent fair, but children should know that their parents always *try* to be fair.

What about the old adage "spare the rod and spoil the child"? Ross Campbell, in his book *How to Really Love Your Child*, replies,

> Yes, I have seen children who were raised by the rod [of punishment] become Christians. But because they were raised primarily by punishment instead of unconditional love, these unfortunate people seldom have a healthy, loving, warm relationship with God. They tend to use their religion punitively against others under the guise of "helping" them. They use biblical commandments and other scriptural statements to justify their own harsh, unloving behavior. . . .
>
> It is possible, of course, for any child to eventually find his way into God's loving arms and to accept His love. With God anything is possible. Unfortunately, a child's chances are markedly diminished if his parents have not given him a loving foundation. . . .
>
> There are two requirements essential to helping a child spiritually: A parent's personal relationship with God, and a child's assurance that he is unconditionally loved.[10]

The most profound biblical teaching on discipline can be summed up in the words of Ephesians 6:4: "Do not provoke your children to wrath, but bring them up in the training and admonition of the Lord." In other words, don't inflict emotional wounds on your children that will make them feel angry and bitter for the rest of their lives. Instead, nurture them. Train them. Meet their emotional needs. When you do that, you are raising them to have a healthy relationship with their loving heavenly Father.

10. Most of all, give your children the gift of your time—and yourself. Spend time alone with your children—focused time, fun time, intimate time. Make eye contact with them as you talk to them about God and His love. Meet your children's emotional as well as spiritual needs. Bedtime is a valuable time for building their image of God, for at bedtime your children are especially eager to cuddle and interact with you. Use those moments to build memories and a sense of truth and security.

Share your spiritual pilgrimage with your children in terms appropriate to their ages and understanding. Talk about how you came to know the Lord, how Jesus is a friend to you, how you can talk to God anytime you want, in any words you want, not just at meals or at bedtime. Let your children hear you praying for them, thanking God for them, and praying for their future. Let them hear you address God as a loving heavenly Father, who loves, forgives, and is the Giver of good gifts.

Pray very specifically for your children's hurts, needs, and fears, no matter how trivial they may seem from an adult perspective. Remember how large those issues loom in the minds and emotions of children.

How to Lose a Son

Randy Sullivan was raised in a respected Christian home in the suburbs. His parents had their careers (Dad was an attorney, Mom a nurse practitioner). They were also very involved in the church (he was an elder, and she was Sunday school superintendent).

Randy had been vaguely unhappy for several years, though he could not articulate *why* he was unhappy. The Sullivans were affluent enough, and there was nothing Randy wanted that he didn't already have. Randy's folks were slow to notice when his grades began to slide and he began staying away from home for long periods of time. After all, they were not home very much themselves.

When, at the age of fifteen, Randy announced he didn't want to go to church anymore, Mr. Sullivan didn't bother to ask his son *why* he didn't want to go. He just gave Randy the same answer he had given many times before: "As long as you're living under my roof, eating my chow, with clothes I paid for on your back, you'll go to church and do anything else I tell you to!"

As his father went into the old refrain, Randy mockingly chimed in on the chorus: "Living under my roof, eating my chow . . ."

Mr. Sullivan then promised to "wipe that smirk" off his son's face. From there, things inevitably escalated into a full-blown shouting match. Later, after things quieted down, Randy's father grumbled to his wife, "Where does he get that stuff? Why does he think all I ever do is yell at him? Lately, it seems I hardly ever talk to him at all, much less yell at him!"

Randy's dad was closer to the truth than he realized, but he still couldn't see it. He had become almost absent as a father, busily taking care of the office business and the church business while neglecting the business of his own home. When did he ever talk to Randy anymore? Only when things went wrong, and then only at the top of his lungs.

Over the next few months, Randy sank even deeper into sullenness and depression. Mr. and Mrs. Sullivan had no idea who his friends were or how he spent his time. They would have been horrified to hear the heavy metal music he was listening to—and the discussions he was having with his friends about the meaning of life.

"Santa Claus, the Easter Bunny, Jesus Christ, what's the difference?" said Randy's friend Scott, who was dressed in black pants and a black Slayer T-shirt. "No more myths for me, man. I create my own reality. You can't find God in church, Randy. The only God there is, is is-ness itself."

"Scott's right, Randy," added Shannon, Scott's girlfriend. With her frosted black hair and heavy eye makeup in shades of bruise black and livid purple, she looked like a refugee from the Addams family. "Your folks still want you to go to church and learn about their Christian God, right? Well, I don't have to visit my god in church."

The three of them—Randy, Scott, and Shannon—were sitting in the basement recreation room of the Sullivans's home, listening to Twisted Sister screaming the lyrics to "Burn in Hell" on the CD player. Randy didn't expect his folks to be home for hours, so he invited Scott and Shannon over for some music and talk. Randy lapped up every word his friends said. The idea of a god who was completely unlike his parents' God captured his imagination. He wanted nothing to do with the God his parents worshiped.

"I worship two kinds of deities," Shannon continued, "the ones whose energies are already a part of me, and the ones who are alien energies from outside myself. Lately, I've been working a lot with Gaia, the earth goddess."

"Church'll just mess up your head, Randy," added Scott. "I get my insight straight from my spirit guides. I concentrate on deep breathing, and I visualize myself inhaling white light. The light pours into me, and I let it flow through me. You should try it, man."

And Randy did try it. Soon, he was receiving messages from spirit guides too. At first, it was exciting to know he had tapped into a power beyond his imagining. But as the weeks passed, he began to feel haunted and afraid. His sleep was troubled by night-terrors and bad dreams. He experienced strange, powerful compulsions—to cut himself, burn himself with cigarettes, or kill himself.

Randy's parents had no idea what he was into until they came home from church one Wednesday night. From somewhere in the house, a stereo was shrieking rock at maximum volume. "Randy!" called Mr. Sullivan as he entered the screaming, shud-dering house. "Randy! Answer me! Where are you?" There was no answer. Looking for the blaring source of the music, the Sul-livans descended the stairs to the rec room and found their son Randy on the floor. He was unconscious.

Mr. Sullivan lifted his son, carried him to the car, and rushed him to the hospital, where his stomach was pumped. He had swal-lowed a large number of Quaaludes along with some liquor his friend Scott had given him. Today, Randy and his parents are in counseling with a Christian psychologist and their pastor. Mr. and Mrs. Sullivan came within a whisker of losing their son—and their son may well have come equally close to losing his eternal soul. God only knows.

Randy is not out of the woods yet—his psychological and emo-tional wounds are too deep for any quick fix. But Randy *is* mak-ing progress. He has begun to look to God for his ultimate reality—not to spirit guides. Randy's parents have resigned from the majority of their time-consuming church duties so they can spend more time with their son. If only they hadn't waited until they nearly *lost* their son to make time to *find* him!

Randy's parents have learned a painful lesson. So has Carrie Bishop. These parents are discovering—just in time and through painful life experiences—that if they want to raise children who have a strong, sound relationship with God, they must

- work on rebuilding their relationship with God.
- communicate honestly with their children and encourage them to communicate honestly.
- forgive and receive forgiveness.
- never use God as a threat.
- respect their children's emotional boundaries.
- build warm memories in their children's hearts.
- become involved in their children's spiritual education.
- discipline with love and consistency.
- give their children the gift of *time*.

"For me, parenting is all about breaking the cycle," says Rick Hanks. "It's about saying, 'The cycle of pain stops with me.' I've made a promise before God that I won't do to my kids what my father did to me. I don't keep that promise perfectly, of course, but it's my goal as a father and I give it my best shot. The payoff for me is when I listen to my children pray, and they just pour out their little hearts to their heavenly Father. Those prayers are so honest and trusting. It's the sweetest sound you'll ever hear."

As a Christian parent, you want your children to experience a close, warm relationship with God. The key to your children's image of God is *the way you live* and *the way you parent*. You are God's earthly representative to your children. God is counting on you—and your children are counting on you—to give them a hug from God every day. Every hug, every kiss, every affirming, tender word you give your children is given on behalf of a loving God. When that becomes the way you view your task as a parent, it will transform your view of parenting from a duty to a *ministry*.

Jesus loves the little children—and He loves them through you and me.

A Letter to God

As you've been reading this book, your heavenly Father has been speaking to you—not through any special words of mine but through the stories and the principles and Scripture in this book. In fact, I am convinced, deep in my heart, that God has *always* been speaking to you and trying to reach out to you.

In the last book of the Bible is a famous passage where Jesus said, "Behold, I stand at the door and knock. If anyone hears My voice and opens the door, I will come in to him and dine with him, and he with Me."[1] This verse is often quoted as a salvation verse—one that invites non-Christians to receive Jesus Christ as their Savior. However, I believe that this verse is directed not only at non-Christians but at believers like you and me. In this verse, Jesus was saying, "Let Me be your Savior," and He was also saying, "Let Me be your Friend."

"If anyone hears My voice and opens the door, I will come in to him and dine with him, and he with Me." Do you see the beautiful image in these words? It is the homey, cozy image of two close friends sitting down for an intimate meal together. Warm emotional hues of trust, friendship, and contentment are embedded in that word picture.

I hope that *this* image of God has been saturating your mind and emotions as you have been reading this book. Such warm and reassuring images are found everywhere throughout the Bible. My goal, in part, has been to pull some of these beautiful biblical pictures of our heavenly Father together in one place and thus enable you to see and experience God in a new and intimate way. Perhaps, in your journey through these past ten chapters, you have encountered at least one story, one principle, one idea, one verse of Scripture, one *key* to help you take just a few steps closer to the warm, trusting friendship with God that is described in the beautiful word picture of Jesus: "I will come in to him and dine with him, and he with Me."

During the writing of this book, I wondered what would be the most appropriate way to close it. As I reread the "Open Letter from God" that opens this book, it came to me: What better way to close this book than to *answer* that letter from God? What could be more appropriate than to pledge ourselves to the lifelong goal of a healed and restored image of God? What could be more healing than to write a love letter and a thank-you letter to our heavenly Father?

So I have written such a letter. At the end of that letter, I've left a place for you to sign your name as a symbol of your commitment to a healed relationship with your heavenly Father. On the blank page following the letter, add your own postscript—any personal thoughts and feelings that I may not have captured in the letter itself. I hope you will return again and again to these pages so that you can renew your commitment to a positive image of God and a healed relationship with God.

So here is that letter. It is a letter from my heart. I hope it speaks for your heart as well.

A LETTER TO GOD

Dear heavenly Father,

It feels so good to call You Father and to know that I am Your child.

I know I've distanced myself from You in the past. But, Father, I was too ashamed, hurt, and afraid to let You love me.

I know now that I didn't have to hide from You or be afraid of you. I know now that You truly are gracious, accepting, and merciful. I also know that You see me exactly as I am. You know the pain, the failures, the disappointments that have distorted my image of You. There is no one who knows me like You do—and there is no one who loves me like You do.

I have to be honest with You. I have a long way to go. I still have areas of distortion in my image of You. I still feel I am just beginning to know who You really are. I am just beginning to put all the diverse and amazing aspects of Your character together into one beautiful picture.

Dear Father, I have made a commitment never to fragment my image of You again. I know that You are God the Father and God the Son and God the Holy Spirit. I accept the truth that the Baby in the manger also created the heavens and the earth. I receive You and acknowledge You as my Creator, my Father, my Savior, my Lord, and my Friend.

I want to learn to trust You completely. I want to feel Your love for me and Your presence with me in a real and intimate way. But I desperately need Your help.

Father, You know that my capacity for trust has been damaged. My intellect and my feelings do not agree on who You really are. So I really need Your grace and Your healing power. I can't heal my emotions and my spirit. Only You have the power to heal.

Dear Father, I ask You to invade my life with Your love. Hold me in Your powerful arms. Teach me to trust You, no matter what comes. Open my eyes to see You clearly. Remove every speck and hint of contamination from my image of You. Let me know You as You really are.

I know that You stand and knock at the door of my life. I hear Your voice calling to me. And, Father, I have always wanted to open the door and let You into my life, to share with You the warm, intimate personal relationship that You talk about in Your Word. I really want that relationship with You more than anything else in the world.

That's why I am making a commitment right here in this letter to open the door and let You in. Father, I commit myself to meet You every day in prayer and in the study of Your Word. I also promise to meet You faithfully in worship at church. Finally, I am deciding to trust You with my life, accept Your love for me, and accept Jesus Christ as my personal Savior, since the Bible says the only way I can know You is through Your Son, Jesus.

Thank You for Your great love for me, and for the gift of Your Son, Jesus, who has saved me from my sins. I love You, Father, and I thank You for knocking again at the door of my life.

I'll close now—but we'll talk again soon.

All my love,
Your child,

_____

[Name]

P.S.

Notes

Chapter 1: The Distorted Image
1. J. I. Packer, *Knowing God* (Downers Grove, Ill.: InterVarsity, 1973), 20.
2. Ibid., 29–30.
3. John 17:3.
4. Mark 15:34.

Chapter 3: Diagnosing Our Distortions
1. See Psalm 143:10.
2. Matthew 19:17.
3. James 1:17.
4. John 14:14.
5. Matthew 5:45.
6. See Romans 6:13, 16; 12:1; 1 Corinthians 6:20; 2 Corinthians 5:15.
7. Revelation 3:20.
8. Matthew 11:28, 30.
9. 1 Peter 1:16.
10. Oswald Chambers, *My Utmost for His Highest* (Grand Rapids, Mich.: Discovery House, 1990), 245.

Chapter 4: Where Distortions Begin
1. John 14:9.
2. Romans 8:28–29.
3. See 2 Timothy 1:7; 1 John 4:18.
4. See 1 Corinthians 14:33.
5. See 1 Peter 5:8.
6. Ephesians 6:4.
7. Bob Millard, *Amy Grant: A Biography* (Garden City, N.Y.: Doubleday, 1986), 21.
8. Ibid., 24.
9. Carl W. Roberts, "Imagining God: Who Is Created in Whose Image?" *Review of Religious Research*, 30 (1989), 383.
10. C. Ellzey, "Relationships Among Acceptance of Self, Acceptance of Others, and Belief in an Accepting God" (Ph.D. diss., Columbia University, 1961), 100.
11. Isaiah 55:11.
12. 2 Corinthians 7:1.
13. Isaiah 26:3, emphasis added.

≈§ NOTES §≈

Chapter 5: The Four-Dimensional Image

1. Revelation 7:17; see also Isaiah 53:7; John 1:29, 36; 1 Peter 1:19; Revelation 5:6, 8, 12–13; 7:10; 15:3; 19:7, 9.
2. Romans 8:16; see also 2 Corinthians 1:22.
3. Romans 8:26.

Chapter 6: God's *True* Image

1. Matthew 22:37; Mark 12:30; Luke 10:27.
2. Galatians 4:6.
3. C. Austin Miles, "In the Garden," copyright 1912, renewed 1940, The Rodeheaver Co., owner. All rights reserved. Used by permission.

Chapter 7: Spiritual Decontamination

1. Job 30:20–21; 38:4; 40:8.
2. Job 42:7.
3. 2 Corinthians 7:1
4. 2 Corinthians 7:1, NIV
5. James 4:8; cf. Acts 17:27–28.
6. Psalm 44:23–26.
7. Philip Yancey, *Disappointment with God* (Grand Rapids, Mich.: Zondervan, 1988), 235.
8. Proverbs 14:10.
9. Ephesians 4:31.
10. Hebrews 12:15.
11. "Learning to Trust," music by David Meece, lyrics by David Meece and Michael Hudson. ©Copyright 1989 by Ariose (a Division of Starsong) and Meece Music (Administered by Word Music, a Division of Word, Inc.) used by permission.

Chapter 8: Reparented by God

1. Romans 12:18.
2. Ephesians 4:32.
3. See Matthew 18:3–4; Luke 18:17.

Chapter 9: Obstacles to Knowing God Intimately

1. See John 15:11; 1 Peter 1:8; 1 John 1:4.
2. 1 Corinthians 13:1.
3. Psalm 4:4.
4. Ephesians 5:22–23.
5. See John 17:5.
6. John 14:7; see also John 14:9.

7. J. I. Packer, *Knowing God* (Downers Grove, Ill.: InterVarsity, 1973), 33–34.

8. John 14:26.

Chapter 10: Giving Your Children a Hug from God

1. Dick Van Dyke, *Faith, Hope and Hilarity: The Child's Eye View of Religion* (Garden City, N.Y.: Doubleday, 1970), 52.

2. Ibid., 41.

3. Ibid., 42.

4. Ibid., 55.

5. Ibid., 42.

6. Dr. Robert Hemfelt, Dr. Frank Minirth, and Dr. Paul Meier, *Love Is a Choice* (Nashville: Thomas Nelson, 1989), 34ff.

7. See Matthew 18:3; 19:14; Mark 10:14–15.

8. See Ephesians 6:4; Titus 2:4.

9. Van Dyke, *Faith, Hope and Hilarity*, 11–12.

10. Ross Campbell, *How to Really Love Your Child* (Wheaton, Ill.: Victor Books, 1977), 126.

A Letter to God

1. Revelation 3:20.

Appendix

The Thirty-Day Image of God Restoration Program

Having taken the step of reading this book and gaining insight into the distortions in your image of God, you are ready to walk through a thirty-day program of restoring God's *true* image in your mind and heart. This program is designed to get you started on a *lifelong process*. I am convinced that once you have spent thirty days building a regular habit of prayer and Bible study, you will have the foundation you need to keep moving forward in your relationship with God.

Think of this thirty-day program as a jump-start. When you attach jumper cables to the terminals of a depleted car battery, you provide the spark to start the car's engine—but you have not restored the battery to full power. To fully restore the battery, you must keep the motor going so that the car's generator can provide a continuous surge of power to the battery.

In the same way, no thirty-day program can fully restore your image of God. It can only "jump-start" your relationship with Him. To fully restore your image of God and relationship with God, you must "keep the motor running." You must continuously draw on the power that God provides through prayer and His Word—not just during the thirty-day jump-start but every day of your life.

This study is divided into five sections. The first seven-day segment cements your commitment to restoring your image of God, and it is called "I Make a Commitment to Change and Growth." The second seven-day segment, "I Explore God's True Image," guides you on a journey of discovery through seven healing facets of God's character. The third seven-day segment takes you deeper into meditating on and immersing yourself in God's Word; it is called "I Bathe My Heart and Mind in Scripture." The fourth seven-day segment, "A New Relationship with God," explores new vistas of your personal interaction with God. The final two-day segment—"I Maintain a Restored Image of God *for Life!*"—launches you on a life's journey of change, growth, and discovery.

So be patient. Be prayerful. Be persistent. If you fall off the program, get right back on again. And once you have finished this thirty-day program, go right into another Bible study program. Many excellent Bible study books and workbooks are available at your local Christian bookstore, or you can create your own program with nothing more than a Bible and your daily journal.

I wish you God's grace as you set forth on the journey of a lifetime!

Dr. Larry Stephens

I Make a Commitment to Change and Growth

Day 1
Where My Distortions Began

Prayer

Heavenly Father, please open the eyes of my understanding. Clear away the cobwebs of hurt or sin or neglect that have clouded my image of You. Give me insight into my feelings. Most of all, please give me a clear sense of who You really are.

Scripture—A Prayer for Restoration

> Restore to me the joy of Your salvation,
> And uphold me with Your generous Spirit.
> Then I will teach transgressors Your ways,
> And sinners shall be converted to You.
> —Psalm 51:12–13

Action

A doctor never treats a patient without first making a diagnosis. Healing begins with a diagnosis of the problem.

After you have prayed to God for insight and have meditated on the Scripture passage above, complete the exercise below. It will help you to identify key areas where you have experienced distortions in your image of God. (Remember that those distortions may have originated with any combination of the following experiences.)

In the box at the left of each category, place an X next to those experiences that have caused distortions in your image of God. In the blank spaces, briefly describe any experiences that have contributed to those distortions.

☐ Experiences in infancy:
(For example, I was adopted. I am afraid God might abandon me like my birth mother.)

197

☐ Early exposure to parents who did not portray God's true nature:
(For example, my dad was critical. I often see God as a critical parent.)

☐ Personality patterns:
(For example, I have an avoidant personality. I distance myself from God.)

☐ False attribution of negative events to God:
(For example, I see poverty, war, and injustice in the world, and I feel God is asleep at the wheel.)

☐ Expectations, moods, and emotions:
(For example, God has not answered a certain prayer I have repeatedly prayed. I feel God is not available.)

☐ Abusive religious experiences:
(For example, a pastor I admired had an affair. God is unreal, or He cannot be trusted.)

☐ Early religious training:
(For example, my mother often said, "God will get you." I see God as a threatening, punishing figure.)

After you have completed this exercise, take five minutes alone with God, lifting these distortions up to Him, asking Him to heal them. Be sure to take time not only to speak but to *listen* to what God is saying to you. Close with the following prayer:

Prayer

Dear heavenly Father, thank You for revealing to me the sources of these distortions in my image of You. Please continue to open my eyes to those factors that hinder my experience with You. Most of all, open my eyes so I can see You clearly. Restore to me the joy of Your salvation. Uphold me with Your loving and generous Spirit. Thank You for beginning a process of healing in my life that will continue until I see You face-to-face and feel Your loving arms around me in eternity.

In the name of Jesus, Amen.

Day 2
Praying for Healing

Prayer

My loving heavenly Father, I know that You are the source of all physical, emotional, and spiritual healing. I ask You to heal my emotions and my spirit. I ask You to heal my image of You. And, Father, I make a commitment right now to work with You and cooperate with You, to do whatever I have to do to become healed in my relationship with You. As a symbol of this commitment, I will sign my name right now:

_____

Thank You for the healing work You have already begun in my life.

Scripture—Prayers and Promises of Healing

> Heal me, O LORD,
>   and I shall be healed;
> Save me, and I shall be saved,
> For You are my praise.
>
> —Jeremiah 17:14

> "But to you who fear My name
> The Sun of Righteousness shall arise
> With healing in His wings;
> And you shall go out
> And grow fat like stall-fed calves.
> You shall trample the wicked,
> For they shall be ashes under the soles of your feet
> On the day that I do this,"
> Says the LORD of hosts.
>
> —Malachi 4:2–3

When Jesus opened the Scriptures in the synagogue at Nazareth, He read this passage from Isaiah, which is a prophecy referring to Jesus and His healing, liberating ministry:

> The Spirit of the LORD is upon Me,
> Because He has anointed Me to preach the gospel to the poor.
> He has sent Me to heal the brokenhearted,
> To preach deliverance to the captives
> And recovery of sight to the blind,
> To set at liberty those who are oppressed,
> To preach the acceptable year of the LORD.
>
> —Luke 4:18–19

Action

Meditate on the Scripture passages above. Read them carefully, and think about what these prayers and promises of God's healing mean to you. When you read words such as,

> Heal me, O LORD,
>   and I shall be healed;
> Save me, and I shall be saved,
> For You are my praise,

personalize the words. Make this prayer *your* prayer, the prayer of your heart. When Jesus said that He came to heal the brokenhearted, savor the truth that He meant *you,* that He came to heal *you.*

Spend a few moments in silence, listening for the message of hope and healing that God is speaking to your heart *right now*. Then close your special time in the presence of God with this prayer.

Prayer

Heavenly Father, it is good to spend time alone with You, praising You and enjoying Your presence. I thank You that You have sent Jesus to heal me, bind up my broken heart, deliver me from bondage to the past, free me from emotional oppression, give me insight and understanding of who You truly are and how much You truly love me. I thank You that, as Luke 9:11 says, Jesus has come to heal all those who have need of healing.

Father, I need Your healing touch in my spirit and my emotions. Heal me, O Lord, and I shall be healed; save me, and I shall be saved.

In the name of Jesus, the Sun of Righteousness, who arose with healing in His wings, Amen.

Day 3
Making a Decision to Trust God

Prayer

Heavenly Father, You know it is not easy for me to trust You. And You know that trust does not come easily for me. But I can never have a healed relationship with You unless I am able to completely trust You. I understand that trusting You requires making a decision and a commitment. So, Father, I want You to know right now that I am *choosing to trust You*. It is a choice I make not with my feelings but with my will. Help me to keep this commitment to You.

Scripture—Making a Decision to Trust God

Trust in the LORD with all your heart,
And lean not on your own understanding;
In all your ways acknowledge Him,
And He shall direct your paths
    [or, He shall make your paths smooth and straight].
                              —Proverbs 3:5–6

But let all those rejoice who put their trust in You;
Let them ever shout for joy, because You defend them;

Let those also who love Your name
Be joyful in You.
For You, O LORD, will bless the righteous;
With favor You will surround him as with a shield.
　　　　　　　　　　　　　　—Psalm 5:11–12

Oh, taste and see that the LORD is good;
Blessed is the man who trusts in Him!
Oh, fear the LORD, you His saints!
There is no want to those who fear Him.
The young lions lack and suffer hunger;
But those who seek the LORD shall not lack any good thing.
　　　　　　　　　　　　　　—Psalm 34:8–10

Action

For years you may have believed that trust is something that you feel, not something that you choose. And it is true that your capacity to trust others and to trust God may have been damaged by past experiences. Still, we all have the God-given ability to *make a decision to trust God*. That is why the Bible contains *commandments* and *admonitions* that we should trust Him. The Bible says, "Trust in the Lord with all your heart," because God knows we have the power to choose.

Perhaps you made a decision long ago never to be vulnerable or allow yourself to be hurt again. Maybe you feel God has let you down. Or maybe you simply have a hard time trusting Someone you cannot touch or hear or see with your physical senses.

God will not force you to trust Him. Rather, He invites you to trust Him of your own free will. You have the choice to receive God, spend time with God, talk to God, listen to God, know God, and trust God.

"But how?" you ask. "How do I make a *choice* to trust God when I don't *feel* like trusting God?"

First, meditate on the Scripture passages above. Think about what God is saying to you about trust. Picture the biblical word pictures in your mind. Read Proverbs 3:5–6 and imagine that as you trust God and thank Him for all that happens in your life, He is making all the paths of your life smooth and straight. Read Psalm 5:11–12 and feel the warmth, security, and trust that come from being surrounded by God as if by a shield. Read Psalm 34:8–10 and taste the goodness of the Lord; savor the blessings that come from trusting in Him.

Second, talk to God. Thank Him for being your shield, your defender, the immovable mountain of your security. Then take a few quiet moments to listen for God's response.

Third, recognize that your feelings may not be aligned with the choice you have made to trust God. In all areas of our emotional and spiritual well-being, we sometimes have to make decisions and commitments when the feelings are not there. Be patient and persistent with your commitment to trust God. If you keep your commitment to trust Him, the feelings of trust will follow and grow.

Prayer

Father, I choose to trust You. I make a commitment not to lean on my feelings or moods or understanding but to lean on the promises You have given me in Your Word. Lord, I thank You for being my defender, my shield, my rock, my fortress. I ask You to continue to build my capacity for trust upon the foundation of this commitment I have made today. Make it like Mount Zion—a solid rock of trust that cannot be moved but abides forever.

In the name of Jesus, Amen.

Day 4
Learning to Trust

Prayer

Dear heavenly Father, thank You for giving me another day in which to learn and grow and know You better. Help me to view this day and all of its challenges as an opportunity to practice my new-found trust in You. Thank You for the peace of mind that comes from trusting You. Uphold me today with Your everlasting strength.

Scripture—Learning to Trust God

You will keep him in perfect peace,
Whose mind is stayed on You,
Because he trusts in You.
Trust in the LORD forever,
For in [Jehovah], the LORD, is everlasting strength.
—Isaiah 26:3–4

The LORD also will be a refuge for the oppressed,
A refuge in times of trouble.

And those who know Your name will put their trust in You;
For You, LORD, have not forsaken those who seek You.
—Psalm 9:9–10

The LORD is my rock and my fortress and my deliverer;
My God, my strength, in whom I will trust;
My shield and the horn of my salvation, my stronghold.
I will call upon the LORD, who is worthy to be praised;
So shall I be saved from my enemies.
—Psalm 18:2–3

Action

Meditate on the Scripture passages above. Think about what it means to trust God with all your needs, all your problems and worries, all the decisions of your life. As you grow in your capacity to trust God, what blessings and benefits will come into your life?

Now, let's get very specific about your life—the areas of your life where you trust God and where you withhold trust from Him. In the following brief exercise, search yourself thoroughly and honestly before listing your answers.

A. List three areas of your life where you feel you trust God without any reservation or hesitation:

 1. _____
 2. _____
 3. _____

B. List three areas of your life where you feel you partially trust God:

 1. _____
 2. _____
 3. _____

C. List three areas of your life where you hold back and either cannot or will not trust God:

 1. _____
 2. _____
 3. _____

Now that you have identified specific areas of your life that need to be given over in trust to God, take time to pray over these areas. Ask God to give you the desire and the will to trust Him with every aspect of your life, every problem, every need, every goal, every issue. Then close with this prayer.

Prayer

Heavenly Father, You know that I am still learning to trust You, and there are areas where I am holding back. I know that I will never know perfect peace until I have entrusted *all* of these areas of my life to You. Help me to do so. As Your Word says in Psalm 16:1, "Preserve me, O God, for in You I put my trust."

In the name of Your Son, Jesus, Amen.

Day 5
Committing to God and Submitting to God

Prayer

Heavenly Father, as I seek to cement this commitment to grow and change in my experience with You, one thing is holding me back. I have a problem with authority and with feelings of rebellion. I don't want anyone to control me. Obviously, that creates a real problem as I seek to build a trust relationship with the ultimate Authority in the universe!

Lord, heal me of my rebelliousness. Heal me of my unhealthy fear of You and of Your sovereignty over my life. Help me to commit to You and submit to You, knowing that You want only the best for my life.

Scripture—What God's Authority Is Like

Come to Me, all you who labor and are heavy laden, and I will give you rest. Take My yoke upon you and learn from Me, for I am gentle and lowly in heart, and you will find rest for your souls. For My yoke is easy and My burden is light.

—Matthew 11:28–30

Choose for yourselves this day whom you will serve, whether the gods which your fathers served that were on the other side of the River, or the gods of the Amorites, in whose land you dwell. But as for me and my house, we will serve the LORD.

—Joshua 24:15

But now having been set free from sin, and having become slaves of God, you have your fruit to holiness, and the end, everlasting life. For the wages of sin is death, but the gift of God is eternal life in Christ Jesus our Lord.

—Romans 6:22–23

Action

Are you reluctant to accept God's authority? Does it grate on you to think of yourself as a "slave to God"? You may be thinking, *I've had enough authority in my life! I don't want anyone to control me or abuse me or boss me around!*

If that is how you feel, get ready for a big surprise: the authority of God is unlike any other authority you have ever known before! God does not control; He leads. God does not force; He invites. God does not boss; He guides. His rod and His staff do not inflict pain; they comfort us.

Whatever abusive earthly authority has filled you with fear and rebellion—whether parents, employers, or religious leaders—the authority of God is completely different. God's authority is perfect, just, compassionate, and merciful. Most important of all, God's authority is *protective*. God wants to preserve you as His child.

In C. S. Lewis's fantasy novel *Perelandra,* there is a sinless woman known simply as the Lady of Perelandra. Though God has established rules, boundaries, and prohibitions on Perelandra, the Lady does not mind submitting to God's authority. "I am His," she says, "and all His biddings are joys." That is what God's authority is like. Since He is perfect, His will for our lives is perfect. All His rules and His biddings are joys to those who truly know and trust Him.

Take a few moments to meditate on the Scripture passages above. Let the true meaning of God's gracious, caring, protective authority seep into your heart and saturate your emotions. Understand that God's yoke is easy, His burden is light. He doesn't bind you and enslave you with chains; He invites you to make a choice: "Choose for yourselves this day whom you will serve." You have complete freedom to choose enslavement to sin if you like—even though the wages of sin is death. But if you choose to be free from sin and to become a slave of God, your life becomes fruitful, leading to eternal life with God!

After meditating on these Scriptures passages, talk to God and listen to what He has to say to you through His Holy Spirit about the blessings of His authority in your life.

Prayer

Lord, I thank You for Your authority in my life. Help me to commit all my ways to You and to submit my will to You, knowing that You love me more completely than I could ever love myself. Thank You for being the kind of gentle, gracious Authority that allows me to choose You. You never forced Yourself on me. You never took away my freedom or my will. You very quietly invited me to come to You, and I eagerly respond to Your invitation. I choose You as my Lord, my God, my Father, and my Friend.

In the name of Jesus, Amen.

Day 6
Talking to God

Prayer

Dear heavenly Father, please help me to understand this amazing process called prayer. Help me to relax in Your presence, to simply have a conversation with You as one friend talks with another. Heal my false ideas about prayer. Open the channels of two-way communication between us. Father, I thank You that though You are infinite, You are also intimate, and You have graciously given me free access and Your complete attention. Help me to sense Your presence with me during this special time we have together.

Scripture—How to Talk to God

Now it came to pass in those days that He [Jesus] went out to the mountain to pray, and continued all night in prayer to God.
—Luke 6:12

Be anxious for nothing, but in everything by prayer and supplication, with thanksgiving, let your requests be made known to God; and the peace of God, which surpasses all understanding, will guard your hearts and minds through Christ Jesus.

—Philippians 4:6–7

O LORD God of hosts, hear my prayer;
Give ear, O God of Jacob! Selah
O God, behold our shield,
And look upon the face of Your anointed.

For a day in Your courts is better than a thousand.
I would rather be a doorkeeper in the house of my God
Than dwell in the tents of wickedness.
For the LORD God is a sun and shield;
The LORD will give grace and glory;
No good thing will He withhold
From those who walk uprightly.

O LORD of hosts,
Blessed is the man who trusts in You!
                                        —Psalm 84:8–12

Action

If Jesus felt such a need of contact with His heavenly Father that He would spend an entire night in the mountains in prayer, how much more do you and I need prayer? Martin Luther once said, "I have so much to do today, I'll need to spend another hour on my knees." Unfortunately for most of us, prayer is the first thing to get crowded out of a fast-paced schedule.

One of the goals in this thirty-day program is to make talking to God such a natural, joyful, and relaxed part of your day that you wouldn't dare miss it! So spend a few minutes meditating on the above Scripture passages dealing with prayer. Then—what else?—*pray!*

Don't bother with using high-sounding language or addressing God as "Thee" or "Thou." Just open your heart and talk to God. Tell Him whatever is on your mind. Talk to Him as a trusted friend, a confidant who will guard every secret, who will listen without rebuking or criticizing, who will love you and accept you no matter what you say or do.

And when you've finished talking—*let God talk to you!* Don't forget that prayer is a two-way conversation.

Prayer

Thank You, Father, for the gift of prayer. Thank You for making me Your child. Thank You for letting me come into Your presence anytime I want to or need to. Thank You for listening to me so attentively and compassionately.

In the name of Your Son, Jesus, Amen.

Day 7
Listening to God

Prayer

Heavenly Father, quiet my thoughts. Help me to be still and listen for Your voice. Speak to me now. I am listening.

Scripture—Listening for God's Voice

Be still, and know that I am God.
      —Psalm 46:10

> O God, You are my God;
> Early will I seek You;
> My soul thirsts for You;
> My flesh longs for You
> In a dry and thirsty land
> Where there is no water.
> So I have looked for You in the sanctuary,
> To see Your power and Your glory.
>
> Because Your lovingkindness is better than life,
> My lips shall praise You.
> Thus I will bless You while I live;
> I will lift up my hands in Your name.
> My soul shall be satisfied as with marrow and fatness,
> And my mouth shall praise You with joyful lips.
>
> When I remember You on my bed,
> I meditate on You in the night watches.
> Because You have been my help,
> Therefore in the shadow of Your wings I will rejoice.
> My soul follows close behind You;
> Your right hand upholds me.
>   —Psalm 63:1–8

Action

Many of us make the mistake of thinking that prayer is just talking to God. Prayer is talking, of course, but prayer is also listening. When we make a petition or ask God a question, how often do we truly listen for His answer? How often do we make time in our prayers for simply being still and savoring the presence of God? How often do we say, "God, show me Your will for this day; I'm listening and ready to carry it out"? How often do we listen for the still small voice of God's Spirit to speak to our hearts, to guide us into truth, to reveal God's character to us?

That is your assignment today. Be still. Be attentive. Listen. Invite the Spirit of God to speak to you in the silence of these moments.

Prayer

Thank You, Father, for speaking directly to me. Help me to remember to take time every day to listen for Your voice.

In Jesus' name, Amen.

I Explore God's True Image

Day 8
God Is Loving

Prayer

Heavenly Father, open the eyes of my understanding. Give me a glimpse into Your heart—the heart of a loving Father. Help me to sense Your deep love for me. Let it saturate my mind, my spirit, and my emotions.

Scripture—Catching a Glimpse of God's Love

> The LORD has appeared of old to me, saying:
> "Yes, I have loved you
>   with an everlasting love;
> Therefore with lovingkindness
>   I have drawn you."
> —Jeremiah 31:3

> Love suffers long and is kind; love does not envy; love does not parade itself, is not puffed up; does not behave rudely, does not seek its own, is not provoked, thinks no evil; does not rejoice in iniquity, but rejoices in the truth; bears all things, believes all things, hopes all things, endures all things. Love never fails.
> —1 Corinthians 13:4–8

> There is no fear in love; but perfect love casts out fear, because fear involves torment. But he who fears has not been made perfect in love. We love Him because He first loved us.
> —1 John 4:18–19

Action

"God is love," the Bible tells us. But do we really know what those words mean? As you meditate on the Scripture passages above, plunge yourself into the refreshing truths these passages relate about the love of God. Think about what it really means that God has loved us with an everlasting love, that He has drawn us to Himself with His lovingkindness, that the amazing love described in 1 Corinthians 13 is precisely the kind of love with which God loves us, that once we truly understand and are perfected in God's love, we have no more fear!

What can we compare God's love to? If you are a parent, imagine your love for your children. Imagine the joy you felt when your children were born, when they took their first steps, when they said their first words. Now multiply those feelings a thousand, a million, a billion times over. . . .

And you still have not plumbed the depths of the love of God, a love so great it compelled Him to carry out a plan in which God the Son became a human being, was born as a baby, grew up, suffered incredible physical pain and alienation from God the Father while carrying our sins on a wooden cross, then *died*. God did all of that out of love for us. How can we ever understand such love?

A children's song describes us as being "all wrapped up in His love"—and so we are. As you pray, picture His loving arms around you, encircling you, protecting you, holding you close to His heart.

Prayer

Dear loving heavenly Father, I have probably never stopped to meditate on Your love before. Now that I have done so, I am amazed at how far and wide and deep Your love for me truly reaches. Thank You!

Before closing, I have just one request to make of You. Please cast out all the fear from my heart and replace it with *love*—with a warm, secure sense of Your love for me; with my responsive and obedient love for You; and with an unconditional, accepting love for others.

In the name of the One who loved me enough to die for me, Jesus Christ, Amen.

Day 9
God Is Forgiving

Prayer

Dear heavenly Father, I know You are a forgiving God. I know it as an intellectual fact, but sometimes I have a hard time feeling truly forgiven in my heart. Help me to feel truly cleansed, free, and forgiven—now and forever.

Scripture—The Freedom of God's Forgiveness

> "Come now, and let us reason together,"
> Says the LORD,
> "Though your sins are like scarlet,
> They shall be as white as snow;
> Though they are red like crimson,
> They shall be as wool."
>
> —Isaiah 1:18

Then the scribes and Pharisees brought to Him a woman caught in adultery. And when they had set her in the midst, they said to Him, "Teacher, this woman was caught in adultery, in the very act. Now Moses, in the law, commanded us that such should be stoned. But what do You say?" This they said, testing Him, that they might have something of which to accuse Him. But Jesus stooped down and wrote on the ground with His finger, as though He did not hear.

So when they continued asking Him, He raised Himself up and said to them, "He who is without sin among you, let him throw a stone at her first." And again He stooped down and wrote on the ground.

Then those who heard it, being convicted by their conscience, went out one by one, beginning with the oldest even to the last. And Jesus was left alone, and the woman standing in the midst. When Jesus had raised Himself up and saw no one but the woman, He said to her, "Woman, where are those accusers of yours? Has no one condemned you?"

She said, "No one, Lord." And Jesus said to her, "Neither do I condemn you; go and sin no more."

> —John 8:2–11

Action

As you meditate on these passages, think about what it truly means to have your sins completely removed from you as far as the east is from the west; what it truly means to have your most blood-scarlet sins turned as white as the powdery blanket on a ski slope; what it truly means to have Jesus, the Son of God, say, "I don't condemn you. You are forgiven. Go and sin no more."

You may identify with the woman caught in adultery. The Bible says she was caught in the very act and dragged out to be publicly shamed and stoned to death. You may have committed some sin that has caused you shame and humiliation. You may feel that people have figuratively "stoned" you. Maybe you feel condemned by family, by acquaintances, or even by fellow Christians—and you may feel that God is standing over you with the biggest, deadliest stone of all!

But the true forgiving character of God is revealed in the response of Jesus to this woman: "Neither do I condemn you." Complete forgiveness! Unconditional love! Unearned and freely given!

No matter what damage has been done to your memories or your reputation, no matter what secret or public shame you carry in your heart, God will never throw stones at you. God has forgiven you.

Meditate on the truth of God's forgiveness in these passages. As you pray, listen for the comforting forgiveness of God's Spirit as He speaks to your heart.

Prayer

Father, thank You for these beautiful word pictures of Your forgiving nature that You have placed in Your Word. Please bring them to my mind whenever I am tempted to feel ashamed and unworthy. Whenever I see snow, remind me that my scarlet sins have been changed to the same dazzling whiteness as that snow. Whenever I see a pile of stones on the ground, remind me that no one can ever throw stones at me because You have removed all shame and condemnation from me. Amen.

Day 10
God Is Gracious and Accepting

Prayer

Gracious heavenly Father, I can't completely understand Your grace and acceptance toward me—but I want to *begin* to understand. Lord, help me make that beginning right now as we talk together and as I read Your Word.

Scripture—God's Grace and God's Acceptance

For all have sinned and fall short of the glory of God, being justified freely by His grace through the redemption that is in Christ Jesus.

—Romans 3:23–24

Jesus said,

> All that the Father gives Me will come to Me, and the one who comes to Me I will by no means cast out.
>
> —John 6:37

> But God, who is rich in mercy, because of His great love with which He loved us, even when we were dead in trespasses, made us alive together in Christ (by grace you have been saved), and raised us up together, and made us sit together in the heavenly places in Christ Jesus, that in the ages to come He might show the exceeding riches of His grace in His kindness toward us in Christ Jesus.

> For by grace you have been saved through faith, and that not of yourselves; it is the gift of God, not of works, lest anyone should boast. For we are His workmanship, created in Christ Jesus for good works, which God prepared beforehand that we should walk in them.
>
> —Ephesians 2:4–10

Action

One of Jesus' traits that really upset His enemies was His accepting and gracious spirit. Jesus socialized with and ministered to the outcasts and sinners of His society—adulterers, prostitutes, lepers, dishonest tax collectors, and more. Jesus' enemies—who were the upper class, the lawyers, and the religious elite of His day—were offended that Jesus criticized them, yet accepted and aided people they considered the lowest class of sinners.

The fact is that everyone Jesus came in contact with was a sinner. The prostitutes were sinners, the tax collectors were sinners—but so were the religious leaders. The problem was that the religious leaders refused to admit it. They clutched their pride and arrogance, denying the truth of their sinfulness.

No matter what sins you have committed, no matter what life-style you have lived, even if you think of yourself as the lowest and worst of all sinners, God is ready to accept you. Don't deny the truth of your sin; don't cling to pride. Admit the truth of who you really are to God, and He will receive you and accept you. You have His guarantee on it. As Jesus said, "The one who comes to Me I will by no means cast out."

As you meditate on these Scripture passages and talk with God, thank Him for His grace and His acceptance toward you.

Prayer

Father, thank You for Your grace. Thank You for receiving me, even though I do not deserve Your love and cannot earn it. I accept it as a gift of Your grace. Help me to leave this special time of prayer and Bible meditation with a sense of being renewed and recharged, ready to do the good works You have prepared for me to do.

In the name of Your Son, Jesus, Amen.

Day 11
God Is Merciful

Prayer

Merciful heavenly Father, You know that I have tended to view You with fear and wariness. I have been afraid of Your anger. I have doubted Your compassion and love for me.

Father, I ask You to cast out my fears. Help me to see the *truth* of Your character—the truth that You are full of compassion; You are gracious and patient; You are abundant in mercy. Speak to my heart through Your Word and Your Spirit.

Scripture—God Is the Father of Mercies

> Oh, gives thanks to the LORD, for He is
>   good!
> Because His mercy endures forever.
> Let Israel now say,
> "His mercy endures forever."
> Let the house of Aaron now say,
> "His mercy endures forever."
> Let those who fear the LORD now say,
> "His mercy endures forever." . . .
> Oh, give thanks to the LORD, for He is good!
> For His mercy endures forever.
>   —Psalm 118:1–4, 29

Blessed be the God and Father of our Lord Jesus Christ, the Father of mercies and God of all comfort.

                         —2 Corinthians 1:3

Action

As you meditate on these passages, picture the mercy of God as a refreshing spring of water flowing in the desert of your hurt and shame. The water of God's mercy is abundant, overflowing, never-ending. When you first found this spring, you wondered if there was enough for one cooling sip. But the more you experience of the flowing streams of God's mercy, the more you realize that there is not just enough for a drink, not just enough to dip your hands in, not just enough to bathe your face in. You can actually *plunge* into the spring of God's mercy and never touch the bottom. Immerse yourself in it. Revel in it.

God's mercy is rich and overflowing. His mercy covered the sin of David when he committed murder and adultery. His mercy covered the sin of the thief who was crucified on the cross next to the cross of Jesus. His mercy covered the sin of Peter's denial of Jesus. His mercy covers our sin. It covers our shame. It covers the pain of broken memories.

As you pray, give thanks to the Lord, for He is good, for His mercy endures forever.

Prayer

Father, throughout my life I have encountered people who are hurt-ful, critical, insensitive, judgmental, and unloving. Those experiences have colored my emotions and caused me to expect *You* to treat me as *they* have treated me. Now I begin to understand that I have been need-lessly afraid of You. Now it seems ridiculous that I should have dis-tanced myself from You when all You ever wanted me to experience was Your love, Your acceptance, and Your mercy.

Thank You for Your mercies to me, which are new and rich every day. In the name of Jesus, who came to earth as a gift of Your mercy, Amen.

Day 12
God Is Personal

Prayer

Father in heaven, I am just beginning to know You as a close and intimate friend. I am just beginning to realize how warm and personal a relationship with You can be. I have been standing away from You, keeping my distance, because of my fears. All along, You have wanted to hold me close and call me by name—and I didn't even know it! Open the eyes of my understanding. Open my heart. Please enable me to know You as I am already known by You.

Scripture—The Face of the Personal God

Then the word of the LORD came to me, saying:
"Before I formed you in the womb I knew you;
Before you were born I sanctified you."

—Jeremiah 1:4–5

O LORD, You have searched me and known me.
You know my sitting down and my rising up;
You understand my thought afar off.
You comprehend my path and my lying down,
And are acquainted with all my ways.

—Psalm 139:1–3

Thus says the LORD:
"Let not the wise man glory in his wisdom,
Let not the mighty man glory in his might,
Nor let the rich man glory in his riches;
But let him who glories glory in this,
That he understands and knows Me,
That I am the Lord, exercising lovingkindness, judgment,
    and righteousness in the earth.
For in these I delight," says the LORD.

—Jeremiah 9:23–24

Jesus said,

I am the good shepherd; and I know My sheep, and am known by My own. As the Father knows Me, even so I know the Father; and I lay down My life for the sheep. And other sheep I have which are not of this fold; them also I must bring, and they will hear My voice; and there will be one flock and one shepherd. . . .

My sheep hear My voice, and I know them, and they follow Me. And I give them eternal life, and they shall never perish; neither shall anyone snatch them out of My hand. My Father, who has given them to Me, is greater than all; and no one is able to snatch them out of My Father's hand. I and My Father are one. . . .

And this is eternal life, that they may know You, the only true God, and Jesus Christ whom You have sent.

—John 10:14–16, 27–30; 17:3

Action

As you meditate on these passages that demonstrate God is a personal God—a God who knows us intimately and invites us to know Him in a personal and intimate way—ask yourself these questions:

- What is God saying to me in these Scripture passages about His involvement in my life and His attentiveness to my needs and wants?
- What does God want me to understand about the kind and quality of relationship He wants to have with me?
- What do these Scripture passages tell me about my fears about God—my fear of abandonment or fear of condemnation or fear of God's anger?
- Is God a force, as many New Agers proclaim? Is God a remote and silent figure out in the sky somewhere? Is He a stern and easily angered critic? Or is He as close and approachable as my most intimate friend?

In Galatians 4:8–9, Paul said that once we did not know God, but now we do know God—and then, significantly, he added this phrase: "Or rather [you] are known by God." Yes, God is personal, He knows us personally, and He invites us to know Him in an intimate way.

Prayer

Dear Father, dear Friend, I thank You for being so close, so approachable, so intimate, so personal. I thank You for drawing near to me so that I can come close to You and know You as a person. I ask You to continue to reveal to me Your face and Your heart. Continue to draw me into a warm and special love relationship with You.

I am Your sheep. I listen for Your voice. Thank You for being my shepherd. Thank You for the gift of eternal life. Thank You for the privilege of knowing You.

In the name of Jesus, Amen.

Day 13
God Is Faithful

Prayer

Heavenly Father, I thank You that You are faithful, unchangeable, and merciful. As I meditate on Your Word and listen to Your Spirit, help me to see Your true and constant nature. Help me to trust You as I gain a greater understanding of Your great faithfulness. Speak to my mind, my emotions, and my spirit. I am listening for Your voice.

Scripture—The Faithfulness of Our Father

Therefore know that the LORD your God, He is God, the faithful God who keeps covenant and mercy for a thousand generations with those who love Him and keep His commandments.
                                        —Deuteronomy 7:9

> Through the LORD's mercies we are not consumed,
> Because His compassions fail not.
> They are new every morning;
> Great is Your faithfulness.
> "The LORD is my portion," says my soul,
> "Therefore I hope in Him!"
>   —Lamentations 3:22–24

> Your mercy, O LORD, is in the heavens;
> And Your faithfulness reaches to the clouds.
> Your righteousness is like the great mountains;
> Your judgments are a great deep.
>   —Psalm 36:5–6

Action

If you have ever been rejected, betrayed, abused, or abandoned, you may struggle with seeing God as Someone you can trust, Someone who is completely faithful and reliable. That is understandable, but your goal is to move beyond these distorted emotions to an image of God corresponding to His *true* image found in the Bible.

As you pray and meditate on these passages, dwell on the beautiful word pictures God paints in His Word. Imagine, as you read Deuteronomy 7:9, the thousand generations of people with whom God has kept His covenant and toward whom He has shown mercy, all the way from

Adam and Eve to *you*. As you absorb Lamentations 3:22–24, picture His mercies and His compassions arriving new every morning, wrapped in a package with a card that reads, "With love from your heavenly Father." As you meditate on Psalm 36:5–6, imagine God's mercy shining like the sun in the heavens, and His great faithfulness towering majestically into the clouds.

Prayer

Father in heaven, I thank You for Your great faithfulness to me. Even before I knew You, You dealt faithfully and mercifully toward me. I thank You that You have kept Your promises to me, even though I have often let You down. I thank You that You have established me and You protect me from the evil one; that You forgive my sins and cleanse me from all unrighteousness and shame; and that Your faithfulness endures to all generations.

In the name of Your Son, Jesus, who was faithful even unto death on the cross, Amen.

Day 14
God Is the Source of Peace

Prayer

Heavenly Father, I all too often experience fear, anxiety, and confusion rather than Your peace. I ask You to show me how to keep my mind stayed on You, how to trust You, and how to receive the peace that comes from truly knowing You. Help me to understand the width and breadth and depth of Your peace as I meditate on these passages from Your Word.

Scripture—The Peace of God

I will both lie down in peace, and sleep;
For You alone, O Lord, make me dwell in safety.
—Psalm 4:8

You will keep him in perfect peace,
Whose mind is stayed on You,
Because he trusts in You.
—Isaiah 26:3

But the fruit of the Spirit is love, joy, peace, longsuffering, kindness, goodness, faithfulness, gentleness, self-control. Against such there is no law.

—Galatians 5:22–23

Be anxious for nothing, but in everything by prayer and supplication, with thanksgiving, let your requests be made known to God; and the peace of God, which surpasses all understanding, will guard your hearts and minds through Christ Jesus.

—Philippians 4:6–7

Action

As you meditate on these passages, ask yourself,

- What issues in my life make me anxious?
- What are the fears plaguing me?
- If my mind is not stayed on God, what is my mind occupied with?
- If I do not trust God, who or what am I trusting in?
- What fruit of the Spirit do I experience right now? What fruit of the Spirit do I lack?

Prayer

Heavenly Father, I know You are the Lord of peace. I know it is Your will for my life that I experience Your peace. I ask You to help me understand the root causes of my anxiety and confusion. Give me the courage to take whatever steps I need to find healing in those areas of my life. Give me grace to trust You more. Give me Your peace.

In the name of the Prince of Peace, Jesus Christ, Amen.

I Bathe My Heart and Mind in Scripture

Day 15
The Truth That Sets Me Free!

Prayer

Heavenly Father, I thank You that in Your great love You have not been silent, but You have spoken through Your Word. Help me to hear and understand what You are saying to me. Give me grace today and through this coming week as I seek to bathe my heart and mind in the truth You have revealed in Your Word. As I study and meditate on the Bible, bring me to a place where I know You—not just know *about* You but know You *intimately* through Your perfect self-disclosure in the Bible.

Scripture—About Scripture

All Scripture is given by inspiration of God, and is profitable for doctrine, for reproof, for correction, for instruction in righteousness, that the man of God may be complete, thoroughly equipped for every good work.

—2 Timothy 3:16–17

Then Jesus said to those Jews who believed Him, "If you abide in My word, you are My disciples indeed. And you shall know the truth, and the truth shall make you free."

—John 8:31–32

How sweet are Your words to my taste,
Sweeter than honey to my mouth!
Through Your precepts I get understanding;
Therefore I hate every false way.
Your word is a lamp to my feet
And a light to my path.

—Psalm 119:103–105

Action

Many people look for the shortcut, the "secret," the special technique for knowing God. But there is no shortcut, no "secret." If we truly want to know God in an intimate way, we must go to the place where He has made His most complete disclosure of Himself: His Word, the Bible. Our relationship with God is based on an understanding of His Word.

In the Bible we learn about Jesus Christ, who is fully God and fully man, who was sent to earth to die for us and to give God a human face. In the Bible we learn about the Holy Spirit, the Comforter, who comes alongside us, giving us insight and guidance while ministering to us in the depths of our spirits.

There is no substitute for spending quality time alone with God in prayer and in His Word. But make sure you also spend time with fellow Christians studying the Bible. Attend worship services and hear God's Word preached and explained. Attend a Sunday school class or midweek Bible class at your church. Join a neighborhood Bible study and dig into God's truth in an intensive way while exchanging insights and experiences with other committed Christians.

Now, as you meditate on these passages that speak of God's revealed truth, ask God to fill your heart with a love for His Word. Ask His Spirit to give you the desire to seek Him with a whole heart. Ask Him to fill your emotions with the honey-like sweetness of the taste of His truth.

Prayer

Heavenly Father, thank You for Your Word. Thank You that You did not leave me in the darkness of my ignorance, but You have given me this lamp, this light for my path. As I continue to bathe my mind, my spirit, and my emotions in the truth that comes from meditating on Your Word, I ask You to open my understanding and my heart. Give me a hunger and a thirst for Your truth. Help me to say, as David said in Psalm 119:127, "I love Your commandments more than gold, yes, than fine gold!"

In the name of the living Word Himself, Jesus Christ, Amen.

Note:

In the next six studies titled "I Bathe My Heart and Mind in Scripture," we will change the format. Instead of having an opening and a closing prayer and an "Action" section, as in the previous devotionals, these studies will consist simply of Scripture.

I encourage you to immerse your mind and your emotions in these beautiful, powerful, healing passages of God's Word. Meditate on them. Pray the words of these Scripture texts to God. Take time in silence to listen to what He is saying to you through His Word and through His Holy Spirit. Let the refreshing truths of God's Word wash over you, cleansing your mind and your heart, driving out the impurities that distort your image of God and your relationship with God.

Then in the weeks and months and years after you have completed this "Thirty-Day Image of God Restoration Program," I hope you will return to these passages of Scripture again and again. As you continue to dwell in the truths of God's Word, you will maintain forward momentum in your growth and healing process, and in your relationship with God.

Day 16
God Chose Me

Scripture

For you are a holy people to the LORD your God; the LORD your God has chosen you to be a people for Himself, a special treasure above all the peoples on the face of the earth. The LORD did not set His love on you nor choose you because you were more in number than any other people, for you were the least of all peoples; but because the LORD loves you, and because He would keep the oath which He swore to your fathers, the LORD has brought you out with a mighty hand, and redeemed you from the house of bondage, from the hand of Pharaoh King of Egypt.

Therefore know that the LORD your God, He is God, the faithful God who keeps covenant and mercy for a thousand generations with those who love Him and keep His commandments; and He repays those who hate Him to their face, to destroy them. He will not be slack with him who hates Him; He will repay him to his face. Therefore you shall keep the commandment, the statutes, and the judgments which I command you today, to observe them.

Then it shall come to pass, because you listen to these judgments, and keep and do them, that the LORD your God will keep with you the covenant and the mercy which He swore to your fathers. And He will love you and bless you and multiply you; He will also bless

the fruit of your womb and the fruit of your land, your grain and
your new wine and your oil, the increase of your cattle and the
offspring of your flock, in the land of which He swore to your
fathers to give you.

—Deuteronomy 7:6–13

Day 17
The Lord Is My Shepherd

Scripture

The LORD is my shepherd;
I shall not want.
He makes me to lie down in green pastures;
He leads me beside the still waters.
He restores my soul;
He leads me in the paths of righteousness
For His name's sake.

Yea, though I walk through the valley of the shadow of death,
    I will fear no evil;
For You are with me;
Your rod and Your staff, they comfort me.
You prepare a table before me in the presence of my enemies;
You anoint my head with oil;
My cup runs over.
Surely goodness and mercy shall follow me
All the days of my life;
And I will dwell in the house of the LORD
Forever.

—Psalm 23

Day 18
God Is My Refuge

*Note: This Scripture passage has been altered slightly. It has been
personalized by turning second-person pronouns (you and your) into
first-person pronouns (me, my, and I).*

Scripture

He who dwells in the secret place of the Most High
Shall abide under the shadow of the Almighty.
I will say of the LORD, "He is my refuge and my fortress;
My God, in Him I will trust."
. . . .
Because I have made the LORD, who is my refuge,
Even the Most High, my habitation,
No evil shall befall me,
Nor shall any plague come near my dwelling;
For He shall give His angels charge over me,
To keep me in all my ways.
They shall bear me up in their hands,
Lest I dash my foot against a stone.
I shall tread upon the lion and the cobra,
The young lion and the serpent shall I trample under foot.

Because I have set my love upon God, therefore He will
deliver me;
He will set me on high, because I have known His name.
I shall call upon Him, and He will answer me;
He will be with me in trouble;
He will deliver me and honor me.
With long life He will satisfy me,
And show me His salvation.

—Psalm 91:1–2, 9–16

Day 19
Praise for God's Mercies

Note: This Scripture passage has been altered and personalized.

Scripture

Bless the LORD, O my soul;
And all that is within me, bless His holy name!
Bless the LORD, O my soul,
And forget not all His benefits:
Who forgives all my iniquities,
Who heals all my diseases,
Who redeems my life from destruction,

Who crowns me with lovingkindness and tender mercies,
Who satisfies my mouth with good things,
So that my youth is renewed like the eagle's.

The LORD executes righteousness
And justice for all who are oppressed.
He made known His ways to Moses,
His acts to the children of Israel.
The LORD is merciful and gracious,
Slow to anger, and abounding in mercy.
He will not always strive with me,
Nor will He keep His anger forever.
He has not dealt with me according to my sins,
Nor punished me according to my iniquities.

For as the heavens are high above the earth,
So great is His mercy toward those who fear Him;
As far as the east is from the west,
So far has He removed my transgressions from me.
As a father pities his children,
So the LORD pities those who fear Him.
For He knows my frame;
He remembers that I am dust.

As for man, his days are like grass;
As a flower of the field, so he flourishes.
For the wind passes over it, and it is gone,
And its place remembers it no more.
But the mercy of the LORD is from everlasting to everlasting
On those who fear Him,
And His righteousness to children's children,
To such as keep His covenant,
And to those who remember His commandments to do them.
—Psalm 103:1–18

Day 20
God Knows Me

Scripture

O LORD, You have searched me and known me.
You know my sitting down and my rising up;
You understand my thought afar off.
You comprehend my path and my lying down,

And are acquainted with all my ways.
For there is not a word on my tongue,
But behold, O Lord, You know it altogether.
You have hedged me behind and before,
And laid Your hand upon me.
Such knowledge is too wonderful for me;
It is high, I cannot attain it.

Where can I go from Your Spirit?
Or where can I flee from Your presence?
If I ascend into heaven, You are there;
If I make my bed in hell, behold, You are there.
If I take the wings of the morning,
And dwell in the uttermost parts of the sea,
Even there Your hand shall lead me,
And Your right hand shall hold me.
If I say, "Surely the darkness shall fall on me,"
Even the night shall be light about me;
Indeed, the darkness shall not hide from You,
But the night shines as the day;
The darkness and the light are both alike to You.

For You have formed my inward parts;
You have covered me in my mother's womb.
I will praise You, for I am fearfully and wonderfully made;
Marvelous are Your works,
And that my soul knows very well.
My frame was not hidden from You,
When I was made in secret,
And skillfully wrought in the lowest parts of the earth.
Your eyes saw my substance, being yet unformed.
And in Your book they all were written,
The days fashioned for me,
When as yet there were none of them.

—Psalm 139:1–16

Day 21
God Is My Loving Father

Scripture

Behold what manner of love the Father has bestowed on us, that
we should be called children of God! Therefore the world does not

229

know us, because it did not know Him. Beloved, now we are children of God; and it has not yet been revealed what we shall be, but we know that when He is revealed, we shall be like Him, for we shall see Him as He is. And everyone who has this hope in Him purifies himself, just as He is pure.

—1 John 3:1–3

No one has seen God at any time. If we love one another, God abides in us, and His love has been perfected in us. By this we know that we abide in Him, and He in us, because He has given us of His Spirit. And we have seen and testify that the Father has sent the Son as Savior of the world. Whoever confesses that Jesus is the Son of God, God abides in him, and he in God. And we have known and believed the love that God has for us. God is love, and he who abides in love abides in God, and God in him.

—1 John 4:12–16

A New Relationship with God

Day 22
My Heavenly Daddy

Prayer

Heavenly Father—my heavenly Daddy—I know intellectually that You are the original and perfect model of all fatherhood. Yet it has been hard for me to relate to You as a Father on a feelings level. Perhaps my image of fatherhood needs healing. Perhaps I have just not understood and appreciated the fatherly love within Your heart. Whatever the reason for this distortion in my Parent-child relationship with You, I pray that You will reach down, lift me up, put me on Your knee, hug me, hold me, tell me I belong to You. Help me to sense Your fatherhood—Your daddyhood—in my life as I meditate and pray right now.

Scripture—Images of a Loving Father

> A father of the fatherless,
> a defender of widows,
> Is God in His holy habitation.
> —Psalm 68:5

Jesus said,

Do not fear, little flock, for it is your Father's good pleasure to give you the kingdom.

—Luke 12:32

Then He [Jesus] said: "A certain man had two sons. And the younger of them said to his father, 'Father, give me the portion of goods that falls to me.' So he divided to them his livelihood. And not many days after, the younger son gathered all together, journeyed to a far country, and there wasted his possessions with prodigal living.

"But when he had spent all, there arose a severe famine in that land, and he began to be in want. Then he went and joined himself to a citizen of that country, and he sent him into his fields to feed swine. And he would gladly have filled his stomach with the pods that the swine ate, and no one gave him anything.

"But when he came to himself, he said, 'How many of my father's hired servants have bread enough and to spare, and I perish with hunger! I will arise and go to my father, and will say to him, "Father, I have sinned against heaven and before you, and I am no longer worthy to be called your son. Make me like one of your hired servants."'

"And he arose and came to his father. But when he was still a great way off, his father saw him and had compassion, and ran and fell on his neck and kissed him. And the son said to him, 'Father, I have sinned against heaven and in your sight, and am no longer worthy to be called your son.'

"But the father said to his servants, 'Bring out the best robe and put it on him, and put a ring on his hand and sandals on his feet. And bring the fatted calf here and kill it, and let us eat and be merry; for this my son was dead and is alive again; he was lost and is found.'"

—Luke 15:11–24

For as many as are led by the Spirit of God, these are the sons of God. For you did not receive the spirit of bondage again to fear, but you received the Spirit of adoption by whom we cry out, "Abba, Father." The Spirit Himself bears witness with our spirit that we are children of God, and if children, then heirs—heirs of God and joint heirs with Christ, if indeed we suffer with Him, that we may also be glorified together.

—Romans 8:14–17

Action

Throughout the Bible, God is presented to us as a loving, protective Father. When Jesus taught His disciples to pray, He began with the words, "Our Father. . . ." When He wanted to reveal God's unconditional love to His followers, He told them the story of a loving father and his lost son. When Jesus was in the Garden of Gethsemane, praying to His heavenly Father before going to the cross, He addressed God as "Abba, Father" (Mark 14:36)—an Aramaic term that literally means "Daddy."

232

As you meditate on these passages about the fatherhood of God, think about the images of earthly fatherhood you experienced in childhood. Can you trace distortions in your image of God to distorted models of fatherhood in your early life or adolescence? If God brings any such sources of distortion to your mind, offer them immediately to your heavenly Father. He will accept your feelings, He will understand, and He will begin to heal you.

As you meditate, reflect on the wonder that you are a joint heir with Christ, and that it is your Father's good pleasure to give you the kingdom. Put yourself into the sandals of the prodigal son, and imagine how he must have felt at every stage of that story—from his "bottoming out" experience in a pigsty far from home to the moment his father hugged him and threw a party in his honor. Do you find elements of your life, your story, expressed in this parable of Jesus? Do you sense the incredible, unconditional fatherly love God has for you, as God is symbolized by the father in this story? Do you sense the longing and grief of His fatherly heart when you go astray or distance yourself from Him?

As you meditate and pray, offer to God any feelings that well up within you, then listen for what your heavenly Daddy wants to say to your heart through His Spirit.

Prayer

Dear God, my Daddy in heaven, thank You for being my Father of choice. You have chosen me, and You have invited me to choose You as well. You have adopted me as Your child. You have loved me with an everlasting, unconditional love. You will never let me go.

You are my "Abba," my Daddy, and I feel the warmth of Your embrace. I sense Your heartbeat of love as You draw me close to You. Father, I ask You to continue to remove my fears and help me experience childlike joy, childlike freedom, and childlike trust in Your presence.

In the name of Your Son, Jesus, Amen.

Day 23
A Fresh Experience of God's Grace

Prayer

Gracious heavenly Father, I need Your grace right now. I have been laboring under a heavy burden—a burden of misunderstanding and apprehension. I have not understood Your grace so I've been trying to do it all myself. Lord, help me to fully grasp the fact that Your yoke is easy and Your burden is light, that You want to give me rest and mercy and grace. Open my understanding and my feelings as I share this time with You, talking to You and listening to Your Word.

Scripture—The Grace of God

But God, who is rich in mercy, because of His great love with which He loved us, even when we were dead in trespasses, made us alive together with Christ (by grace you have been saved), and raised us up together, and made us sit together in the heavenly places in Christ Jesus, that in the ages to come He might show the exceeding riches of His grace in His kindness toward us in Christ Jesus. For by grace you have been saved through faith, and that not of yourselves; it is the gift of God, not of works, lest anyone should boast.

—Ephesians 2:4–9

Seeing then that we have a great High Priest who has passed through the heavens, Jesus the Son of God, let us hold fast our confession. For we do not have a High Priest who cannot sympathize with our weaknesses, but was in all points tempted as we are, yet without sin. Let us therefore come boldly to the throne of grace, that we may obtain mercy and find grace to help in time of need.

—Hebrews 4:14–16

Action

In these passages we catch a glimpse of the amazing *freedom* of God's grace. We are free from sin. We are free from the law. We are free of fear. Because of the grace of God, we are free of the pressure to be perfect. God does not demand perfection; rather, He invites us to love Him and He encourages us to do our best.

Because of God's grace, we do not have to live in a tangled maze of complex rules, such as the scribes and Pharisees imposed on the people of Jesus' day. Unfortunately, however, many of us needlessly impose impossible rules, standards, and demands on ourselves in complete contradiction to the grace of God. God is patient with us; are we patient with ourselves? God allows us to make mistakes; are we accepting of ourselves when we fall short of perfection?

As you meditate on these Scripture passages, search the specific areas of your life that you have not yet yielded to God's grace. Identify the areas and then offer them up to God for healing by His grace.

Prayer

Lord, I thank You for Your grace in my life. I truly have received grace upon grace through the gift of Your Son, Jesus. Thank You for giving me free access to Your throne of grace. Have mercy on me. I trust You, Father, because of Your grace, and I know that You will supply all my needs according to Your riches in glory.

In the name of Jesus, who saves me by His grace, Amen.

Day 24
Perfect!

Prayer

Heavenly Father, I know—mentally, intellectually—that You are a perfect God and all Your works are perfect. But I have to confess that there are times when I feel You have made a mistake in my life. Father, I need healing in my image of Your holy perfection. Please guide me to the truth about Yourself as I pray and meditate on Your Word.

Scripture—Our God Is a Perfect God

> For I proclaim the name of the LORD:
> Ascribe greatness to our God.
> He is the Rock, His work is perfect;
> For all His ways are justice,
> A God of truth and without injustice;
> Righteous and upright is He.
> —Deuteronomy 32:3–4

> I beseech you therefore, brethren, by the mercies of God, that you present your bodies a living sacrifice, holy, acceptable to God, which is your reasonable service. And do not be conformed to this world, but be transformed by the renewing of your mind, that you may prove what is that good and acceptable and perfect will of God.
> —Romans 12:1–2

Every good gift and every perfect gift is from above, and comes down from the Father of lights, with whom there is no variation or shadow of turning.

—James 1:17

Action

We live in such an imperfect and unholy society that it is easy for us to forget what words like *perfect* and *holy* really mean. We are surrounded by violence, poverty, immorality, and declining standards. In view of the woeful imperfection of this world, many people are tempted to believe that the world must be run by a woefully imperfect God. Nothing could be further from the truth!

The world was created in perfection by a perfect God, who looked upon all He had created and then called it "good." The world was distorted and filled with pain by a thing called *sin*. God's perfect world was made subject to imperfection when sin entered creation through the first man and woman.

If we are to learn to trust God, we must separate this imperfect world from our perfect God. His ways are perfect. His will is perfect. He is the Author of every good and perfect gift.

As you meditate on and pray over these passages from God's Word,

- thank Him for His perfection and holiness.
- ask Him to reveal to you His good and acceptable and perfect will.
- thank Him for His perfect love.

Prayer

Heavenly Father, I praise You because You are perfect. I offer myself as a living sacrifice to You and ask You to use my life to demonstrate before a watching world that You and Your will and Your ways are good, acceptable, and altogether perfect.

In Jesus' holy name, Amen.

Day 25
Knowing Jesus Means Knowing God

Prayer

Dear heavenly Father, I thank You for sending Jesus, not only because He has saved me from my sins but because through knowing the

Son, I also come to know the Father. The fact that You are one God expressed in three persons is a mystery beyond my understanding. Yet I accept that all Jesus is revealed to be in the Scriptures, *You are*. Open my understanding as I read, pray, listen, and learn from You.

Scripture—Jesus and the Father Are One

Thomas said to Him, "Lord, we do not know where You are going, and how can we know the way?"

Jesus said to him, "I am the way, the truth, and the life. No one comes to the Father except through Me. If you had known Me, you would have known My Father also; and from now on you know Him and have seen Him."

Philip said to Him, "Lord, show us the Father, and it is sufficient for us."

Jesus said to him, "Have I been with you so long, and yet you have not known Me, Philip? He who has seen Me has seen the Father; so how can you say, 'Show us the Father'? Do you not believe that I am in the Father, and the Father in Me? The words that I speak to you I do not speak on My own authority; but the Father who dwells in Me does the works. Believe Me that I am in the Father and the Father in Me, or else believe Me for the sake of the works themselves."

—John 14:5–11

Let this mind be in you which was also in Christ Jesus, who, being in the form of God, did not consider it robbery to be equal with God, but made Himself of no reputation, taking the form of a servant, and coming in the likeness of men. And being found in appearance as a man, He humbled Himself and became obedient to the point of death, even the death of the cross. Therefore God also has highly exalted Him and given Him the name which is above every name, that at the name of Jesus every knee should bow, of those in heaven, and of those on earth, and of those under the earth, and that every tongue should confess that Jesus Christ is Lord, to the glory of God the Father.

—Philippians 2:5–11

Action

As you meditate on these truths about Jesus, thank God for expressing Himself to you in human form—the form of a humble servant, obedient unto death. Are there aspects of God's character that you have fragmented in your mind? Do you assign the "good" traits of God to Jesus and the "bad" traits to God the Father? I encourage you to take those distortions and fragmented pieces of your image of God and offer them to Him in prayer. Ask Him to show you that Jesus and His Father are one.

If this is a problem area in your image of God, I encourage you, once you have completed this "Thirty-Day Image of God Restoration Program," to begin a study of the Gospels—Matthew, Mark, Luke, and John—which contain the account of Jesus' life, ministry, message, death, and resurrection. In those four books of the Bible, you will find the character of God represented through the life of Christ. You will meet God in human form.

Prayer

Father in heaven, I thank You for revealing Yourself to me through the person of Your Son, Jesus. I want to see Jesus—not with my physical eyes as Thomas did but with the eyes of faith—and like Thomas, I want to be able to say with conviction as I meet Him, "My Lord and my God!"

Thank You for the gift of Your Son, who is the human expression of Your nature and Your love. In His name I pray, Amen.

Day 26
The Comforter

Prayer

Heavenly Father, I thank You for Your Spirit whom You have sent to be my guide and my comforter. I ask that You would reveal Your true nature and character to me through Your Spirit. Give me a sensitive, listening heart so that I can hear what the Spirit has to say to me during this time of study, meditation, and prayer.

Scripture—The Holy Spirit

Jesus said,

> But the Helper, the Holy Spirit, whom the Father will send in My name, He will teach you all things, and bring to your remembrance all things that I said to you.

—John 14:26

APPENDIX

But as it is written:

> "Eye has not seen, nor ear heard,
> Nor have entered into the heart of man
> The things which God has prepared
>   for those who love Him."

But God has revealed them to us through His Spirit. For the Spirit searches all things, yes, the deep things of God. For what man knows the things of a man except the spirit of the man which is in him? Even so no one knows the things of God except the Spirit of God.

Now we have received, not the spirit of the world, but the Spirit who is from God, that we might know the things that have been freely given to us by God. These things we also speak, not in words which man's wisdom teaches but which the Holy Spirit teaches, comparing spiritual things with spiritual.

—1 Corinthians 2:9–13

By this we know that we abide in Him, and He in us, because He has given us of His Spirit.

—1 John 4:13

Action

Many Christians spiritually shortchange themselves. They go through life without ever truly realizing the power that has been given to them—power from God to enable them to live fruitful, abundant lives for Him, power through the Holy Spirit. Many Christians drift through their lives with a vaguely dissatisfying relationship with God. To them, God is like a distant relative. They know where He lives and some facts about His life, but they do not relate to Him in an intimate way. They do not access His power. They do not rely on Him for insight and guidance.

If you have committed your life to Jesus Christ, you already have the Holy Spirit living within you. He is there twenty-four hours a day, 365 days a year. You have all of the Holy Spirit you need. If you don't feel the power and activity of the Spirit in your life, you don't need to get more of the Spirit. You need to let the Spirit have more of you!

You need to become more aware of His presence. You need to ask for the Spirit to fill you and speak to you and empower you. He speaks in a very still, small voice. That is why prayer is not just talking; you must also quiet yourself and listen for what the Spirit has to say to you.

239

After you have prayed and meditated on these few passages about the Holy Spirit, take a few minutes to be still and to listen to what the Spirit has to say to you through your spirit, mind, and emotions.

Prayer

Father, I thank You for Your Spirit, who is already within me, uniting my heart to Yours. I ask You to remind me to listen to what He has to say to me as I continue to seek healing and restoration in my image of You. I invite Your Spirit to invade every area of my life. I ask You to reveal to me the gifts the Spirit has given me so that I can fully serve You. I open my life to the cleansing and revitalizing work of the Spirit so that I can experience love, joy, peace, longsuffering, kindness, goodness, faithfulness, gentleness, self-control—the fruit of Christlike character that the Spirit has come to produce in my life.

In the name of Your Son, Jesus, Amen.

Day 27
Taking the Risk of Faith

Prayer

Father, I am still learning to trust You. Increase my faith. Help me to grow in the assurance that I can take risks for You, that I can dare to do great things for You, and You will always be there for me. As we meet together today, help me to understand the mystery of faith.

Scripture—Keeping Your Eyes on Jesus

Immediately Jesus made His disciples get into the boat and go before Him to the other side, while He sent the multitudes away. And when He had sent the multitudes away, He went up on a mountain by Himself to pray. And when evening had come, He was alone there.

But the boat was now in the middle of the sea, tossed by the waves, for the wind was contrary. Now in the fourth watch of the night Jesus went to them, walking on the sea. And when the disciples saw Him walking on the sea, they were troubled, saying, "It is a ghost!" And they cried out for fear.

But immediately Jesus spoke to them, saying, "Be of good cheer! It is I; do not be afraid."

And Peter answered Him and said, "Lord, if it is You, command me to come to You on the water."

So He said, "Come." And when Peter had come down out of the boat, he walked on the water to go to Jesus. But when he saw that the wind was boisterous, he was afraid; and beginning to sink he cried out, saying, "Lord, save me!"

And immediately Jesus stretched out His hand and caught him, and said to him, "O you of little faith, why did you doubt?" And when they got into the boat, the wind ceased. Then those who were in the boat came and worshiped Him, saying, "Truly You are the Son of God."

—Matthew 14:22–33

Now faith is the substance of things hoped for, the evidence of things not seen. For by it the elders obtained a good testimony. By faith we understand that the worlds were framed by the word of God, so that the things which are seen were not made of things which are visible. . . .

By faith Noah, being divinely warned of things not yet seen, moved with godly fear, prepared an ark for the saving of his household, by which he condemned the world and became heir of the righteousness which is according to faith.

By faith Abraham obeyed when he was called to go out to the place which he would afterward receive as an inheritance. And he went out, not knowing where he was going. . . .

Therefore we also, since we are surrounded by so great a cloud of witnesses, let us lay aside every weight, and the sin which so easily ensnares us, and let us run with endurance the race that is set before us, looking unto Jesus, the author and finisher of our faith, who for the joy that was set before Him endured the cross, despising the shame, and has sat down at the right hand of the throne of God.

—Hebrews 11:1–3, 7–8, 12:1–2

Action

As you read these passages about taking the risk of faith, try to identify with the people you read about. Picture yourself sitting in the boat with the disciples or stepping out in faith on the water, as Peter did, or taking your eyes off Jesus and sinking, as Peter also did. Picture yourself living the adventure of faith with Noah and Abraham, described in Hebrews 11. Then consider this: Are you willing to step out in faith in your life right now? If not, what holds you back? In what specific areas of your life do you need to develop greater faith and trust in God?

Prayer

Heavenly Father, help me to trust You more. Help me to know where You want me to go and what You want me to do. Increase my faith. Increase my courage. Plant in me the desire to dare great things for Your sake.

In Jesus' name, Amen.

Day 28
Ask, Seek, Knock

Prayer

Heavenly Father, You are the Giver of all good gifts. Now, as I meet You in prayer and meditation on Your Word, I ask for only one gift: insight from Your Spirit into the beautiful mystery of prayer.

Scripture—Asking and Receiving

Jesus said,

Ask, and it will be given to you; seek, and you will find; knock, and it will be opened to you. For everyone who asks receives, and he who seeks finds, and to him who knocks it will be opened.

Or what man is there among you who, if his son asks for bread, will give him a stone? Or if he asks for a fish, will he give him a serpent? If you then, being evil, know how to give good gifts to your children, how much more will your Father who is in heaven give good things to those who ask Him!

—Matthew 7:7–11

Now this is the confidence that we have in Him, that if we ask anything according to His will, He hears us. And if we know that He hears us, whatever we ask, we know that we have the petitions that we have asked of Him.

—1 John 5:14–15

Action

Consider these questions about prayer:

- What does Jesus really mean when He invites us to "ask . . . seek . . . knock"?
- When do you usually pray?
  _____ At a regular time each day
  _____ When I have to make a major decision
  _____ When I get into trouble
  _____ When I get sick or my life is in danger
  _____ When I want something from God
  _____ When someone I care about has a major need
- When you pray, what do you usually ask God for? In other words, what is your priority in prayer?
- In 1 John 5:14–15, what is the important condition God places on His answers to our prayers? (Hint: it's a phrase that begins with the word *according*.)
- How do these verses change the way you look at prayer?

As you ask, seek, and knock in your prayer time with God, be open to whatever way God chooses to answer that prayer, and be open to whatever time frame He thinks is best.

Prayer

Father in heaven, as I look back over my prayer life, I have to confess there have been times when I have asked for things that were not according to Your will. In my human frailty and willfulness, I have asked for a serpent and a stone, for gifts that would have been bad for me, and I have sulked when You have given me good gifts instead. I have asked and knocked, demanding that You answer my prayer on my terms, according to my timetable.

Father, help me to realize that the purpose of prayer is not to bend Your will to mine but to align my will with Yours. Help me to pray as I ought to.

Not my will, but Yours be done, in the name of Jesus, Amen.

I Maintain a Restored Image of God *for Life!*

Day 29
Putting My Restored Image of God to the Test

Prayer

Lord, I have some work to do today—an inventory of my image of You. I ask You to give me insight into my feelings and experiences. Help me to be honest with myself and with You. Let me feel Your assurance that You accept my honest feelings, my honest answers, and that this is all part of the process of becoming healed and restored in my relationship with You.

Scripture—Continuous Renewal in the Relationship with God

> But those who wait on the LORD
> Shall renew their strength;
> They shall mount up with wings like eagles,
> They shall run and not be weary,
> They shall walk and not faint.
> —Isaiah 40:31

> Create in my a clean heart, O God,
> And renew a steadfast spirit withing me.
> —Psalm 51:10

Action—Image of God Inventory

Now that you have spent four weeks in daily study, prayer, and meditation on God's Word, it's time to take inventory of the current condition of your image of God. Make a copy of this blank inventory before you start, so you can take it again later.

APPENDIX

Assets	Liabilities
☐ I tend to trust God.	☐ I tend to doubt God.
☐ I tend to approach God.	☐ I tend to distance myself from God.
☐ I feel close to God.	☐ I feel wary around God.
☐ I read my Bible and pray daily.	☐ I have a hard time maintaining a consistent devotional life.
☐ I seek God's true image in the Bible.	☐ I form my image of God on the basis of my feelings.
☐ I see God as holy and perfect.	☐ I feel God sometimes makes mistakes.
☐ I base my image of God on Jesus.	☐ I base my image of God on my experiences.
☐ I feel God is merciful.	☐ I am apprehensive about God's condemnation.
☐ I feel free and forgiven.	☐ I struggle with feelings that I am not forgiven.
☐ I feel God hears and answers my prayers.	☐ I don't know if God really hears my prayers.
☐ I enjoy going to church and worshiping God.	☐ I don't enjoy the worship experience.
☐ I can share anything with God and say anything to God.	☐ I am careful not to say anything to God that might make Him angry.
☐ God is my Father and my Friend.	☐ God is powerful and remote.

This inventory is divided into two columns—"Assets" and "Liabilities." For each line, place a check in one column. This inventory is between you and God, so be thorough and honest. Check the description that most accurately characterizes your behavior and feelings right now.

Take time to pray over this inventory. Offer any items in the "Liability" column to God, asking Him to work with you to bring about healing and restoration. Don't be hard on yourself for any "Liability" answers. Accept yourself right where you are—just as God accepts you. Your goal is not attaining instant perfection but getting started on a lifelong program of growth and change.

Make an appointment with yourself to retake this inventory (say, three or six months from now), and check on the progress you are making in your experience with God.

Prayer

Heavenly Father, I have come a long way, but I still have a long way to go. Thank You for standing with me in this lifelong healing process. Thank You for restoring me and renewing my spirit, day by day. Thank You for being patient with me as I slowly build a new and more accurate image of You.

In the name of Jesus, Amen.

Day 30
Maintaining God's True Image for Life!

Prayer

Dear heavenly Father, I have made it to Day 30. Even though this is a tremendous milestone in my relationship with You, I realize that this "Thirty-Day Image of God Restoration Program" is the beginning, not the end, of my healing process. Help me to continue moving forward in my relationship with You.

Scripture—Continuing to Trust God

Trust in the LORD forever,
For in [Jehovah], the LORD, is everlasting strength.
—Isaiah 26:4

The LORD also will be a refuge for the oppressed,
A refuge in times of trouble.
And those who know Your name will put their trust in You;
For You, LORD, have not forsaken those who seek You.
— Psalm 9:9–10

Cause me to hear Your lovingkindness in the morning,
For in You do I trust;
Cause me to know the way in which I should walk,
For I lift up my soul to You.
Deliver me, O LORD, from my enemies;
In You I take shelter.
Teach me to do Your will,
For You are my God;
Your Spirit is good.
Lead me in the land of uprightness.
Revive me, O LORD, for Your name's sake!
For Your righteousness' sake bring my soul out of trouble.
— Psalm 143:8–11

Action

Maintaining your new image of God is a lifelong experience. It requires a commitment to trusting God, studying His Word, and living in His presence every day.

So don't stop here—keep moving ahead! Continue your journey deeper into the joy and the abundant life God created you to have. In closing, let me share with you ten principles for maintaining an accurate image of God for life. I call these principles. . . .

The Ten Keys to a Restored Image of God

Key 1: Do not evaluate God on the basis of your understanding. Your understanding is finite; God is infinite. "Trust in the LORD with all your heart," declares Proverbs 3:5, "and lean not on your own understanding." The goal is to continually expand the limits of your understanding of God's ways, not reduce Him until He fits within the boundaries of your thinking. Whatever happens in life, you must seek to respond with an attitude that says, "Lord, I trust You," rather than one that says, "Lord, explain this so I will understand."

Key 2: Be careful not to base your image of God on negative experiences in your life, past or present. People, acting out their sinful free will, may have hurt you. Living in a world that has been corrupted by sin may have hurt you. But God does not hurt you. God is a healer. He loves you. He is on your side.

Key 3: Be careful not to base your image of God on the model, behavior, or ideas of others.   People will let you down. Christians will let you down. Teachers, pastors, evangelists, authors, doctors, and mentors are all human and fallible. You can learn a lot from watching and interacting with other people, but you should never base your image of God on other people. The only valid sources for determining God's true image are the Bible, Jesus Christ, and the guidance of the Holy Spirit.

Key 4: Be careful not to base your image of God on your feelings—particularly your negative feelings.   Remember that feelings are always real, but they are not always true. Emotions go up and down, but God—and the truth about God—never changes. Your image of God must be grounded in biblical truth, not in your variable and unreliable feelings.

Key 5: Make a commitment to trust God, unequivocally and unconditionally.   Again, I remind you of the counsel of Scripture: "Trust in the LORD with all your heart." Let's face it. You may not *feel* like trusting God right now. At this point, don't worry about your feelings. What matters now is that you've made a conscious *decision* to trust God. So base all your future behavior on that decision, not on your feelings.

Here's a basic piece of advice that I have relied on whenever my feelings began to get in the way of the actions I wanted to take: *it's easier to act your way into a new way of feeling than to feel your way into a new way of acting.* In other words, concentrate on living your life as if you trust God, and the feelings of trust will follow. As someone once said, "You have to fake it till you make it." Do it even if you don't feel like it. Pretty soon, you'll be surprised to discover that the feelings are there as well.

Key 6: Evaluate your image of God on a regular basis, and make conscious, deliberate adjustments whenever you detect distortions.   I suggest using the diagnostic tools—the checklists and inventories in this book—to help you evaluate your relationship with God on a regular basis.

Key 7: Recognize and accept the biblical truth that Jesus is God and the character of God is the character of Jesus Christ. Make a commitment *not* to fragment your image of God but to embrace the fact that Jesus and God the Father and the Holy Spirit are one.

Key 8: Make a commitment to read your Bible and pray daily and habitually, regardless of whether you feel like it. This is another area of your spiritual life where you may have to "fake it till you make it." Prayer and Bible study are spiritual disciplines, and it takes daily commitment to turn a discipline into a habit. I guarantee, however, that if you make it a priority to meet God daily in prayer and Bible study, a time will come when the feelings will be there. At that point, if you skip a day of fellowship with the Lord, you will feel that something important is missing from your life.

Key 9: Don't allow your personality to dictate your experience with God. Different personality types tend to experience God in different ways. Your personality type can be a hidden source of distortion in your image of God. If you recognize that the doubt you feel is due to your obsessive-compulsive tendencies, you can make allowances for those tendencies, and the doubts will likely not produce as much anxiety within you. If you feel resentment toward what you perceive as God's attempt to control you, you may remember that, after all, you have an independent personality and it's part of your personality makeup to feel that way. Once you realize that your personality is getting in the way of your experience with God, you can say to yourself, "God isn't really that way. I've just been perceiving Him that way because of this personality issue. Now that I understand the real source of my distortion, I can correct the problem by focusing on God's *true* image in the Bible."

Key 10: Seek healing in your self-image. You may have a tendency to project your self-image onto God. If you have a negative self-image, you tend to confuse your feelings about yourself with the way God truly feels toward you. As a result, you experience distortion and pain in your relationship with God. You feel judged and unworthy. But if you accept yourself unconditionally, you tend to feel accepted by a loving God. You feel forgiven and loved.

I invite you to seal your commitment to lifelong growth and healing by signing your name in the space below. By signing your name, you signify that you commit yourself to a conscious, diligent effort to restore and strengthen your relationship with God every day for the rest of your life. As part of that commitment, you pledge to continually return to these "Ten Keys to a Restored Image of God." You pledge to review them and renew them in your life. If that is the desire of your heart right now, sign your name here:

Prayer

Thank You, heavenly Father, for these past thirty days of enrichment, insight, and growth in my relationship with You. I believe I have turned a corner in reshaping my image of You so that it better conforms to Your true image in the Bible. I commit myself to trusting You, spending time in Your Word, meeting You every day in prayer. I love You, my Lord, my Friend, my Father, my Savior, my Refuge. I love You because You first loved me.

Thank You for this special access that You have given me by Your grace. I can hardly wait till the next time we meet, just You and me together. Until then, all of these things I have asked You and committed to You and shared with You are offered in the name of Jesus, the perfect human expression of who You are.

Amen.

END